William Shakespeare's

Making Sense of Othello!

A Students Guide to Shakespeare's Play

Includes Study Guide, Biography, and Modern Retelling

BookCaps™ Study Guides

www.bookcaps.com

Cover Image © tomorrowfriday - Fotolia.com

© 2013. All Rights Reserved.

Table of Contents

STUDY GUIDE 5
- *Historical Context* 6
- *Plot* 7
- *Themes* 9
  - Race 9
  - Stereotypes and Prejudices 9
  - Manipulation and Deceit 9
  - Love and Chastity 9
  - Marriage 9
  - Jealousy 10
  - Revenge 10
  - Military Life and Politics 10
  - Christianity 10
  - Witchcraft 10
- *Characters* 11
  - Othello 11
  - Desdemona 11
  - Iago 11
  - Emilia 11
  - Roderigo 11
  - Cassio 12
  - Bianca 12
  - Brabantio 12
  - The Duke of Venice 12
  - Montano 12
  - Lodovico 12
  - Gratiano 12
  - Clown 13
- *Chapter Summary* 14
  - Act I 15
  - Act II 20
  - Act III 25
  - Act IV 31
  - Act V 36

THE LIFE AND TIMES OF WILLIAM SHAKESPEARE 40
- *The Times Shakespeare Lived In* 41
- *Shakepeare's Family* 43
- *Shakespeare's Childhood and Education* 45
- *Shakepeare's Adulthood* 47

MODERN VERSION OF THE PLAY 51
- *Characters* 52
- *Act I* 53
  - Scene I. Venice. A street. 54
  - Scene II. Another street. 73

2

Scene III. A council-chamber.	85
ACT II	125
Scene I. A Sea-port in Cyprus. An open place near the quay.	126
Scene II. A street.	159
Scene III. A hall in the castle.	161
ACT III	200
Scene I. Before the castle.	201
Scene II. A room in the castle.	209
Scene III. The garden of the castle.	210
Scene IV. Before the castle.	265
ACT IV	290
Scene I. Cyprus. Before the castle.	291
Scene II. A room in the castle.	327
Scene III. Another room In the castle.	357
ACT V	370
Scene I. Cyprus. A street.	371
Scene II. A bedchamber in the castle: DESDEMONA in bed asleep; a light burning.	389
ABOUT BOOKCAPS	**437**

Study Guide

Historical Context

Shakespeare was born in 1564 to middle-class parents in England. He received limited schooling and married in 1582 to an older woman. In 1590, Shakespeare left his family and moved to London to start his career, and soon became immensely successful. At the height of his career, he helped build the Globe Theatre to accommodate the popularity of his plays. Because of the high demand for new entertainment, Shakespeare wrote a total of 37 known plays and numerous poems.

One of Shakespeare's more popular tragedies, Othello was first performed for King James I in 1604, although the exact year it was written is not known. The story, like many of Shakespeare's works, is based on another tale. In 1565, a writer nicknamed Cinthio wrote a short story about a nameless Moor wed to a beautiful lady. Driven mad by jealousy because of his ensign's manipulations, and taking a handkerchief as proof of adultery, the Moor kills his wife and is sent into exile. Shakespeare took the bare plot of this story in order to forge his own creation. He altered the plot and characters in order to better explore the themes of race and stereotypes prevalent during that time period.

When Othello was written, the term "Moor" was used to refer to Africans and others who had darker skin. In 1601, three years before Othello was performed, Queen Elizabeth deported all the Moors from England for several reasons, but one of them was the stereotype that they were wild and more savage than their white counterparts. Using Othello, Shakespeare breaks these stereotypes. Although Othello is referred to as a bestial man in the beginning of the play, when the audience first sees him they form an opinion of an intelligent, respectable man. By turning Othello into a noble figure, and making the primary villain of the play a white man, the play explores these stereotypes and makes a social statement. In the original story, the Moor is not a hero, but Shakespeare turns Othello into a tragic hero with his actions and eventual suicide.

Othello was published in print for the first time in 1622. After his death Shakespeare quickly became known as England's best playwright and remains highly influential to this day. Because so many facts about Shakespeare's life are unknown, there are some who think that Shakespeare was a woman, or that someone else actually wrote the plays. However, there is no hard evidence to back these conspiracies up. While people may always argue about Shakespeare's true identity, his plays have become an important part of literary history.

Plot

In Venice, Iago and Roderigo are plotting. Iago wants revenge against Othello, a Moor who is his superior. Roderigo wants to sleep with a Desdemona, whom Othello has just married. They go to Brabantio's window, a senator and Desdemona's father and wake him up. They tell him his daughter has run off, and when he goes to check Iago leaves. Brabantio finds out his daughter is gone and demands that she be found.

Meanwhile, Othello is summoned to a midnight call by Cassio on behalf of the Duke. Brabantio and Roderigo come up and order Othello arrested. They agree to go before the Duke and let him decide. At the palace, the Duke is talking with his councilors. The Turks have amassed a fleet and are planning on attacking Cyprus. The Duke is glad to see Othello because he needs a good commander. Brabantio brings forth his case, claiming Othello stole his daughter with witchcraft. Othello tells how Desdemona fell in love with him after hearing his tales of exotic lands and battles. The Duke refuses to arrest Othello, telling him to command in Cyprus instead. Othello agrees, on the condition that Desdemona go with him. Iago convinces Roderigo to tell all his land and come with them in pursuit of Desdemona. He is dishonest and is using Roderigo for money.

In Cyprus, a tempest destroys the Turkish fleet. Desdemona, Iago, Cassio and Othello all arrive safely. They are greeted by Montano, who is giving his rule to Othello. During these exchanges, Iago reveals that he plans to accuse Desdemona of sleeping with Cassio. The city celebrates and Iago gets Cassio drunk. He convinces Roderigo to enrage Cassio, which he does, and Cassio tries to kill him. Instead, he hurts Montano. When Othello comes to see what the fuss is about, he strips Cassio of his rank. Iago advises Cassio to plead with Desdemona to get back in Othello's good graces.

The next day, Cassio follows Iago's advice and speaks with Desdemona, who promises to help him. Iago times it so that he and Othello walk by as they are talking, and Cassio leaves. Othello recognizes him, and Iago plants suspicions in Othello's mind that Desdemona loves him. Desdemona enters, and notices that Othello is acting queer. He says he has a headache, and she wipes his forehead with her handkerchief. Othello waves it away and it falls to the floor, where it is picked up by Emilia, Iago's wife. Iago has asked her to steal the handkerchief, although she does not know why. When she gives it to him, the next part of his plan is set into motion.

Othello comes to Iago, enraged at the nagging in his head, and demands proof of Desdemona's infidelity. Iago tells him that Cassio has her handkerchief, and Othello takes his word for it. He vows to kill Cassio and Desdemona. The next day Othello asks Desdemona to use her handkerchief, and she cannot produce it. He claims it was a token from his father to his mother and contained ancient magic. When he leaves, Emilia recognizes that he is jealous, but Desdemona convinces herself nothing is wrong. Cassio meets his mistress, Bianca, and gives her the handkerchief he found in his room to copy.

The next day, Iago tells Othello to hide while he talks to Cassio about Desdemona. Instead of Desdemona, Iago asks Cassio about Bianca the prostitute, knowing that he will laugh and joke. Seeing this, Othello has no more doubts. A messenger named Lodovico enters with order for Othello to return to Venice and for Cassio take his place in Cyprus. Desdemona is happy, and Othello hits her. Lodovico is bewildered, as Othello does not act like the man he once knew.

Othello goes to question Emilia, who swears Desdemona is innocent. He questions Desdemona but does not believe her. Desdemona asks Iago for help in figuring out what is wrong. Roderigo approaches Iago because he realizes he is being duped. Iago, however, convinces him to kill Cassio.

That night, Othello sends Desdemona to bed. On the streets, Roderigo stabs Cassio, who is wearing armor. Cassio stabs Roderigo and Iago stabs Cassio. Iago then pretends to "find" Cassio and kills Roderigo before calling for a stretcher. Othello smothers Desdemona in their bed, and Emilia comes in with news that Roderigo is dead. She finds Desdemona and calls out murder. Several men enter, and through talking Emilia figures out that it was her husband who was lying to everyone. Othello despairs and lunges for Iago, who stabs his wife. Emilia dies, Iago escapes, and Othello is locked in the room.

When the men bring Cassio and Iago in, the truth of everything is revealed. Lodovico announces that Othello will be taken to Venice for trial and that Iago will be tortured. Othello begs them to tell everyone that he was a man who loved too much, and threw away something precious. He stabs himself with a hidden weapon and dies kissing Desdemona.

Themes

Race

One of the main explorations of the play was Shakespeare's exploration of Othello, a Moor, or black man. The simple act of making Othello an African instead of a Venetian allowed the play to have many different levels, turning the otherwise typical tragedy into one of Shakespeare's more famous plays. Interestingly enough, not only did Shakespeare make Othello the tragic hero, but he made the major villain a seemingly honest white man. By doing this, he moves away from the stereotype of the time of the black man being the villain and switches the roles.

Stereotypes and Prejudices

If it were not for the stereotypes and prejudices commonly held by the people in Shakespeare's time, then Othello's race would be of no consequence to the play. In examining the interactions of characters and Othello's race, Shakespeare touches on many of the common stereotypes held at the time, mostly those concerning how Moors were full of rage and passion and were in general more bestial than white men. At the beginning of the play, Othello defies these stereotypes with his calm, rational demeanor. However, after Iago's meddling, Othello takes on the prejudices of his race.

Manipulation and Deceit

The only deceitful character in the play is Iago. He is the main reason for most of the conflict in the play, as he uses his extreme powers of manipulation to cause it. He is so good at manipulating others and seeing exactly how they react that, at times, the other characters feel like dominos Iago has set up to fall perfectly. Manipulation allows Iago to get the others to do his dirty work for him, and he himself takes almost no active role other than being in the right place at the right time and telling people exactly what he wants them to hear.

Love and Chastity

Closely intertwined, love and chastity play a prominent part in Desdemona and Othello's relationship. It is hard for the other characters to believe that two people who are so different could love each other. However, in the beginning, their love seems genuine and mutual. It is only when Desdemona's chastity is threatened, however, that Othello ceases to love her. To him, her chastity is more important than her love, or rather, if she is not chaste, she is not capable of love. Desdemona as well values her chastity, and claims she would not give it up for all the world.

Marriage

Throughout the play, there are several scenes, which mimic the marriage vows or marriage ceremony itself. Oddly enough, the play does not show Othello and Desdemona's actual marriage ceremony, or even say for sure whether or not their marriage was consummated. There is, however, a scene shown in which Othello and Iago engage in marriage-like vows while kneeling, when Othello promises to have revenge. Another almost-wedding scene occurs on the night Desdemona is killed. She has the wedding sheets put on her bed, and the two have one final kiss of death.

Jealousy

Jealousy is the primary reason Othello became obsessed. Iago and Emilia both refer to jealousy as a "monster" that eats away at men, and in Othello's case this proves to be true. Once Iago so much as puts the suspicions in his head, Othello cannot believe that Desdemona is innocent. The idea consumes him, and jealousy transforms him from a calm, rational man into a vengeful murderer. It blinds him to all Desdemona's goodness and kindness until all he can see her as is a whore. It is not just Othello who is jealous, but Iago as well is suspicious because he believes the Moor has slept with his life, and it is his unfounded jealousy that drives his actions.

Revenge

Both Iago and Othello are motivated by revenge in the play. Iago wants revenge on the Moor due to his jealousy for the man, and also seeks revenge on characters such as Cassio, who did not slight Iago directly but rather were more handsome and more wealthy than he. Othello seeks revenge on both Cassio and Desdemona for their supposed love affair. In no instance during the play does revenge end well. Iago gets his revenge, but is doomed to a life of painful torture. Othello gets his revenge, but after he finds out he falsely killed his wife he kills himself.

Military Life and Politics

Desdemona is drawn to Othello because of his life not only as an exotic, but as a soldier. When she requests to be sent to Cyprus with Othello, she claims that she knew she married a soldier and accepted war as part of that. Othello is proud of his political accomplishments, and Iago is jealous of them. Several of the deceits in the play involve false political information or gaining or changing ranks in the military. The military represents order and serves as the backdrop for Venice. When the characters travel to Cyprus, however, this order is upset, and a political struggle ensues.

Christianity

There are many Christian allusion in Othello, centered around the figures of Jesus, Judah and the devil. Iago is referred to most often as the devil, because of his scheming, although it is ironic because is his a Caucasian man with an honorable reputation. He is also referred to as Judas, however, because of his betrayal of Othello. Othello is most often referred to as Jesus. Christianity is present throughout the play, and symbolizes western religion and civilization.

Witchcraft

Witchcraft, representative of paganism and the opposite of Christianity, is brought into the play by Othello. Because he is African, other characters associate him with witchcraft and other magical, primal forces. Brabantio accuses Othello of stealing his daughter using witchcraft, falling into the stereotype that Moors are barbarians. Othello reacts rationally to this accusation, yet it becomes clear that he considers magic part of his past. The handkerchief, the most important symbol in the play, was made by an ancient witch and was dyed with the blood of virgins. Othello takes its power seriously, showing that he is torn between the European world and his ancestors.

Characters

Othello

The tragic hero of the play, Othello is a respectable Moor high up in the Venetian military. He falls in love with Desdemona and marries her in secret. Although his love in genuine, he is poisoned by suspicions and jealousy planted in his head by Iago. Because of this, he transforms from a rational man into a man driven solely by passion and rage. After he realizes his mistakes, he kills himself, thereby keeping his more noble aspects and letting him die an honorable death. Shakespeare uses Othello to explore many racial stereotypes and prejudices that existed in their society.

Desdemona

Desdemona is a beautiful and virtuous young woman. She turns down many conventional suitors to marry Othello in secret, and she fell in love with him because of unusual past and his bravery. Desdemona proves to be an independent and strong young woman, capable of holding her own. However, she holds her chastity and virtue above all else. She represents the perfect traditional wife of the time, totally obedient and faithful to her husband despite her independent nature. Even when Othello smothers her, she does not blame him but continues to love him.

Iago

The main villain in the play, Iago spends most of his time manipulating and lying to the other characters, playing them like a master puppeteer. He is fueled by unfounded jealousy of Othello and other characters whose status is higher than his own. He himself admits his motives are confused: he suspects Othello slept with his wife, he lusts after Desdemona, Cassio is more handsome, Othello doesn't deserve to have a higher position as Moor. His jealousy causes all the conflict in the play, and Iago is eventually captured for his crimes and doomed to spend the rest of his life in a torture chamber.

Emilia

Emilia is Iago's wife and does not becomes important until the end of the play. She travels to Cyprus to act as Desdemona's hand-maid, and spends all her time with the young bride. She is not as virtuous as Desdemona and has a more realistic view of the world. She helps Iago unwittingly by snatching Desdemona's handkerchief, but is shocked and outraged when Iago turns out to be the one behind all the trouble. She denounces her husband and proclaims Desdemona's loyalty and virtue until her dying breath.

Roderigo

A young Venetian gentleman who is madly in love with Desdemona. Really, he just wants to sleep with her, but because of this Iago uses Roderigo as a tool. He convinces Roderigo that he is his ally and tells him to sell all his land for money and jewels. Roderigo travels to Cyprus in pursuit of Desdemona, although she doesn't even know his name. Eventually he realizes that he is being duped by Iago, but by then he is penniless. Iago kills him to prevent ruining his schemes.

Cassio

Othello's young, handsome lieutenant. He is always polite to women, and because of his new position he inspires Iago's jealousy. Iago sets Cassio up to be stripped of his rank and turns Othello against him with suspicions of an affair. Cassio is good-natured and courteous, does not drink much, and loves Othello. When he is kicked out of the army, he goes to Desdemona to beg her help. Eventually, when all comes to light, he forgives Othello for his actions and thinks he is an honorable man, even in death.

Bianca

Bianca is Cassio's mistress or prostitute—it is never stated clearly which. She sleeps with Cassio and wishes to be his legal wife, though Cassio would never marry her. Bianca is the only promiscuous woman in the play and serves as a scapegoat for her immoral lifestyle. In reality though, she comes across as a moral woman who has a certain pride in herself, no different from any of the other women in the play. Just as Othello defies his stereotypes as a Moor with his actions, so too does Bianca with her stereotype as a whore.

Brabantio

A senator of Venice, Brabantio is Desdemona's father and a powerful man with a good reputation. He is outraged when he learns of his daughter secret marriage, and is convinced that Othello seduced her with magic or witchcraft of some sort. He eventually gives his reluctant consent for their marriage but dies of grief shortly after.

The Duke of Venice

Othello's superior, the Duke has an immense respect for the Moor. He looks past his skin color to see that Othello is a good, strong man, and sends him to Cyprus to rule because of his trustworthiness. Although the Duke only appears in one scene, he is the only character to totally dispel the stereotypes to which Othello is subject. He refuses to punish Othello for practicing witchcraft and treats him as an equal.

Montano

Othello's predecessor in Cyprus, Montano welcomes Othello to the city with open arms. He is injured by Cassio during his drunken rage and taken off in a stretcher.

Lodovico

Lodovico is a politician from Venice, and a kinsman to Brabantio. He comes with a message for Othello to return to Venice and Cassio to take his place of command in Cyprus. Lodovico, as the first character entering from the outside, is shocked at the change that has taken place in Othello. In the end, it is Lodovico who dispenses judgment and wraps up the situation and the play, vowing to take Othello's tale back to Venice.

Gratiano

Another gentleman who appears at the end of the play, Gratiano is Brabantio's brother and, therefore, Desdemona's uncle. He witnesses the end of their tragedy, and reveals to the audience that Brabantio is dead of grief. After Othello commits suicide, Lodovico names Gratiano the Moor's heir because of his relation to Desdemona.

Clown

A jester that occasionally acts as a messenger throughout the play.

Chapter Summary

Act I

Act I, Scene I

The setting opens on Venice, with two men, Rodrigo and Iago walking down the street. Roderigo is a young gentleman, and Iago is a captain in the military. They are arguing - Roderigo is upset because he has been paying Iago to woo the lady Desdemona, however, Desdemona has eloped with Othello, Iago's superior (and an African). Rodrigo questions Iago's loyalty, but Iago assures him that he hates Othello, who gave an unworthy man a promotion that Iago was up for. He reveals that he only pretends to be loyal to Othello, so that he can scheme behind "the Moor's" back.

The two men arrive at the lady Desdemona's house. They know that she has eloped with Othello, and plan on rousing her father in order to bring shame on Othello while freeing Desdemona's affections. They yell up, calling "thief" until Desdemona's father, senator Brabantio, opens the window to see what is going on. He is angry at being woken in the middle of the night and does not believe that he has been robbed. Iago shouts cruel sexual insults up at him, telling him that his daughter is off having sex.

Eventually, Brabantio begins to believe them and leaves the window to check and see if his daughter is in the house. Iago, not wanting to be identified because he must appear loyal to Othello, says farewell to Roderigo and goes to Othello. Brabantio, finding his daughter's room empty, comes downstairs, lamenting his bad fortune. Roderigo tells him that he thinks the two are married, and Brabantio is even more upset. He asks Roderigo to show him where they are so he can retrieve his daughter and promises Rodrigo that he will reward him for his trouble.

Act I, Scene II

On another Venetian street, Othello, Iago and other attendants are walking and carrying torches. Iago is relating to Othello how he overheard a rude ruffian bashing Othello's name in front of Senator Brabantio's house. Iago is trying to get Othello riled up with his story, but Othello remains calm and collected. Iago also warns him that Brabantio, knowing of Othello's elopement with his daughter, will be searching for him. They see torches approaching, and Iago urges Othello to hide in the house. Othello, however, stands his ground. He believes he has nothing to be ashamed of, and knew what he was getting into when he married Desdemona for love.

Cassio, Othello's newly promoted lieutenant, enters with officers. Othello greets them and asks for news. Cassio tells him that the Duke is requesting Othello's presence at a meeting and hints that it must be urgent to be meeting so late at night. He also says that Brabantio has search parties out looking for Othello. Othello agrees to go with Cassio and says he must get something out of his house before they go. He exits.

Cassio asks Iago what is going on, and Iago tells him that Othello is married. When Cassio wants to know who the woman is, Iago is interrupted before he can tell him by Othello coming back from the house. Just then, they see another group headed towards them.

Brabantio, Roderigo and officers enter with torches and weapons. They spot Othello and Brabantio orders the officers to take him down. They draw weapons on both sides, and a conflict seems unavoidable. However, Othello calmly talks to the senator and tells him that his status commands more respect than his weapons, and politely asks him to put them down. Brabantio goes into a rant, demanding to know where his daughter is and what witchcraft Othello used on her to get her to fall in love with him. It is inconceivable to Brabantio that his daughter could fall in love with a "savage" black man unless put under some sort of spell, and once again orders Othello subdued.

Othello says he does not want to fight and asks Brabantio where they will take him in order to address the serious charges laid against him. Brabantio says to prison, but Othello wants to go see the Duke since his presence at the meeting is wanted anyway. Brabantio, sure that the Duke will take his side and punish Othello, agrees. He remarks that if things like this are allowed to go unpunished, that the "slaves" shall become the rulers. They exit.

Act I, Scene III

The Duke and several Senators are in the council chamber. Many Turkish ships have been seen offshore, leading the senators to believe that they plan on attacking Cyprus. There are conflicting reports about the numbers, but do doubt that it is a large fleet. A sailor calls and enters with news that the ships are headed for Rhodes instead of Cyprus. The Duke asks his senators what they think about this change, and they think it is a ruse. Rhodes is not as valuable and more easily defended than Cyprus, so it would make no sense for them to attack there. Another messenger enters, this time with news that fleet from Rhodes joined the Turkish fleet and now both fleets are headed towards Cyprus.

Just then, Brabantio, Othello, Iago, and Roderigo enter. The Duke greets Othello and tells him straightaway that he is needed to defend Cyprus. Only after noticing Othello does the Duke notice Brabantio, who tells the Duke that he has a personal emergency that needs solving. Curious, the Duke asks him what is the matter. Brabantio explains that his daughter has been stolen from him through the use of spells and witchcraft. The Duke thinks this is awful and tells Brabantio that he can punish the criminal in any way he wants. When he finds out it is Othello, however, the Duke demands to know more information.

Othello admits that he did marry Brabantio's daughter. As a soldier, he admits that he does not have a way with words, but promises to tell the Duke his tale. He claims that he won Desdemona over and that they are truly in love. Brabantio speaks up again, claiming that his daughter, a shy and innocent maiden, could have never fallen for such a fearful looking man without being cursed. The Duke says that Brabantio needs proof of witchcraft, and another senator asks Othello is he subdued Desdemona in any way. In response, Othello asks them to send for Desdemona herself in order to ask for her honest opinion. If she claims that he forced her in any way, he will consider his life forfeit and take any punishment necessary. The Duke agrees to this, and Othello sends Iago to fetch Desdemona.

While they are waiting for Desdemona's arrival, the Duke wants to hear the rest of Othello's story. Othello begins telling the group of how he met Desdemona when she listened to his stories of war and valor. He used to tell them to her father, stories about how he used to be a slave, how he bought his freedom, about the cannibals he has seen, and other exotic tales. Othello claims that she listened to every word he said and was fascinated by it. She fell in love with because of his fascinating life and bravery, and he fell in love with her because of her strong feelings towards him. He says that if his stories were magic, then that was all the witchcraft he used.

After Othello is done telling his story, Iago returns with Desdemona. The Duke, after hearing Othello's tale, believes that even his daughter would be won by such a story and consoles Brabantio. Brabantio, however, still thinking his daughter was forced, asks her to whom she owes obedience. Desdemona is torn between her father and her husband, but admits that she is in love with Othello and most loyal to him. After hearing the words from his daughter, Brabantio gives up. He reluctantly gives consent to the marriage and remarks that he is glad he has no other children because they are so much trouble. The Duke tries to comfort him by saying that what's done is done and that he can make the best of the situation, but Brabantio still seems unhappy.

With the personal matters over, the discussion turns to the matter of the upcoming war. The Duke wants Othello to defend Cyprus from the invaders and wants him to leave as soon as possible. Othello agrees to defend his country, but requests that the Duke make proper arrangements for his new wife. When the Duke suggests she live at her father's while Othello is at war, both Othello and Brabantio disagree. Desdemona speaks up, saying that she would like to remain with her husband despite the danger that might be involved. Othello asks the Duke to allow this, promising him that Desdemona will not distract him from the important battle. The Duke relents and leaves after giving Brabantio a hint that goodness in a person is more important than the color of their skin. When the

Duke leaves Brabantio warns Othello that Desdemona has lied to him, and may lie to her new husband, as well. Othello orders Iago to make arrangements for Desdemona, and leaves with his new wife.

The only people left in the room are Iago and Roderigo, who is so depressed at what he just witnessed he says he might as well drown himself. Iago calls him an idiot, and Roderigo asks him what he should do. Iago advises him that Othello and Desdemona's marriage cannot last long, and says that Desdemona will soon tire of her new husband. He tells Roderigo to sell his lands and get all his assets in cash. After he has done this, he should bide his time and steal Desdemona away when she becomes bored and seeks a new lover. They plan on meeting the next morning at Iago's house, and Roderigo, easily swayed by Iago's words, goes to sell his land.

Alone, Iago reveals his true plan. He hates Othello and is going to steal money from the "fool" Roderigo. He plans to manipulate Othello by planting suspicions of Desdemona's infidelity. He decides to pin the rumors on Cassio, Othello's lieutenant, in order to kill two birds with one stone. Cassio is handsome; therefore, it would be easy to believe that he would have an affair with Desdemona. Plus, with Cassio out of the way, Iago will be in a prime place to grab his position. He thinks that because of Othello's honest nature he will be easy to manipulate, and vows to put his devious plan into motion.

Act II

Act II, Scene I

At a seaport in Cyprus near the water, Montano and two gentlemen enter. There has been a veritable tempest, and Montano theorizes that the Turkish fleet could not have survived the storm. They can't see any ships yet, so they don't know for sure, but the gentlemen agree. A third gentleman enters with news that the Turkish fleet is indeed destroyed. Cassio's ship has just come to shore, but Othello's ship is still out at sea. Cassio brings news that Othello has been chosen by the Duke to rule Cyprus for the time being. Montano is glad at this news as he has a high opinion of Othello. The gentleman also relates that Cassio seemed upset because he was worried Othello's ship would not make it to Cyprus safely.

Cassius enters, asking the heavens to spare Othello on his dangerous journey. Just then, a sail is seen on the horizon, and a gun is fired, the signal that the ship is friendly. As a gentleman exits to see whose ship has arrived, Montano asks Cassio if the rumors are true that Othello has married. Cassio says they are, and praises his wife's qualities. The gentleman returns with news that it was Iago's ship that arrived, with Desdemona onboard. Cassio once again hopes that Othello's ship makes it so that Desdemona and Othello can be reunited.

Desdemona, Emilia (Iago's wife), Iago and Roderigo enter. Cassio tells the men to bow to Desdemona as she is the wife of the new ruler of Cyprus. He tells her that Othello has not arrived, and another sail is seen along with the gunshot. Cassio greets Emilia next, kissing her and apologizing to Iago as it is courtesy where he comes from. Iago makes a joke about Emilia being a loudmouth, and Desdemona comes to her defense. Iago is persistent, however, and insinuates that women are lazy around the house and sluts in bed.

Desdemona has jokingly gone along with the conversation and asks him what is good about women. She asks about ugly, pretty, stupid, and intelligent women. In Iago's opinion, all of them are the same. During the conversation, Cassio kisses Desdemona's hand, and Iago says in an aside that he plans to use Cassio's courteous ways with women in order to remove him from his station.

A trumpet is heard, and Iago recognizes it as Othello's. Just then, Othello and his attendants enter. Othello and Desdemona greet each other passionately, and express thanks that they were not injured during the tempest. They kiss, and Iago says in an aside how he will ruin their happiness. Othello and Desdemona exit to go to the castle, leaving Iago and Roderigo to talk.

Iago tells Roderigo that Desdemona is in love with Cassio. Roderigo does not believe him, but Iago goes on about how handsome Cassio is and how Desdemona could not be physically attracted to Othello. He calls Cassio a knave and talks bad about him. Roderigo defends Desdemona, sure that she is a moral woman. In response, Iago says that if she were a moral woman she never would have wed Othello. He then points out how Cassio kissed Desdemona's hand. Roderigo says that was merely a courtesy, but Iago insists that their body language was too intimate. He convinces Roderigo to quarrel with Cassio that evening in order for Iago to have something to spread negative rumors about. He hopes to sway the public opinion, and also touch Othello on a personal note when he thinks Cassio is interested in his wife.

Roderigo leaves, and Iago tells the audience his plan once again. His motives seems a bit more confused, however, as he admits that part of him is in love with Desdemona instead of merely jealous of Cassio's promotion. He is under the suspicion that both Othello and Cassio have slept with his wife, and wants to get revenge on them "wife for wife". He plans on acting extremely loyal to Othello until he gains his complete trust, and then take his revenge.

Act II, Scene II

A herald walks down the streets of Cyprus proclaiming that Othello will be holding a celebration. The occasion will be the destruction of the Turkish fleet, as well as his new marriage. The festivities will start at five o'clock the next day.

Act II, Scene III

In the castle, Othello, Desdemona and Cassio are talking. Othello asks Cassio to take guard duty during the night and not to let anyone get too rowdy, and Cassio readily agrees. He bids Cassio goodnight and leaves with Desdemona, presumably to consummate their marriage.

Iago enters and remarks that Othello has gone to bed early to spend time with his new wife, saying that she is beautiful. Cassio agrees that she is "exquisite" but Iago keeps insinuating that she is a temptress and wild in bed. Cassio says she is perfect and beautiful, but modest too. When Iago cannot get Cassio to seem romantically interested in Desdemona, he asks him to have a drink for celebration. Cassio refuses, saying that he has already had one glass and is feeling drunk. Iago badgers him until he relents and invites other gentlemen and officers in for a night of revelry. To himself, Iago says that if he gets Cassio drunk that it will be easy for Roderigo to pick a fight with him.

Montano as well as several other gentlemen and servants carrying wine come up. Cassio has already had some more, but Iago urges Cassio and everyone else to keep drinking. Iago begins singing drinking songs, and Cassio remarks that his songs are good. He tries to convince everyone that he isn't drunk (even though he obviously is) and gets ready to leave. When he is out of earshot, Iago remarks casually to Montano that Cassius is a good man, but has problems with alcohol. Montano thinks they should tell Othello about his lieutenant's drinking problem, but Iago says he would never do such a thing.

Roderigo enters, and Iago, speaking so that only Roderigo can hear, tells him to follow Cassius outside in order to start the fight. A minute later, cries of "Help!" are heard, and Roderigo comes rushing back in, Cassius following and cursing. When Montano sees that Cassius might hurt the other man, he tries to restrain him. Cassius turns on Montano and they begin fighting. Iago tells Roderigo to go outside and raise the alarm. He then pretends to try and stop the fight. Bells ring outside, calling a state of alert.

Othello enters and demands to know what is going on. Montano is severely wounded, and faints. Iago urges everyone to stop fighting and reminds them of their sense of duty. Othello is angry and gets on to everyone for being so rowdy. He wants to know the truth of what is going on and turns to Iago, who claims not to know. He then turns to Cassio, who also cannot answer. Finally, he asks Montano, who tells Othello to ask Iago. Reluctantly, Iago admits that Cassius chased a man into the room, and when Montano rushed to defend him, Cassius turned on him. He claims to then have gone outside and tried to stop the man from sounding the alarm and frightening the villagers, but he was too late. When he returned, everyone was fighting. Iago tries to make excuses for Cassius by saying that he had too much to drink and that the man must have done something to provoke him.

Othello praises Iago for his "honesty" and thinks that he is softening the truth in order to protect Cassio. He strips Cassio of his rank in punishment for his behavior. Just as this is done, Desdemona comes in and asks what is going on. Othello sweeps the matter aside and tells her to go back to bed. Everyone exits except for Iago and Cassio.

Iago asks Cassio if he is hurt, and he replies that he is hurt in a way that no doctor can fix. When Iago expresses pity, Cassio reveals that it is his reputation that is ruined. Iago, pretending to be Cassio's confidant, comforts him while he despairs over his actions. Cassio does not even remember what started the fight, and is confused as to why he acted the way he did. Iago tells Cassio that he can still get his place back and recommends that he plead to Desdemona, who has a great influence over Othello and also has a kind heart. Cassio thinks this is a good idea, and thanks Iago for his advice. He exits.

To himself, Iago remarks that it is ironic that he plays the part of the devil when he tells Cassio to do something that would actually work. Were not Iago planning on interfering, talking to Desdemona would actually be the best way to get back into Othello's good graces. However, he plans to make sure Othello sees Cassio and Desdemona spending time together, all the while whispering in his ear that Desdemona is betraying him with the handsome young man. Iago is relying on Desdemona's goodness for his plan to succeed. The more she tries to help Cassio, the more Othello will be suspicious of her. Iago congratulates himself on the brilliance of his plan.

Roderigo enters, and he doesn't seem happy. He complains that he has been beat up and spent nearly all his money, and still has nothing to show for it. Iago tells him to have patience and convinces him to stay in Cyprus until the plan has been fully realized. Roderigo exits, and Iago reveals the rest of his plan. He is going to have Emilia make sure that Desdemona accepts Cassio's help, and also make sure that he knows when they are meeting so he can bring Othello there to see them together.

Act III

Act III, Scene I

Before Othello's castle, Cassio asks some nearby musicians to play some music in the hopes of putting Othello in a good mood. The musicians begin playing, and a clown enters. He makes a few witty jokes before telling the musicians that Othello sent him to stop their playing. He says that unless they are capable of playing music that can't be heard, then they need to leave. When the musicians have left, Cassio gives a piece of gold to the clown, asking him to give Desdemona the message that someone wishes to speak with her. The clown agrees and leaves.

Iago enters, and Cassio greets him. Cassio reveals that he has stayed up the rest of the night, and, following Iago's advice, asked to see Desdemona in order to plead his case. Iago offers to send his wife, who is attending Desdemona, to see Cassio. Iago leaves, and Cassio remarks that Iago is a kind and honest man.

As promised, Emilia enters. She tells Cassio that Othello and Desdemona have been discussing what happened. Othello still bears love for Cassio, but Montano is an influential man in Cyprus so it would not be wise to reinstate the one who injured him. Desdemona was pleading on Cassio's behalf. When Cassio hears this, he asks Emilia if he can speak to Desdemona alone. Emilia invites him into the castle.

Act III, Scene II

Inside the castle, Othello and Iago are talking with some gentlemen. Othello hands Iago some letters to give to the pilot, asking him to do Othello's duties in the senate. After giving these orders, Othello decides that he wants to walk around the castle to make sure everything is going well.

Act III, Scene III

In the garden, Desdemona, Cassio and Emilia are talking. Desdemona gives assurance to Cassio that she will do everything she can in order to reinstate him. Emilia agrees and adds that her husband Iago is worried about Cassio's predicament "as if it were his own". Cassio is grateful and vows to be Desdemona's servant in all matter. He hopes that Othello loves him still and that he won't forget their friendship while Cassio is away. Desdemona tells Cassio that she won't give Othello a chance to forget him as she will constantly bring him up until he is reinstated. By doing this, Desdemona is falling right into Iago's plan.

Emilia sees Othello coming, and Cassio gets ready to leave. Desdemona asks him to stay and talk to Othello, but Cassio is nervous and insists on going. When Cassio exits, Iago, walking beside Othello, makes a negative remark. Othello thinks he saw Cassio leave Desdemona, but Iago assures him that Cassio would never slink away in guilt, skillfully putting the insinuation that he is in Othello's mind. Desdemona greets her husband and tells him that she has just been talking with Cassio, and asks Othello to call him back so they can reconcile. Othello vaguely replies that he will call on Cassio "some other time", and Desdemona insists on having an exact meeting set up. She goes on, trying to persuade him, until Othello gives in but asks her to leave.

Desdemona takes Emilia with her when she exits the stage. Othello remarks that he loves Desdemona with his soul and that he could never stop loving her. Iago asks Othello if Cassio knew Desdemona before she and Othello were married. Othello tells him that Cassio often acted as a messenger between the two lovers, and asks why Iago wants to know such information. Iago says that he had no reason, but Othello does not believe him. He becomes convinced that Iago knows something that he is not telling Othello about Cassio. Because of Iago's reputation for honesty, and Othello's trust in him, he will automatically believe anything Iago tells him.

Iago won't tell Othello anything specific, but warns him to beware of jealousy. Othello assures Iago that he would never give in to such a thing as jealousy, and demands to know the meaning of Iago's evasions. Next, Iago hints at Desdemona's dishonesty by pointing out that she lied to her father, thereby insinuating that she might lie to Othello, as well. The reason he gives for telling Othello anything at all is because he loves Othello. He places doubts in Othello's head by hinting that she is going against her nature in marrying him. Iago refuses to say anything more and begins to walk away.

To himself, Othello wonders why he married, and remarks that surely Iago knows more than he was willing to say. Iago turns back and tells Othello not to worry about anything. He says that Cassio should be reinstated, and cautions Othello to keep an eye on both Cassio and Desdemona. Once again, Iago exits. When he is gone for good, Othello puzzles over what Iago has told him. If it were not for Iago's reputation for honesty, Othello would not believe his pauses and insinuations. However, because he has no reason to doubt Iago he begins to suspect that his wife has cheated on him.

Desdemona and Emilia enter again, and Desdemona reminds Othello that it is time for dinner. Othello replies, but faintly, and Desdemona asks him if he is well. He complains of a headache in the center of his forehead, and Desdemona tries to tie his head with her handkerchief. Othello, however, brushes the handkerchief away, saying it is too small, and it falls to the floor. He leaves and Desdemona follows. Emilia stays behind and picks up the dropped handkerchief. It was Othello's first token to his lady, and Iago has asked her many times to steal it, though Emilia does not know why.

Just then, Iago comes in. Emilia teases him by saying she has something for him. Iago calls her foolish, until she produces the handkerchief. Iago wants to know where she found it and snatches it from her. He tells Emilia to leave, and when she does he talks to himself, letting the audience know his plan. He is going to leave the handkerchief in Cassio's room and use it as proof of Cassio and Desdemona's affair. He realizes that Othello has already begun to doubt Desdemona's loyalty, and so his plan is ready to move forward.

Othello enters the scene in a rage. Iago asks him what is the matter, and it becomes clear that the suspicions Iago planted in Othello's mind have taken hold. Othello rants that he would have been happy if Desdemona slept with his whole army as long as he didn't know about it or suspect it. He calls Iago a villain and demands that Iago produce proof to back up his suspicions. Iago does not think they can catch the two having sex, but tells Othello that he has circumstantial evidence to back up his claims. Othello demands to hear everything.

Iago makes up a story, saying that he bunked with Cassio and overheard him talking in his sleep to Desdemona, and worrying about being caught. This infuriates Othello even more, but Iago cautions that it was just a dream and did not point directly to anything going on. However, he asks Othello if Desdemona ever had a handkerchief with strawberries on it, and Othello replies that it was he who gave it to her. Iago claims to have seen Cassio wiping his face with such a handkerchief, and this is all the proof Othello needs.

He vows to get revenge and says that he will never look back. He kneels to finish his vow to the heavens, and Iago kneels beside him. Iago vows to be Othello's faithful servant and to do anything commanded of him. They rise, and Othello's first command to Iago is to make sure that Cassio is dead within the week. Iago swears this will be done, but asks Othello to spare Desdemona. At the mention of her name, Othello damns the "lewd minx" and says he must make plans to kill her. He names Iago his new lieutenant, and Iago says he is Othello's forever.

Act III, Scene IV

Desdemona and Emilia are talking outside the castle. Desdemona, seeing the Clown, asks if he knows where Cassio is sleeping. The clown uses puns to evade her questions, but eventually promises to take Cassio the message that all will be well. He leaves, and Desdemona turns her thoughts to other matters. She is upset that she has lost the handkerchief that Othello gave her, and asks Emilia if she knows where it is. Of course, Emilia is the one who picked it up, but she tells Desdemona nothing. Desdemona remarks that she would have rather lost a purse of gold and that such a situation would be enough for any man, but Othello to suspect her of infidelity. Emilia asks if Othello is jealous, but Desdemona is certain that he is not capable of being so.

Othello enters and greets Desdemona politely. In an aside, he remarks that it is hard to pretend to love her now. He takes her hand and says it is moist. She says it is nothing, but Othello hints that a sweaty hand is a sign of rebellion. Desdemona says this is true because she rebelled against her father to marry Othello. Now, Othello changes the subject and asks to see her handkerchief. She hands him one, but not the one he gave her. He demands to know where it is, but Desdemona says she does not have it with her.

Angrily, Othello tells her the story of the handkerchief's origin. It was made by an old witch for Othello's mother. As long as Othello's mother kept it with her, his father would stay in love with her. If she lost it or gave it away, however, she would lose his love. Hearing this, Desdemona despairs. She tries to hide the truth that she lost it from Othello, but he insists, more and more loudly, that she produce it. In order to distract him, she tries to get him to think about Cassio instead. They talk over each other, getting more and more frustrated before Othello leaves as suddenly as he came.

Emilia sees that Othello has been struck by jealousy, and Desdemona remarks that she has never seen him in such a mood before. Cassio and Iago enter. Iago is in the middle of urging Cassio to once again speak to Desdemona when they see the two women. Desdemona tells Cassio that he has asked for her help at a bad time, as Othello is angry for some unknown reason and will not listen to anything she has to say. Iago is curious about this news and expresses sympathy for Desdemona, saying that he has never seen Othello upset. He leaves to go check on Othello, leaving Cassio alone with the women.

Desdemona makes excuses for Othello's behavior, saying that surely he was upset about something else, and she happened to come across him at a bad time. Emilia still thinks his attitude is related to jealousy, but Desdemona continues to think the best of Othello. She decides to seek him out once more and tells Cassio to wander around close by in case he is called for. Desdemona and Emilia exit.

Bianca enters, Cassio's mistress, and greets him. She was on the way to his house and complains that he has not visited her in over a week. Cassio tells her that he has been depressed and that many things have gone wrong. He begs her forgiveness, and, giving her Desdemona's handkerchief, asks her to copy the pattern. Bianca immediately assumes that it was given to him by another woman, but Cassio assures her it was not. He found it in his room, and assumed that, because of its nice quality, someone would be looking for it. However, he likes the pattern, so he wants to have it copied before he gives it up. He wants Bianca to leave in case his general comes around, and he promises to see her soon.

Act IV

Act IV, Scene I

Before the castle, Othello and Iago are talking. The scene begins in the middle of a conversation, with Iago torturing Othello with thoughts of his wife kissing another man, or lying naked with another man in bed. He turns the subject to the handkerchief, remarking that, as a love token, a woman can give a handkerchief as well as receive one. Othello does not want to be reminded of the handkerchief, but Iago keeps on until his sentences become utterly incoherent and he falls into a trance of rage. To himself, Iago comments that his "medicine" is working well.

Cassio enters, and Iago makes an excuse for Othello's trance-like state, saying he has had an epileptic fit. He advises Cassio to leave until Othello is gone, for fear of making him angry with his presence. Cassio leaves and Othello snaps out of his trance. When Iago asks him if he hurt his head, Othello thinks Iago is mocking him. Iago assures him that he is not, and tells Othello that Cassio stopped by. He tells Othello to go hide while Iago calls Cassio back and asks him to recount the story of how Cassio slept with Desdemona.

Othello withdraws and Iago reveals his true intentions. While Othello is watching, Iago will ask Cassio about his prostitute, Bianca. When Cassio talks about her and her dreams of marriage he cannot help but laugh. Iago knows that, seeing this, Othello will assume Cassio is talking about Desdemona. Cassio enters and brings up the subject of Bianca, and Cassio, falling into Iago's trap, laughs and gestures about how she hangs on to him in public and begs him to marry her. Othello interrupts their lines with frequent asides about how angry he is at Cassio's behavior. Iago beckons Othello closer while Cassio talks about how "she" is always making eyes at him and hanging all over him in public.

Just then, Bianca herself enters. She is angry at Cassio and has changed her mind about copying the pattern of the handkerchief. She is convinced that it is the love token of another woman and gives it back to him. In the exchange, Othello recognizes it as the handkerchief he gave Desdemona. Bianca tells Cassio to join her at supper, or she will never talk to him again. She storms out, and Cassio goes after her, afraid she will cause a scene in the streets.

Othello emerges after they are out of sight, in a rage at what he thinks he has seen. Iago remarks that Desdemona gave her handkerchief to Cassio, and then Cassio gave it to his whore. Othello is angry, but interjects with thoughts about how sweet, intelligent and talented Desdemona is. Obviously, her image has now been torn in his mind. One is a promiscuous shrewd, and the other the noble lady he fell in love with. Iago, seeing Othello waver, reminds him to stay on track. Othello asks where he can find some poison, but Iago tells him it would be better to strangle Desdemona on their bed where she committed her crime. Othello likes this idea.

Offstage, a trumpet sounds. Lodovico, a messenger from Venice, and Desdemona enters. Lodovico has a letter for Othello and gives it to him. Othello begins to read, and Lodovico asks Iago and Desdemona how Cassio is doing. Desdemona tells him that Othello and Cassio have had a falling-out, one that she is sure Lodovico can fix. She comments that she is trying to do all she can to restore Cassio in Othello's eyes, because of the fondness she has for Cassio. Hearing this, Othello loses his cool entirely. When Desdemona asks him what is wrong, he strikes her. Desdemona beings to leave, saying she did nothing to deserve that.

When she walks away, Lodovico asks him to call her back because she is crying. Othello tells her to stop, and she does, but he only calls her names until she leaves for good. Othello exits as well after inviting Lodovico to dine with him that evening. When Othello is gone, Lodovico is shocked at his behavior. He never thought he would see the stable, calm Othello get angry, much less strike his own wife. He asks Iago if Othello has lost his mind, and Iago, always hinting, merely tells Lodovico to watch him and see how he behaves. Lodovico leaves, expressing sorrow that he misjudged Othello so profoundly.

Act IV, Scene II

Inside the castle, Othello is questioning Desdemona's maid, Emilia, for information about her affair. Even though asked repeatedly, Emilia is insistent that Desdemona is loyal to Othello and defends her vigorously. Othello, realizing he will get nothing to validate his suspicions from Emilia, asks her to bring in Desdemona. Emilia leaves, and Othello makes an excuse about Emilia being a "simple bawd" who would readily lie.

Desdemona enters with Emilia, and Othello sends Emilia outside to guard the door. When she is gone, Othello immediately begins accusing Desdemona of committing adultery, calling her a whore and refusing to listen to her pleas. She has no idea what he is talking about and tries to calm him down. She swears on heaven that she is innocent of being with another man, but when she does this Othello just gets angrier. He is weeping and yelling, oblivious to reason. Hearing all the name-calling, Emilia enters the bedroom. Othello walks out of the room, throwing money at his wife like she was a common prostitute.

After Othello is gone, Emilia tries to comfort Desdemona and asks her what is wrong. Desdemona is in shock, and can't even cry she is so confused. Desdemona asks Emilia to get out her wedding sheets and summon her husband, Iago. Emilia goes and fetches Iago, who asks Desdemona what is wrong, though he knows full well what the problem is. Seeing that Desdemona is still too shocked to answer, Emilia relates to Iago how Othello entered angrily and called Desdemona a whore and worse. Iago feigns shock and asks how Othello came about such an idea. Emilia has a theory that some "villain" has been pouring falsehoods into Othello's ear for his own gain. Iago tries to silence her in vain. Desperate, Desdemona asks Iago how she will gain back her husband's love. He assures her that Othello is just under political stress and tells her to go to dinner.

After Desdemona and Emilia exit, Roderigo enters. He is angry because he is beginning to suspect that Iago has been deceiving him. He complains that every day Iago makes something up to trick him, but that isn't going to work anymore. He gave Iago a fortune worth of jewels to give to Desdemona. Since she never gave anything in response, he is going to assume she does not want to be with him, and he will go ask her for the jewels back. Since Iago took the jewels for himself, his whole scheme could be ruined if Roderigo talked to Desdemona face to face. So, thinking quick on his feet, Iago tells Roderigo that if he has not slept with Desdemona by the following night that he can kill Iago.

Intrigued, Roderigo wants to know more. Iago tells him that Cassio is set to replace Othello in Cyprus, while Othello is being sent to Mauritania. In fact, Othello is going to be sent back to Venice. However, the thought of Desdemona being taken away to such a faraway place causes Roderigo to listen to Othello for a little longer. Iago asks Roderigo to help him kill Cassio so that Othello cannot leave Cyprus. Roderigo wants more information about how the plan is going to lead to him sleeping with Desdemona, and Iago promises to give him all the information he wants.

Act IV, Scene III

That evening in the castle, Othello, Lodovico, Desdemona and Emilia are walking together. Othello is going to walk with Lodovico, and he orders Desdemona to go to bed and dismiss Emilia. Othello and Lodovico leave, and Emilia remarks that Othello seems to have calmed down some. Desdemona tells her Othello's orders, and when Emilia balks at leaving Desdemona alone with Othello, Desdemona says they must not displease him. Angry, Emilia remarks that it would be better if Desdemona had never met the man, but Desdemona still loves Othello despite his anger towards her.

Desdemona is thoughtful, and she cannot get a certain song out of her mind. The song is called "willow" and was sung by a woman named Barbara whose love went mad and left her. Barbara died of grief from her broken heart while singing this song. Changing the subject, Desdemona remarks that Lodovico is a "proper man" and she and Emilia talk about that for awhile. However, Desdemona cannot get the song out of her head and begins singing. It is a sad song about lost love.

When Desdemona is done singing, she says her eyes itch, and thinks that is a sign that she will soon be crying. She seems to have some idea of her fate, although she does not know exactly what will happen. Instead of fighting against it, however, she calmly resigns herself to it. She asks Emilia how a woman could ever cheat on her husband. Emilia can understand why, which repulses Desdemona. She claims she would not cheat on Othello "for all the world" but Emilia says she would cheat on Iago, using the logic that having the whole world would make up for the offense. She goes on to say that women are people, the same as men, and that they have their needs and desires. When women cheat, she says, it is because their men have treated them falsely. Not wanting to hear any more, Desdemona sends Emilia away so she can get ready for bed.

Act V

Act V, Scene I

On the streets of Cyprus, Iago and Roderigo are getting ready to ambush Cassius. Iago tells Roderigo to stand behind a bulkhead and strike when Cassius walks by. Roderigo agrees, but wants Iago to stay nearby in case something happens. Iago will do this, but retreats a little farther back. Once he is far enough away, Iago talks to himself. Either Cassio or Roderigo's death would benefit Iago immensely, and it would be best if both died. If Roderigo dies, he cannot ruin Iago's scheme by going to Desdemona. If Cassio dies, it will satisfy Iago's jealousy of those who are more handsome/rich than he.

Cassio enters, and Roderigo recognizes his walk. He jumps out and stabs Cassio, however, Cassio is wearing armor. He is unhurt and takes out his own sword to stab Roderigo who falls to the ground. While Cassio is focused on Roderigo, Iago comes up behind him and slashes his leg with a knife. Cassio also falls to the ground and both wounded men begin calling for help. Othello hears Cassio cry out and is glad that Iago kept his word. Now that he thinks Cassio is dead, he leaves to go kill Desdemona.

As Othello exits, Lodovico and Gratiano enter. They hear the cries of the wounded men, but it is dark and they fear it might be a trap. Iago comes up with a light and goes to "investigate". He "discovers" Cassio, who says the man lying near him was his assailant. Iago goes over to Roderigo and stabs him. Roderigo has time to curse Iago before he dies. Lodovico and Gratiano come over and try to figure out what happened.

While they are talking, Bianca enters and is distressed at Cassio's injury. Iago tells the two men that Bianca, a whore, obviously has something to do with what happened. They call for a stretcher to carry Cassio, still moaning, off. While they are loading him up, Cassio tells the men that he did not know Roderigo and knows of no reason why he would be attacked. Hearing this, Iago once again turns to Bianca, already treating her as if she were guilty. She grows pale and nervous, and Iago tells the other men it is because of her guilt. He knows Cassio had dinner at Bianca's house, but Bianca insists she loved Cassio and had nothing to do with the attack.

Emilia, hearing the commotion, enters. Iago explains the situation, saying it was Cassio's fault for spending time with a prostitute. Without knowing Bianca, Emilia turns on her and begins calling her names. Bianca tells Emilia that she is just as moral as Emilia is, and resents being treated that way. Iago gets everyone to leave, and he goes to tell Othello and Desdemona about what happened.

Act V, Scene II

Desdemona is asleep in her bedroom with a light burning by the bedside. Othello enters, talking to himself, hardening himself for what he is about to do. He decides not to spill any of her blood or mar her perfect skin. He gets closer to her and has regrets, kissing her one last time. The kiss is so sweet that he kisses her twice more, and she begins to stir. Desdemona sees Othello and asks him to come to bed with her. Othello, however, does not move, but rather asks her if she has prayed. She has, and he tells her he would not want to kill her without her having the chance to cleanse her soul.

Desdemona is alarmed when he mentions killing her but is not afraid yet. She asks Othello what she could have done to make him angry, and Othello tells her cryptically to think on her sins. She says her only sin is loving him too much, and that is not something she should be killed for. Othello demands to know why she gave her handkerchief to Cassio, but she denies ever doing so. She begs Othello to find Cassio and ask him about the matter, but Othello tells her that Cassio is on his deathbed. Realizing that she and Cassio have been betrayed, both to their deaths, Desdemona begins to cry. Othello takes her tears as proof of her affair with Cassio and gets even angrier. Desdemona begs Othello to put off killing her for a day, or even an hour, but Othello will not listen and begins to smother her.

Outside, Emilia is shouting for Othello to come to the door. Still in the middle of strangling Desdemona, Othello tells Emilia to wait. Once he feels Desdemona stop moving, he gets up and closes the curtains of the bed before letting Emilia in. Emilia brings news that Roderigo is dead, and Cassio is recovering. Othello is upset that his revenge did not go as planned. Suddenly, Desdemona whispers from the bed that she has been "falsely murdered". Hearing her cry, Emilia opens the curtains to find Desdemona near death. Before she dies, Desdemona absolves Othello of the blame, saying she did it to herself.

Once Desdemona is truly dead, Emilia turns angrily to Othello. She asks him what happened, and he gladly tells her that he was the one who killed Desdemona, and remarks that she kept on lying all the way to her grave. He says that Emilia should not be surprised because her husband knew everything. Shocked, Emilia keeps repeating "my husband!". After doing this several times while Othello is trying to explain Desdemona's betrayal, Emilia tells him he has been deceived. She stands up for Desdemona, even in her death, by saying that she was the truest, most loyal woman in the world. Enraged all over again, Othello threatens to kill Emilia. Emilia, however, is not afraid. Now that she knows the true nature of her husband nothing can scare her. She begins crying murder as loud as she can.

Her cries bring Montano, Gratiano and Iago into the room. Emilia mocks Iago for causing so much murder to be done on his account. Montano and Gratiano want to know what is going on. Emilia asks Iago if he told Othello that Desdemona was an adulterer. He says he did, and labels Cassio as her lover. Calling him a liar, Emilia becomes angry. Iago tells her to stop talking, but she won't. She cries "villainy" and begs all the men to listen to her. When Emilia tells them that Othello killed Desdemona, Othello defends himself by saying she was not loyal. Gratiano says off-handedly that he is glad her father died of his grief and did not live to see Desdemona's fate.

Othello, still on the defensive, gives his evidence of Desdemona's affair, saying he saw Cassio with her handkerchief. At this, Emilia realizes what she has done and falls into despair. Realizing everything could be ruined, Iago puts his sword against Emilia in warning. Gratiano is shocked that he would threaten to hurt his own wife, but Iago does not withdraw his sword. Emilia, not afraid, tells Othello that she found the handkerchief on the ground and gave to Iago since he had asked for it hundreds of times. Iago begins cursing Emilia and calling her a whore.

Othello, finally realizing he has been deceived, runs at Iago. Iago manages to stab his wife and run out of the room before Othello can get to him. Emilia realizes she has received a fatal wound, and requests that she be put next to her mistress. Gratiano and Montano go after Iago, after setting a guard outside Othello's door with orders for him not to leave or he will be killed.

Emilia, near death, begins singing Desdemona's "willow" song. She swears one last time that Desdemona was chaste before dying. Othello knows he has a weapon hidden in the chamber, a sword, and finds it. With the sword hidden, he calls to Gratiano outside his door. Gratiano warns Othello not to leave the room and comes inside to see what he wants. Othello tells him he has a weapon and begins a monologue. He recognizes he is at his journey's end and looks at Desdemona lying on their bed before giving in to despair.

Lodovico, Montano, Cassio still in his stretcher, and Iago, prisoner, enter. When they bring Iago forth, Othello manages to stab him before they wrench his sword away. Iago taunts Othello, saying he is wounded but won't die. Lodovico remarks that he is sorry to have seen Othello fall so low and being manipulated by a villain like Iago. Othello apologizes to Cassio for scheming to have him killed, and asks to know why Iago hated Othello so much that he wanted to hurt him. Iago vows not to answer and says no more in the play. Gratiano says that Iago will be tortured for his crimes.

To provide Othello with the answers he seeks, Lodovico reveals that he found several letters on Roderigo's person. The letters make clear that Iago manipulated Roderigo into killing Cassio for his own purposes and that his scheming went back all the way to the beginning. Othello wants to know one more thing of Cassio - how he came to have Desdemona's handkerchief. Cassio says he found it in his room one day, which supports Emilia's story.

After hearing everything, Lodovico declares that Othello must step down as ruler of Cyprus and go to Venice for trial. Cassio will rule in Othello's place. Othello, knowing he is going to die, asks the men to speak of him without anger, and to describe him as "one who loved too much, and not wisely". He compares himself to a clueless Indian who throws a valuable pearl back into the river, not knowing what it is. After saying this, he stabs himself with a hidden weapon, falling upon Desdemona and kissing her one last time before he dies.

Cassio feared that Othello would try to kill himself, and is not surprised. Lodovico tells Iago that his torture will be terrifying. To Gratiano, Desdemona's uncle, he gives the Moor's possessions as his heir. Lodovico vows to tells what happened in Cyprus with a heavy heart.

The Life and Times of William Shakespeare

The Times Shakespeare Lived In

The Elizabethan London that William Shakespeare arrived in was much different than it is today. Significantly, the population was much smaller. Today, seven and a half million people live in the area known as Greater London. In Shakespeare's time the population was around 200,000 – this still made it an enormous metropolis for the time period and it was the leading city in Europe.

In the sixteenth century London suffered from an extremely high death rate – more people died in the city than were born. It was only the steady influx of newcomers from other English counties and immigrants from Europe that helped London's population grow. The bubonic plague was still a large factor in death counts in the city – in fact many people fled the urban area when the many epidemics rolled through. Shakespeare himself probably returned at times to Stratford when it was healthier to do so. The life expectancy in London at the time was thirty-five years; this seemingly short life expectancy would be lengthened if one survived childhood – many children did not make it to their fifth birthday.

London was a crowded and dirty place – it is not surprising that disease was rampant. The houses were built close together and the streets were very narrow – in many cases only wide enough for a single cart to navigate. There was no indoor plumbing and it would be another three hundred years before a sanitary way of disposing of sewage was built for the city of London.

Shakespeare was born into a time of religious upheaval. The Catholic Church came under pressure from the second Tudor ruler, Henry VIII, to annual his first marriage to Catherine of Aragon. Upon the death of his brother Arthur and Henry's ascendancy to the heir to the English throne, he had married his brother's widow in 1509. Over the years Catherine had given birth to only one surviving heir – a daughter Mary. Twenty-four years later, Henry asked for a divorce so he could marry the young Anne Boleyn. The Pope refused and in 1534 Henry broke from the Church, establishing the Church of England. The throne went to Henry's son Edward VI in 1547 but upon the boy's death in 1553, his half-sister Mary, daughter of Henry and Catherine, became Queen. She was a devout Catholic, and plunged the country back into a period of dissension and conflict, which included persecution and death for Protestants and the re-establishment of the Roman Catholic Church.

Queen Mary's death changed the religious *status quo* in England once again when Queen Elizabeth I came to the throne in 1558. The Catholic Church was once again banned, and the Church of England resurrected in its stead.

England also faced a turning point in its very political existence during Shakespeare's "lost years", those years before his arrival in London when his little is known about his life. In 1588, after Elizabeth I had condemned her cousin Mary, Queen of Scots, to death for conspiracy Spain decided to attack Britain in retaliation for the Roman Catholic Mary's death. The Catholic powers were increasingly fearful of the Protestant movement and with England's break from the Church of Rome now seemingly the final stroke in their relationship, it looked as though Catholicism itself was under threat. Spain rose of fleet of ships to sail upon England and it was thought to be unbeatable. However several factors led to English victory – strategic mistakes on the Spanish side and poor weather were among them. England emerged triumphant, its confidence strong, and the Church of England firmly entrenched. Queen Elizabeth I, known as "Gloriana" always serves as a backdrop to any story of Shakespeare's life. An interesting development during her reign was the acceleration of literacy in Elizabethan England – by the end of her reign, it stood at 33% (probably for males only) and was one of the highest rates in the world.

Queen Elizabeth's reign ended in 1603, when she died in her sleep at the age of sixty-nine. Her cousin's son, James I of Scotland became England's king. He was devoutly Protestant so there was no change in the official Church, and indeed by the beginning of the 17th century, few English citizens had ever attended a Catholic mass.

James enthusiastically supported drama and in particular, Shakespeare's company. Over the next thirteen years, before William's death, the playwright's company would perform for the King one hundred and eighty seven times. It was the time of Shakepeare's greatest dramatic output.

Much information on the London theatres of the day has been gleaned from the journal and business papers of Philip Henslowe, who owned the Rose and Fortune theatres. For his papers we can extrapolate what life for actors and playwrights would have been like during Shakespeare's time. We also know something of the Fortune Theatre's building – the contract to build it has survived. These records were used to build the copy of the Globe Theatre that stands on the banks of the Thames River today. Other information has come from existing diaries and letters that survived the time – mostly from visitors to the city who found the whole experience interesting enough to record.

Shakepeare's Family

William Shakespeare, the son of John Shakespeare and Mary, née Arden, was born in the village of Stratford-upon-Avon in the English county of Warwickshire. Stratford is northwest of London, situated somewhat south of England's center. Shakespeare was born quite possibly on 23 Apr in 1564 – his baptism in the family's parish church on April 26 suggests this. Children in that day and age were often baptized on the third day after their birth.

William was John and Mary's third known child – and the first to survive infancy. His two older sisters, Joan and Margaret, both died before he was born. Of the five younger children (Gilbert, a second Joan, Anne, Richard, and Edmund) Anne died at the age of eight but William's other siblings lived into adulthood. Only the second Joan was to reach what we would consider a good old age – she died in 1646 at the age of seventy-seven.

William's background on his paternal side was, like most of the English of his day, humble. Earlier relatives were not gentry in the least but simple tenant farmers who worked in the parish of nearby Arden. The meaning of the name Shakespeare has long been shrouded in mystery – the rarity of the surname indicates that it probably originated with one man several hundred years before William's birth. Evidence shows that the first Shakespeare was born somewhere north of Warwickshire. By 1389 an Adam Shakespeare was a tenant farmer at Baddesley Clinton in Warwickshire – unfortunately early parish records were not compelled to be kept until not long before William's time so it is not known for sure if he was a direct ancestor. In 1596 William's father John applied for a family coat of arms, citing that his grandfather had been granted land in northern Warwickshire for service under Henry VII in the War of the Roses. Historians believe this was probably a valid claim, but no records have come to light that prove it.

William was the grandson of Richard Shakespeare, a tenant farmer at Snitterfield in Arden who was not a wealthy man but did leave a will in which he named John Shakespeare as administrator, which would indicate he was the eldest surviving son. By the time of Richard's death in 1560, John had been living at nearby Stratford-upon-Avon since 1550. Records show that John had his first house in Henley Street in Stratford by 1552 and had acquired the house next door and one in Greenhill Street by 1556. John's trade was that of a glove-maker and he also worked as a wool dealer and an animal skin-cutter. He may have also worked as a butcher - it would seem that he was a man who was not afraid of work and had some ambition to better himself.

Around 1557 John Shakespeare married Mary Arden, the daughter of the owner of the Snitterfield estate where his father Richard Shakespeare farmed. Mary was the youngest of the eight daughters of Robert Arden – apparently Robert had a hand in marrying his daughters off and John must have seemed a likely prospect at the time – certainly on the social scale the Ardens would have been higher than the Shakespeares.

On his mother's side at least, William's roots in the area were deep. Just to the north of the River Avon is the village of Arden, from which Mary's family undoubtedly took their name. Surnames were beginning to be "set" about four hundred years before William's birth; it is probable that that branch of the family had been in the area for at least that long.

William's grandfather Robert Arden was a man of some means, at least locally. He owned several estates, including the one where Richard Shakespeare was a tenant farmer. The Ardens were Roman Catholic – England at the time was seesawing between the old Catholic Church and Protestantism. Although the marriage is not found in a surviving record, it is likely that it took place at Aston Cantlow where Mary's father had been buried in

1556 and the ceremony would have been a Catholic one, as Mary Tudor, who had brought Catholicism back to England as the official church, was on the throne. Not long before William's birth in 1564 Elizabeth I became Queen of England and the country made the final break with Roman Catholicism, and the local parish church became part of the new Church of England.

Shakespeare's Childhood and Education

William Shakespeare's accepted birth date of April 23, 1564 has long been open to dispute, but the month and year are probably correct. There are two reasons April 23rd is the sentimental favorite: it is St. George's Day in England (George is the country's patron saint) and Shakespeare died on the same date fifty-two years later. Baby William was baptized on the 26th of April in the parish church of Stratford-upon-Avon and as infants in Tudor times were traditionally baptized on the third day following their birth, historians have happily settled on the 23rd as his date of birth.

William was the third of eight known children born to John Shakespeare and Mary (Arden) Shakespeare, and the first to survive infancy. In fact young William's first year was overshadowed by the spectre of the Black Death, now known more prosaically as the bubonic plague. About 10% of the residents of Stratford died that year and the Shakespeares' must have felt relief their young family's survival. The plague was to continue to be a problem for England's citizens during the Elizabethan era. William was to lose his younger sister, eight-year-old Anne, to the disease. Quite possibly his older sister Margaret, a one-year-old baby, died of the Black Death as well, as it swept through the area in 1563. The survival of William, as the first born son, and after the deaths of older sisters Joan and Margaret, no doubt gave him a special place in the Shakespeare family.

William's childhood home, in Henley Street, Stratford, is still standing and is a typical Tudor structure with decorative half timber and small windows. In Shakespeare's time the house would have had a thatched roof. Henley Street led out of town and William apparently spent much time as a boy wandering and playing the countryside near at hand. He undoubtedly spoke the local dialect and though his own speech was probably more refined due to his education - and undoubtedly influenced by his mother, who came from a higher social stratum than the Shakespeares – William retained a good "ear" for dialectic speech which is evident in his plays and apparently retained his Warwickshire accent until his death.

William's life as a youngster was rural. His father was a craftsman and a tradesman – a glover and maker of leather goods – and records show that neighbors included a tailor and a haberdasher. But also nearby was a blacksmith – who's trade in those times would have been mostly horses – and shepherds lived nearby. As William rambled around the countryside he would have come into contact with the rural inhabitants of various occupations and he would have been well versed in the area's flora and fauna. It is very likely that he knew all the local fairy stories and tales of ghosts, witches, and hobgoblins, which England's rural denizens of the era were particularly fond of these stories. William's later writings show that he was well acquainted with the terms and practices of the rural pursuits of hunting and fishing – like most of his male contemporaries of the time, the young William probably spent many a happy hour engaged in these activities.

As the son of an alderman, William was entitled to a free education. His father John had become an alderman when William was just a baby – John was appointed to replace another alderman who got himself into trouble with the town council. By 1568 he was elected as an alderman and three years later was chief alderman and deputy to the local bailiff (the town's top magistrate). John was involved in local politics for many years, and although his fortunes and position faltered in later years, his son William was guaranteed the best education Stratford could offer.

William's learning took place at King's New School – which is still operating as a boy's school today. The school was originally granted a charter in 1553 by the learned young King Edward VI – a number of schools were erected in his name. It is thought the school was the last of the King Edward Schools as the adolescent Edward died only nine days after its charter was granted. It was familiarly known as the King's New School, and sometimes shortened even more to New School. Today it is known as King Edward VI School (or K.E.S.) and while no records exist from Shakespeare's time, it is generally accepted that William was a pupil and would have begun his education there around 1570 about the time he turned six years old.

The average school day for the middle class boys of Stratford was not an easy one. Students arrived early in the morning, not long after dawn, and remained in school until 5 PM. Breaks were given for meals. The boys also attended school on Saturdays. Church attendance was part of the school day, and much time was given over to the learning of the classical languages and translating classical texts. The Roman poet Ovid made a strong impression on young William. Classical mythology is evident in William's later works and no doubt their influence can be traced back to those formative days in Stratford's New School.

William probably left school around the age of fifteen. What he did then has not been documented but in the normal course of things, he would have worked for his father, at least for a time. He may have also been a school master – his facility with words and his sharp intellect would have made him a good candidate – but perhaps it was simply not his avocation and as time would prove, writing was. Within a few years, though, William was married. Marriage at eighteen in those days was relatively rare – physical maturation coming later to the young of that era compared to today. William, however, had been courting an older woman, and as nature took its course, Anne Hathaway became pregnant. Pregnant brides were common among the rural population – in fact many believed that fertility should be proven before heading for the altar! William Shakespeare and Anne Hathaway were married by license and as William was under twenty-one, he had to obtain his father's consent to marry. The actual parish where their wedding ceremony took place is not known, though it may have been in Shottery, Anne's home parish.

Shakepeare's Adulthood

By the time William Shakespeare was twenty-one years old, he had become the father of three children. His wife Anne gave birth to daughter Susanna in May 1583 and to twins Judith and Hamnet early in 1785. William does appear in an existing legal record for Stratford concerning property owned by his parents in 1786. Unfortunately very little else is on record for the years before he appears in London.

William most likely remained in Stratford for the first few years of his marriage and his knowledge of leather indicates that he probably worked with his glove-making father after he left school. The story that he had been a school master or tutor has long been conjectured. A story of William teaching in a more the Catholic-friendly county of Lancashire has been bandied about. None of the stories have any real evidence to back them up, however.

William and Anne lived in the house on Henley Street with his parents. It is hard to conceive that he would have deserted his wife and children when the latter were so young – William came from a comfortable solidly middle class family and he would have likely been taught to fulfill his responsibilities. Shakespeare may have spent his working career in London, and hints of philandering came forth, but he always remained faithful to Stratford and returned often and in middle age, he returned for good. How happy or unhappy he and Anne were together is simply not known. The fact that no children were born to Anne after the twins arrived may speak volumes – but it may also simply be that the birth of twins rendered her unable to have more children. That William did send home much of his acquired wealth in London does at least indicate that he had not entirely deserted his family responsibilities – but whether it was done out of love or duty, we do not have any way of knowing. The years between 1585 and 1592 are considered Shakespeare's "lost years". Simply put, there is no hard evidence of what William was doing during those years.

We also know little about William's wife Anne – she was one of seven children of Richard Hathaway, a yeoman farmer. She was left a small sum of money in his will when he died the year before her marriage and she was to come into this inheritance upon her marriage. The house she grew up in, known as Anne Hathaway's Cottage, is now open to the public, but is more than a mere cottage, having twelve rooms. It is about a mile from the center of Stratford. Anne's gravestone is still in existence as well, and from it her approximate date of birth is calculated – it records that she died in 1623, aged sixty-seven. No verified portraits of her exist and there is no known written description of what she looked like. Some Shakespearean experts believe that Sonnet 145 was written for Anne – the sonnet only really makes sense when the reader understands the wordplay with "hate" and "away" – close enough to mimic her surname, Hathaway.

What were William's influences before he arrived in London to make his way in the world of drama? Certainly he had enjoyed a classical education as a lad and some historians that theorized that he was somehow exposed to more in his late teens and twenties – even if only as a schoolmaster. As for the world of the stage, despite Shakespeare living in a somewhat isolated and rural area, it was quite common for bands of actors to be traveling the countryside plying their trade. These plague haunted years drove many people out of London and into the healthier countryside and actors had to make a living too. They were not above staging performances wherever they could gather enough people to pay the entrance fee. Actors were usually required to have a patron and many wore a badge that identified him as such – this kept the local authorities from looking upon actors as a liability to their parishes. The companies were often sponsored by men of means and even by the nobility. The first acting company created in the reign of Queen Elizabeth I (who came to the throne in 1558) was Lord Leicester's Men in

1574 – the Earls of Sussex and Oxford also had companies by 1582. There was rivalry between the companies and apparently, the Lord Mayor of London disliked the acting groups intensely. Unfortunately, few records for the acting companies have survived.

At least one acting company, The Queen's Men, put in more than one appearance at Stratford in 1589 – and if William was still living there, he very well could have attended their performances. Again, precisely why Shakespeare went to London is not known – but he may have simply been seduced by the theatre life and combined with his love of words it would have seemed the perfect home for him. Again, conjecture comes into deciding Shakespeare's life (one theory has it that William had clung to the old Catholic ways and went to northern England where there was more toleration) but his reasons for going to London remain a mystery. Fortunately for the literary world, he *was* drawn to the theatre and left a stunning literary legacy.

What did William do once he reached London? Again, we don't know for sure, as there are few employment records that have survived from centuries past. Shakespeare did appear in the London in the late 1580's and if he was immediately attracted to the theatre, he would have headed to Southwark, on the south side of the Thames, where many of the restrictions of the city of London did not apply. The entertainment industry of its day was free to do as they wanted there. A tradition has survived down through the centuries that William first got a job holding horses outside the theatre and then moved up to be a prompter's assistant. It is known that within a few years William was "becoming Shakespeare" and was writing.

With so many blanks to fill in his life and so very little solid evidence of Shakespeare's very existence at this point, how is it known that he was writing by 1592? It is thanks to one Robert Greene, another London writer. Greene published an attack on William, accusing him of plagiarism and calling him an "upstart crow". Greene parodied some lines from the history play *Henry VI Part III* and intimated that Shakespeare was stealing from his competition. Greene died soon after this, but the publisher of the attack apologized in print – which indicates that William, still a young man at twenty-eight, had enough of a reputation or at least enough gall, to demand a retraction.

If *Henry VI Part III* had already been written by 1592, there is a good chance that Parts I and II had already been penned as well. This accomplishment would have been remarkable for such a young man, and one who had not attended university as well. His lack of higher education seemed to be an issue with some of his contemporary writers – snobbism not being exclusive to the modern world. Fellow writers, who looked at Shakespeare critically and no doubt enviously, included Christopher Marlowe and Thomas Nashe.

Henry VI Part III was not William's first play. *The Two Gentlemen of Verona* was written sometime between 1588 and 1590. Although it is difficult to determine exactly when many of his early plays were written, it is thought that *A Comedy of Errors* might have been his first comedic play and could have been written as early as 1591. In 1594, Shakespeare created Titus Andronicus, his first attempt at tragedy.

There is nothing in the scant surviving records to suggest that William worked for a theatrical company during his early years in London. It is very likely he worked as a freelance writer, as many of contemporaries of the time did. Looking again at his private life, it is possible that during his early years he was returning home to Stratford at regular intervals.

It is thought that during his early years, he worked with other writers to produce collaborative works. *Sir Thomas More*, a historical play about the martyred Thomas More who was executed by Henry VIII, was co-written with Anthony Munday and Henry Chettle, the latter being the very publisher who retracted Robert Greene's accusation of plagiarism in 1592. Experts believe this was written during Shakespeare's early period.

It is known that it didn't take long for William's work to attract the interest of several different theatrical companies. *Titus Andronicus* was first performed by Sussex's Men. Pembroke's Men also performed several of William's plays and at least two known performance venues are on record – The Inns of Court and the Bankside Rose playhouse. Some Shakespearean historians believe that William had joined the Queen's Men on tour before he arrived in London – some of his later plays are similar to plays they performed in the mid 1580's.

The theatres of London were not a stable entity in the 1590's. Once again, the pall of the plague hung over the city in the summer of 1592. The Puritans, a Protestant faction that had gained some power in the Elizabethan era, despised what they saw as the licentiousness of theatre life and pressured the city to shut down acting venues in London and Southwark. They blamed the theatres for spreading the Plague. The theatres remained closed for two years.

Whether William remained in London for the duration of the Plague years is unknown, but it is known that he turned to writing poetry. In 1593 the rather racy poem *Venus and Adonis* appeared and was dedicated to Henry Wriothesley, the Earl of Southampton. The Earl was a patron of the arts – he supported several poets and often attended the theatre. Shakespeare may have looked upon him as opportunity knocking; after all, having a patron was easier that freelancing. It has been conjectured that Shakespeare's poems were written to Wriothesley as expressions of love and passion; many have conjectured that Shakespeare had homosexual or bisexual leanings. This could be or it might just be that Shakespeare saw an opportunity and wrote what Wriothesley wanted. Without solid evidence, it is impossible to know.

Shakespeare also dedicated the more serious and tragic poem *The Rape of Lucrece* to Wriothesley in 1594. It was about a Roman married woman who is raped by a Roman prince – she then commits suicide. The Rape of Lucrece was not quite as successful as Venus and Adonis but by now Shakespeare's reputation as a writer was established.

William returned to play writing once the Plague had died down again by the fall of 1594. A new theatrical company was formed by Lord Hunsdon (who was Queen Elizabeth's Lord Chamberlain), and called the Chamberlain's Men. Evidence has survived that indicate that Shakespeare was part of the company. Richard Burbage was also part of Chamberlain's Men – he became the company's star actor and would be the lead in many of the Shakespeare plays that they performed. Many of the actors who belonged to the company also had a financial stake in it.

The Chamberlain's Men did well from the start. They first performed for theatre-owner Philip Henslowe in 1594 and were on the bill at Court later that year over the Christmas season. The Chamberlain's Men main rival in London's theatre world was the Admiral's Men and between the two of them, they put on all theatrical performances in the city.

Lord Chamberlain's Men now had a base at the Shoreditch Theatre on the London side of the Thames River. This was an important factor for the rest of William's career – it now settled down to something of permanence. Shakespeare was an asset to the company – he brought in his body of work that could serve as part of the company's repertoire for years to come. William produced about two plays a year until he left London to live out his final days in Stratford.

The first Shakespeare play that was a success after the Plague years was *Richard III*, another history play that chronicled the downfall of the Plantagenet royal house and opened the door for the rise of the Tudor dynasty. No doubt this play was popularly supported by the monarch and her Court of the time. Three other well-regarded and often performed plays were thought to have been written during William's first years with the Chamberlain's Men

– *A Midsummer Night's Dream*, *Romeo and Juliet*, *Love's Labour Lost*, and *Richard II*. The variety of comedy, tragedy, and history plays reflect Shakespeare's talent and versatility. Around this time Shakespeare garnered high praise from a fellow writer Francis Meres. Meres made reference to William's sonnets, which were not actually published for another eleven years.

Tragedy struck the Shakespeare family in 1596 when William and Anne's only son Hamnet. In 1597 William, obviously enjoying some material success with his writing career, purchased a larger house in Stratford, New Place, the second largest estate in the parish. Shakespeare still spent much of his time in London but as the years went on, he returned to Stratford more and more. The playwright was not only a creative type – he had a keen business sense, as well, or possibly good advisors. He invested in property, and by 1599 he was part owner of the Globe Theatre, forever afterward associated with Shakespeare.

After the Globe Theatre was built in 1599 Shakespeare became a prominent member of the King's Men – the company was sponsored by the King himself, James I, when he ascended the throne in 1603. The company was commanded to produce and perform plays "for our (the King's) solace and pleasure". Shakespeare produced a great body of work over the next ten years. The Globe burned down during a performance of Henry VIII (a fired canon caused the thatched roof to catch fire). No one was killed, and the Globe was rebuilt soon after. At about this time, after investing in the new theatre, Shakespeare retired to spend most of his time in Stratford. He died at New Place on his 52nd birthday. He was survived by his wife, two daughters, two sons-in-law, and a grandchild. His wife Anne outlived him, dying in 1623. One of the few official documentation of Shakepeare's to have survived is his will – in which he left his wife "his second-best bed" (by law, she would have also inherited one-third of his estate). William and Anne were survived by their two daughters, both married and who would leave descendants.

Modern Version of the Play

Characters

DUKE OF VENICE

BRABANTIO, a Senator.

Other Senators.

GRATIANO, Brother to Brabantio

LODOVICO, Kinsman to Brabantio

OTHELLO, a noble Moor, in the service of Venice

CASSIO, his Lieutenant

IAGO, his Ancient

RODERIGO, a Venetian Gentleman

MONTANO, Othello's predecessor in the government of Cyprus

CLOWN, Servant to Othello

Herald

DESDEMONA, Daughter to Brabantio, and Wife to Othello

EMILIA, Wife to Iago

BIANCA, Mistress to Cassio

Officers, Gentlemen, Messenger, Musicians, Herald, Sailor, Attendants, &c.

Act I

Scene I. Venice. A street.

Enter RODERIGO and IAGO

RODERIGO

Tush! never tell me; I take it much unkindly

Be quiet! Don't tell me this – I am already annoyed

That thou, Iago, who hast had my purse

That you, Iago, who already uses my money

As if the strings were thine, shouldst know of this.

As if it were yours, knows about this.

IAGO

'Sblood, but you will not hear me:

My god, you won't listen to me.

If ever I did dream of such a matter, Abhor me.

If I even so much as dreamed this were true, which I didn't, then go ahead and hate me.

RODERIGO

Thou told'st me thou didst hold him in thy hate.

You told me that you hated him.

IAGO

Despise me, if I do not. Three great ones of the city,

You can hate me if I was lying: I do hate him. Three of the city's noblemen

In personal suit to make me his lieutenant,

Approached him personally and asked him to make me his next-in-command,

Off-capp'd to him: and, by the faith of man,

Even took their hats off to him. Moreover, I promise you,

I know my price, I am worth no worse a place:

I know my own value and that I deserve that position.

But he; as loving his own pride and purposes,

But he, because he is prideful and loves his own reasons most,

Evades them, with a bombast circumstance

Avoided their request with puffed up speech

Horribly stuff'd with epithets of war;

Full of military jargon and patriotic quotes,

And, in conclusion,

And, finally,

Nonsuits my mediators; for, 'Certes,' says he,

Rejected the noblemen, saying, "In fact,

'I have already chose my officer.'

I have already chosen my lieutenant."

And what was he?

Who did he choose?

Forsooth, a great arithmetician,

None other than the great statistician

One Michael Cassio, a Florentine,

Michael Cassio, from Florence,

A fellow almost damn'd in a fair wife;

A man almost cursed with such a beautiful wife,

That never set a squadron in the field,

A man who never moved troops in combat

Nor the division of a battle knows

And knows less of how an actual battle plays out

More than a spinster; unless the bookish theoric,

Than an unmarried woman – unless you count theories he read in books

Wherein the toged consuls can propose

That any gown-wearing politician can explain

As masterly as he: mere prattle, without practise,

As well as he can. He speaks simply to speak, and has no actual fighting

Is all his soldiership. But he, sir, had the election:

To back up his military life. But it is he, Roderigo, who was chosen:

And I, of whom his eyes had seen the proof

And as for me, whose bravery and talent he saw

At Rhodes, at Cyprus and on other grounds

At Rhodes and Cyprus and all over,

Christian and heathen, must be be-lee'd and calm'd

On Christian ground and foreign land, I must act calm

By debitor and creditor: this counter-caster,

In front of this accountant. So Cassio, this numbers-man,

He, in good time, must his lieutenant be,

Will become his lieutenant,

And I--God bless the mark!--his Moorship's ancient.

While I – how stupid – must hold the flag for the Moor general.

RODERIGO

By heaven, I rather would have been his hangman.

I swear, I would rather be his executioner.

IAGO

Why, there's no remedy; 'tis the curse of service,

And there is no cure for it all. It's the curse of the military life:

Preferment goes by letter and affection,

Promotions come from how liked one is,

And not by old gradation, where each second

And not from simple hierarchy where one

Stood heir to the first. Now, sir, be judge yourself,

Moves up to the next rank. Now, Roderigo, you tell me

Whether I in any just term am affined

If I am in any position

To love the Moor.

To love and respect the Moor general.

RODERIGO

I would not follow him then.

If it were me, I would not serve him.

IAGO

O, sir, content you;

Now don't be hasty:

I follow him to serve my turn upon him:

I serve under him now, but for my own purposes –

We cannot all be masters, nor all masters

After all, we cannot all be leaders, and leaders

57

Cannot be truly follow'd. You shall mark

Cannot all be followed. Take note

Many a duteous and knee-crooking knave,

Of the servant who bows and does his duty,

That, doting on his own obsequious bondage,

Who fully attend to their obedience, their slavery,

Wears out his time, much like his master's ass,

And in the end is worn out like his master's donkey,

For nought but provender, and when he's old, cashier'd:

Both working for nothing but their food, and then terminated when too old.

Whip me such honest knaves. Others there are

We should punish such obedient servants. But there are others

Who, trimm'd in forms and visages of duty,

Who know how to give the appearance of obedience

Keep yet their hearts attending on themselves,

While focusing on themselves.

And, throwing but shows of service on their lords,

They give a performance of doing their duty to their masters

Do well thrive by them and when they have lined their coats

And in reality prosper by quietly stealing

Do themselves homage: these fellows have some soul;

And thus working for themselves. Servants like this are gutsy and bold,

And such a one do I profess myself. For, sir,

And I admit I am one like that. To be sure,

It is as sure as you are Roderigo,

As sure as your name is Roderigo,

Were I the Moor, I would not be Iago:

If I were in the Moor's position, I would not want to switch places with Iago.

In following him, I follow but myself;

By serving him, I am really serving myself –

Heaven is my judge, not I for love and duty,

God knows I do not serve him for love or duty,

But seeming so, for my peculiar end:

But just make it look like that while serving my own goals.

For when my outward action doth demonstrate

If I ever act in such a way

The native act and figure of my heart

That shows my inner self

In compliment extern, 'tis not long after

Then before long I would be in danger:

But I will wear my heart upon my sleeve

One who wears his heart on his sleeve

For daws to peck at: I am not what I am.

Leaves it open for birds to peck at it. I am not who I appear to be.

RODERIGO

What a full fortune does the thicklips owe

That thick-lipped Moor is lucky

If he can carry't thus!

If he can go through with this!

IAGO

Call up her father,

Speaking of which, call after her father

Rouse him: make after him, poison his delight,

And wake him. Annoy him, spoil his happiness,

Proclaim him in the streets; incense her kinsmen,

Shout at him in the streets, anger his and his daughter's family

And, though he in a fertile climate dwell,

Until it seems like, though he lives in a temperate climate,

Plague him with flies: though that his joy be joy,

He is plagued with flies. Though his joy may be real,

Yet throw such changes of vexation on't,

If it changes because of the confusions we put on it,

As it may lose some colour.

It may lose some of its brightness.

RODERIGO

Here is her father's house; I'll call aloud.

Here is her father's house; I'll call for him.

IAGO

Do, with like timorous accent and dire yell

Do it as if you are frightened and yell

As when, by night and negligence, the fire

As if a fire started from negligence at night

Is spied in populous cities.

Has been spotted in a city full of people.

RODERIGO

What, ho, Brabantio! Signior Brabantio, ho!

Brabantio! Mister Brabantio, hey!

IAGO

Awake! what, ho, Brabantio! thieves! thieves! thieves!

Wake up, Brabantio! Thieves are in your house!

Look to your house, your daughter and your bags!

Look around you and protect your daughter and your possessions!

Thieves! thieves!

Thieves! Thieves!

BRABANTIO *appears above, at a window*

BRABANTIO

What is the reason of this terrible summons?

Why are you shouting all of this?

What is the matter there?

What is the matter?

RODERIGO

Signior, is all your family within?

Sir, if your family at home?

IAGO

Are your doors lock'd?

61

And have you locked your doors?

BRABANTIO

Why, wherefore ask you this?

Why? Tell me why you are asking.

IAGO

'Zounds, sir, you're robb'd; for shame, put on your gown;

For God's sake, sir, you have been robbed! Put your nightgown on.

Your heart is burst, you have lost half your soul;

Your heart is broken and you have lost a part of your soul

Even now, now, very now, an old black ram

For now, right now, a black ram

Is topping your white ewe. Arise, arise;

Is riding your white female sheep. Get up, get up;

Awake the snorting citizens with the bell,

Wake up the sleeping people with the bell

Or else the devil will make a grandsire of you:

Or it will be too late and the devil will give you grandchildren.

Arise, I say.

Get up, I say.

BRABANTIO

What, have you lost your wits?

Have you gone crazy?

RODERIGO

Most reverend signior, do you know my voice?

My respected sir, do you recognize my voice?

BRABANTIO

Not I what are you?

No, who are you?

RODERIGO

My name is Roderigo.

I am Roderigo.

BRABANTIO

The worser welcome:

Even worse:

I have charged thee not to haunt about my doors:

I have asked you not to come near my house

In honest plainness thou hast heard me say

And very honestly told you

My daughter is not for thee; and now, in madness,

That my daughter is not for you. Now, as if you are crazy,

Being full of supper and distempering draughts,

After dinner and likely drunk

Upon malicious bravery, dost thou come

With the evil courage a drunkard has, you come here

To start my quiet.

And disturb me.

RODERIGO

Sir, sir, sir,--

Sir, sir, sir—

BRABANTIO

But thou must needs be sure

Let me be clear:

My spirit and my place have in them power

I have the desire and the connections that can

To make this bitter to thee.

Make this turn out very poorly for you.

RODERIGO

Patience, good sir.

Please wait, good sir.

BRABANTIO

What tell'st thou me of robbing? this is Venice;

Why are you telling me my house is being robbed? This is Venice –

My house is not a grange.

I do not live out in the country.

RODERIGO

Most grave Brabantio,

Respectable Brabantio,

In simple and pure soul I come to you.

I have come with pure intentions and a simple message.

IAGO

'Zounds, sir, you are one of those that will not

For God's sake, sir, you are so stubborn that you will not

serve God, if the devil bid you. Because we come to

turn to God if even the devil asks you to. We come

do you service and you think we are ruffians, you'll

for your benefit and yet you think we are troublemakers;

have your daughter covered with a Barbary horse;

so instead of listening, an African horse will mount your daughter.

you'll have your nephews neigh to you; you'll have

Your nephews will neigh at you, you will have

coursers for cousins and gennets for germans.

racing horses for cousins, and all of your close relatives will become horses.

BRABANTIO

What profane wretch art thou?

Who are you, you rude pervert?

IAGO

I am one, sir, that comes to tell you your daughter

I am someone, sir, who has come to you to tell you that your daughter

and the Moor are now making the beast with two backs.

and the Moor general are having sex, like animals.

BRABANTIO

Thou art a villain.

You are an evil person.

IAGO

You are--a senator.

And you are a senator and statesman.

BRABANTIO

This thou shalt answer; I know thee, Roderigo.

Since I know you, Roderigo, you must respond to this.

RODERIGO

Sir, I will answer any thing. But, I beseech you,

Sir, I will tell you anything. But, please,

If't be your pleasure and most wise consent,

If you are pleased and contented with this arrangement,

As partly I find it is, that your fair daughter,

As I think you might be, that your beautiful daughter

At this odd-even and dull watch o' the night,

At this late hour of the night,

Transported, with no worse nor better guard

Has left with no regular guard

But with a knave of common hire, a gondolier,

But with just hired commoner, a boatman,

To the gross clasps of a lascivious Moor--

To the disgusting embrace of the lustful Moor –

If this be known to you and your allowance,

If you already know this and are allowing it

We then have done you bold and saucy wrongs;

Then we have done you a very great evil in coming here.

But if you know not this, my manners tell me

But if you do not know this, I think

We have your wrong rebuke. Do not believe

You are wrongly accusing us. You should not think

That, from the sense of all civility,

That, opposite of any sort of politeness,

I thus would play and trifle with your reverence:

I would disturb you and mess with you.

Your daughter, if you have not given her leave,

Your daughter, if you have not allowed her to leave,

I say again, hath made a gross revolt;

I will repeat, has disgustingly rebelled against you

Tying her duty, beauty, wit and fortunes

By giving her respect, beauty, intelligence, and wealth

In an extravagant and wheeling stranger

To an extravagant and tricky man who is a stranger

Of here and every where. Straight satisfy yourself:

Here and everywhere. Now see for yourself:

If she be in her chamber or your house,

67

If she is still in her room or in your house,

Let loose on me the justice of the state

Then punish me as the state allows

For thus deluding you.

For tricking you.

BRABANTIO

Strike on the tinder, ho!

Someone light a match!

Give me a taper! call up all my people!

Give me a candle! Wake my servants!

This accident is not unlike my dream:

What you have told me is similar to a dream I have had –

Belief of it oppresses me already.

Believing it as possible already haunts me.

Light, I say! light!

Give me a light, I say! A light!

Exit above

IAGO

Farewell; for I must leave you:

Goodbye, I must go

It seems not meet, nor wholesome to my place,

Since it is not good, or right since I serve him,

To be produced--as, if I stay, I shall--

To be seen – which I will if I stay here –

Against the Moor: for, I do know, the state,

As against the Moor. Especially because I know that the senator,

However this may gall him with some cheque,

However this may offend and upset him,

Cannot with safety cast him, for he's embark'd

Cannot easily get rid of him, since the Moor is leaving

With such loud reason to the Cyprus wars,

With clear and understood reason to Cyprus for the wars.

Which even now stand in act, that, for their souls,

Even now these wars are raging and the statesmen

Another of his fathom they have none,

Do not have another general like him

To lead their business: in which regard,

To lead their war efforts. I admit this

Though I do hate him as I do hell-pains.

Even though I hate him as I would the fires of hell.

Yet, for necessity of present life,

So it is necessary for now

I must show out a flag and sign of love,

That I carry his flag and act like I love him,

Which is indeed but sign. That you shall surely find him,

Which as I said is only an act. So that you definitely find him tonight,

Lead to the Sagittary the raised search;

Take the search party to the Arsenal

And there will I be with him. So, farewell.

And I will already be there with him. Goodbye.

Exit

Enter, below, BRABANTIO, and Servants with torches

BRABANTIO

It is too true an evil: gone she is;

And what's to come of my despised time

Is nought but bitterness. Now, Roderigo,

Where didst thou see her? O unhappy girl!

With the Moor, say'st thou? Who would be a father!

How didst thou know 'twas she? O she deceives me

Past thought! What said she to you? Get more tapers:

Raise all my kindred. Are they married, think you?

RODERIGO

Truly, I think they are.

Truly, I think they are.

BRABANTIO

O heaven! How got she out? O treason of the blood!

Fathers, from hence trust not your daughters' minds

By what you see them act. Is there not charms

By which the property of youth and maidhood

May be abused? Have you not read, Roderigo,

Of some such thing?

RODERIGO

Yes, sir, I have indeed.

BRABANTIO

Call up my brother. O, would you had had her!

Call for my brother. Oh, now I wish you married her!

Some one way, some another. Do you know

Some go one way, some go another. Do you know

Where we may apprehend her and the Moor?

Where we will find her and the Moor?

RODERIGO

I think I can discover him, if you please,

I think I know where he is. Please,

To get good guard and go along with me.

Get a good party of your guards and come with me.

BRABANTIO

Pray you, lead on. At every house I'll call;

I beg you to lead us. I will call at every house –

I may command at most. Get weapons, ho!

I can at least command men to join. Hey, arm yourselves!

And raise some special officers of night.

And XXX

On, good Roderigo: I'll deserve your pains.

Go forward, good Roderigo. You will be rewarded for your hard work.

Exeunt

Scene II. Another street.

Enter OTHELLO, IAGO, and Attendants with torches

IAGO

Though in the trade of war I have slain men,

Though I have killed men in war,

Yet do I hold it very stuff o' the conscience

I think it is the makeup of a good character

To do no contrived murder: I lack iniquity

To not commit murder. I lack the evil

Sometimes to do me service: nine or ten times

That would sometimes help me. Nine or ten times

I had thought to have yerk'd him here under the ribs.

I thought to simply stab him through his ribs.

OTHELLO

'Tis better as it is.

It is better that you didn't.

IAGO

Nay, but he prated,

No, he swore

And spoke such scurvy and provoking terms

And said such nasty and offensive things

Against your honour

Against you

That, with the little godliness I have,

That, with all the patience I could muster,

I did full hard forbear him. But, I pray you, sir,

I listened to him say. But, I must ask, sir,

Are you fast married? Be assured of this,

Are you securely married? Because you should know

That the magnifico is much beloved,

That Brabantio is very respected and loved –

And hath in his effect a voice potential

He has a voice worth potentially

As double as the duke's: he will divorce you;

Twice the duke's. He will force you to divorce

Or put upon you what restraint and grievance

Or will try to punish you according to

The law, with all his might to enforce it on,

The law, with all his strength,

Will give him cable.

As much as the law allows.

OTHELLO

Let him do his spite:

He can do his worst:

My services which I have done the signiory

All that I have done for the government

Shall out-tongue his complaints. 'Tis yet to know,--

Will outweigh his complaints against me. This is not known about me –

Which, when I know that boasting is an honour,

If it is ever honorable to boast

I shall promulgate--I fetch my life and being

Then I will let it known widely – but my life

From men of royal siege, and my demerits

Comes from a royal line, and my worth

May speak unbonneted to as proud a fortune

Can show that I have as great a wealth and position

As this that I have reach'd: for know, Iago,

As the woman I've married. And know this, Iago:

But that I love the gentle Desdemona,

Unless I loved Desdemona,

I would not my unhoused free condition

I would never have ruined my bachelorhood and freedom

Put into circumscription and confine

By adding the fence of marriage –

For the sea's worth. But, look! what lights come yond?

Not for an ocean's amount of money. But wait, what are those lights?

IAGO

Those are the raised father and his friends:

Those belong to the angry father and his friends.

You were best go in.

You should go inside and out of sight.

OTHELLO

Not I, I must be found:

No, I will let them come to me.

My parts, my title and my perfect soul

My qualities, my rank, and my lack of wrongdoing

Shall manifest me rightly. Is it they?

Will prove me in the right. Is that them?

IAGO

By Janus, I think no.

Actually no, I don't think so.

Enter CASSIO, and certain Officers with torches

OTHELLO

The servants of the duke, and my lieutenant.

It is the duke's servants and my new lieutenant, Cassio.

The goodness of the night upon you, friends!

I hope you are well, friends!

What is the news?

Why do you come?

CASSIO

The duke does greet you, general,

The duke has sent us to greet you, general,

And he requires your haste-post-haste appearance,

And he requests your presence right away,

Even on the instant.

Immediately.

OTHELLO

What is the matter, think you?

Do you know what the matter is?

CASSIO

Something from Cyprus as I may divine:

I think it is something about Cyprus,

It is a business of some heat: the galleys

And it seems to be important. The warships

Have sent a dozen sequent messengers

Have sent a dozen messengers

This very night at one another's heels,

Tonight, one after another,

And many of the consuls, raised and met,

And many of the statesmen have woken and are here

Are at the duke's already: you have been hotly call'd for;

With the duke. You were quickly asked for

When, being not at your lodging to be found,

And when you were not at found at your home,

The senate hath sent about three several guests

Three different groups were sent

To search you out.

To find you.

OTHELLO

'Tis well I am found by you.

It's good you are the one who found me.

I will but spend a word here in the house,

I have to spend a minute here in this house,

And go with you.

And then will go with you.

Exit

CASSIO

Ancient, what makes he here?

Officer, what business does he have here?

IAGO

'Faith, he to-night hath boarded a land carack:

Truly, tonight he has boarded a large ship full of treasure,

If it prove lawful prize, he's made for ever.

And as long as it is and remains legal, he will be a made man forever.

CASSIO

I do not understand.

What are you talking about?

IAGO

He's married.

He's married.

CASSIO

To who?

To who?

Re-enter OTHELLO

IAGO

Marry, to--Come, captain, will you go?

Why, to – My captain, shall we go?

OTHELLO

Have with you.

Yes, let's go.

CASSIO

Here comes another troop to seek for you.

Here comes another group looking for you.

IAGO

It is Brabantio. General, be advised;

It is Brabantio. Be careful, general,

He comes to bad intent.

Because he intends you harm.

Enter BRABANTIO, RODERIGO, and Officers with torches and weapons

OTHELLO

Holla! stand there!

Hello, stay there!

RODERIGO

Signior, it is the Moor.

Sir, it is the Moor.

BRABANTIO

Down with him, thief!

Get that thief!

They draw on both sides

IAGO

You, Roderigo! come, sir, I am for you.

Roderigo, come towards me, I'll fight you.

OTHELLO

Keep up your bright swords, for the dew will rust them.

Keep your swords in their sheaths so the dew does not rust them.

Good signior, you shall more command with years

Good sir, the years you have served the government will make me respect you

Than with your weapons.

More than fighting you will.

BRABANTIO

O thou foul thief, where hast thou stow'd my daughter?

O you evil thief, where have you hidden my daughter?

Damn'd as thou art, thou hast enchanted her;

Since you are a damned soul, I know you put a spell on her.

For I'll refer me to all things of sense,

All good and common sense says that,

If she in chains of magic were not bound,

Unless she were enchanted through magic,

Whether a maid so tender, fair and happy,

A woman so gentle, beautiful, and happy,

So opposite to marriage that she shunned

A woman who was against marriage so much that she turned away

The wealthy curled darlings of our nation,

The wealthy noblemen of our nation,

Would ever have, to incur a general mock,

This woman would never do something others would see fit to make jokes at

Run from her guardage to the sooty bosom

Like run from her home to your black breast.

Of such a thing as thou, to fear, not to delight.

Someone like you should be feared, not enjoyed.

Judge me the world, if 'tis not gross in sense

The whole world may judge me if it's not obvious

That thou hast practised on her with foul charms,

That you have practiced evil magic on her

Abused her delicate youth with drugs or minerals

And taken advantage of her naive youth through drugs

That weaken motion: I'll have't disputed on;

That make one unable to move. I would go to court over the matter;

'Tis probable and palpable to thinking.

It's what most likely happened.

I therefore apprehend and do attach thee

Therefore, I will take you and see that you are tried

For an abuser of the world, a practiser

As a criminal, a practicer

Of arts inhibited and out of warrant.

Of dark magic.

Lay hold upon him: if he do resist,

Take him: if he resists arrest

Subdue him at his peril.

Then forcefully hold him down.

OTHELLO

Hold your hands,

Do not touch me,

Both you of my inclining, and the rest:

Neither you on my side or the rest of you.

Were it my cue to fight, I should have known it

If it were necessary to fight, I would not

Without a prompter. Where will you that I go

82

Need someone to tell me. Where do you want me to go

To answer this your charge?

In order to respond to your accusations?

BRABANTIO

To prison, till fit time

To prison until the time

Of law and course of direct session

That the law sees fit to take you to court

Call thee to answer.

And ask you to testify.

OTHELLO

What if I do obey?

And if I obey,

How may the duke be therewith satisfied,

Then how will the duke react,

Whose messengers are here about my side,

Since he sent these messengers

Upon some present business of the state

On urgent, national business

To bring me to him?

To bring me to him?

First Officer

'Tis true, most worthy signior;

It's true, worthy sir:

The duke's in council and your noble self,

The duke has called a meeting and you, too,

I am sure, is sent for.

I am sure, are asked to attend.

BRABANTIO

How! the duke in council!

What? The duke has called a meeting!

In this time of the night! Bring him away:

This late at night! Take him away.

Mine's not an idle cause: the duke himself,

This is not some simple affair: the duke himself

Or any of my brothers of the state,

And all of the other senators

Cannot but feel this wrong as 'twere their own;

Will feel how wrong this is, as if it happened to them.

For if such actions may have passage free,

If actions like this go unpunished,

Bond-slaves and pagans shall our statesmen be.

Then slaves and pagans will become our rulers.

Exeunt

Scene III. A council-chamber.

The DUKE and Senators sitting at a table; Officers attending

DUKE OF VENICE

There is no composition in these news

Nothing about these messages

That gives them credit.

Makes me think that they are credible.

First Senator

Indeed, they are disproportion'd;

Yes, they give conflicting reports.

My letters say a hundred and seven galleys.

My letters say there are a hundred and seven warships.

DUKE OF VENICE

And mine, a hundred and forty.

And mine says a hundred and forty.

Second Senator

And mine, two hundred:

Mind says two hundred.

But though they jump not on a just account,--

But though they give conflicting numbers –

As in these cases, where the aim reports,

Since it is often when one is reporting an estimate

'Tis oft with difference--yet do they all confirm

For there to be different numbers – they all report

A Turkish fleet, and bearing up to Cyprus.

That a Turkish fleet is moving to Cyprus.

DUKE OF VENICE

Nay, it is possible enough to judgment:

Right, that seems well confirmed.

I do not so secure me in the error,

I am not so taken by the inconsistency

But the main article I do approve

That I miss the bigger issue, which

In fearful sense.

Frightens me.

Sailor

[Within] What, ho! what, ho! what, ho!

Hello! Hello!

First Officer

A messenger from the galleys.

Another messenger from the warships.

Enter a Sailor

DUKE OF VENICE

Now, what's the business?

86

What have you come to tell us?

Sailor

The Turkish preparation makes for Rhodes;

The Turkish fleet is heading to Rhodes, not Cyprus –

So was I bid report here to the state

This was what I was ordered to report to the government

By Signior Angelo.

By Sir Angelo.

DUKE OF VENICE

How say you by this change?

What do you make of this change?

First Senator

This cannot be,

This cannot be true

By no assay of reason: 'tis a pageant,

By any argument. It's a show

To keep us in false gaze. When we consider

To distract us. We must remember

The importancy of Cyprus to the Turk,

The importance of Cyprus to the Turks.

And let ourselves again but understand,

This will force us to recognize

That as it more concerns the Turk than Rhodes,

That it is more important than Rhodes –

So may he with more facile question bear it,

Especially because the Turks can more easily take it

For that it stands not in such warlike brace,

Since it is not equipped with defenses

But altogether lacks the abilities

And lacks the preparations and forces

That Rhodes is dress'd in: if we make thought of this,

That Rhodes has. These things considered,

We must not think the Turk is so unskilful

We must not think that the Turks are so incompetent

To leave that latest which concerns him first,

That they would put off what they should do first,

Neglecting an attempt of ease and gain,

That they would not take a place so easily taken as Cyprus

To wake and wage a danger profitless.

And instead would attack a dangerous place like Rhodes.

DUKE OF VENICE

Nay, in all confidence, he's not for Rhodes.

I agree, the Turks are certainly not heading to Rhodes.

First Officer

Here is more news.

Another messenger is coming.

Enter a Messenger

Messenger

The Ottomites, reverend and gracious,

The Turks, my revered and gracious leader,

Steering with due course towards the isle of Rhodes,

Went to the island of Rhodes

Have there injointed them with an after fleet.

Where they have joined with another fleet.

First Senator

Ay, so I thought. How many, as you guess?

I thought so. How many ships, do you think?

Messenger

Of thirty sail: and now they do restem

Thirty ships, and now they are turning around

Their backward course, bearing with frank appearance

To their original course and clearly seem to

Their purposes toward Cyprus. Signior Montano,

Be heading to Cyprus. Sir Montano,

Your trusty and most valiant servitor,

Your trustworthy and brave servant,

With his free duty recommends you thus,

Sent me to give you this report and asks for reinforcements,

And prays you to believe him.

And asks you to believe him.

DUKE OF VENICE

'Tis certain, then, for Cyprus.

That settles it: the Turks are going to Cyprus.

Marcus Luccicos, is not he in town?

Is Marcus Luccicos here in town?

First Senator

He's now in Florence.

No, he's in Florence.

DUKE OF VENICE

Write from us to him; post-post-haste dispatch.

Write to him and send it immediately, as fast as possible.

First Senator

Here comes Brabantio and the valiant Moor.

Here comes Brabantio and Othello, the courageous Moor.

Enter BRABANTIO, OTHELLO, IAGO, RODERIGO, and Officers

DUKE OF VENICE

Valiant Othello, we must straight employ you

Brave Othello, we must order you to go

Against the general enemy Ottoman.

Against the Turkish enemy.

To BRABANTIO

I did not see you; welcome, gentle signior;

I did not see you there – welcome, good sir.

We lack'd your counsel and your help tonight.

We have lacked your insight and help tonight.

BRABANTIO

So did I yours. Good your grace, pardon me;

And I lacked yours. Please, your grace, forgive me:

Neither my place nor aught I heard of business

It was not from hearing of this war business

Hath raised me from my bed, nor doth the general care

That made me get out of bed, nor was it general worry over the city

Take hold on me, for my particular grief

That woke me. My personal grief

Is of so flood-gate and o'erbearing nature

Is so overbearing, like a flood,

That it engluts and swallows other sorrows

That it overtakes and swallows all other sorrows and concerns

And it is still itself.

Without being satisfied.

DUKE OF VENICE

Why, what's the matter?

What has happened?

BRABANTIO

My daughter! O, my daughter!

My daughter! O, my daughter!

ALL

Dead?

Dead?

BRABANTIO

Ay, to me;

Yes, she is dead to me at least.

She is abused, stol'n from me, and corrupted

She has been abused, stolen from me, and corrupted

By spells and medicines bought of mountebanks;

By black magic and drugs given to her by deceivers.

For nature so preposterously to err,

Nature itself could not have made such a preposterous mistake,

Being not deficient, blind, or lame of sense,

Since she is not mentally ill, or blind, or paralyzed,

Sans witchcraft could not.

So it must be the fault of witchcraft.

DUKE OF VENICE

Whoe'er he be that in this foul proceeding

Whoever the criminal is

Hath thus beguiled your daughter of herself

Who has tricked your daughter

And you of her, the bloody book of law

And taken her from you, you will use the full, deadly laws

You shall yourself read in the bitter letter

To prosecute him in its harsh solutions

After your own sense, yea, though our proper son

As you see fit – even if it were my own son

Stood in your action.

Who did what you have said.

BRABANTIO

Humbly I thank your grace.

I humbly thank you, your grace.

Here is the man, this Moor, whom now, it seems,

Here is the criminal: this Moor, who, it seems,

Your special mandate for the state-affairs

Your national interest problems

Hath hither brought.

Have brought here.

ALL

We are very sorry for't.

We are sorry to hear this.

DUKE OF VENICE

[To OTHELLO] What, in your own part, can you say to this?

How do you respond to this, Othello?

BRABANTIO

Nothing, but this is so.

He can say nothing, it is true.

OTHELLO

Most potent, grave, and reverend signiors,

Powerful, serious, and revered sirs,

My very noble and approved good masters,

My noble and good masters,

That I have ta'en away this old man's daughter,

That I have taken this old man's daughter from him

It is most true; true, I have married her:

Is true: I have married her.

The very head and front of my offending

The offenses Brabantio mentioned

Hath this extent, no more. Rude am I in my speech,

Are true only in this. I am not a skilled speaker

And little bless'd with the soft phrase of peace:

And do not know how to talk peacefully and smoothly:

For since these arms of mine had seven years' pith,

Since I was seven years old, and these arms had seven years of muscle,

Till now some nine moons wasted, they have used

Until nine months ago, I have used these arms

Their dearest action in the tented field,

For action in the battlefield.

And little of this great world can I speak,

I can't say much about this great world

More than pertains to feats of broil and battle,

Unless it is about war and battle,

And therefore little shall I grace my cause

And therefore I will only say a little

In speaking for myself. Yet, by your gracious patience,

In speaking for my defense. But, by your patience, gracious Duke,

I will a round unvarnish'd tale deliver

I will tell you straightforwardly the story

Of my whole course of love; what drugs, what charms,

Of how we fell in love – including the drugs, magic charms,

What conjuration and what mighty magic,

Spells, and darks arts,

For such proceeding I am charged withal,

Since that is what I am charged of using,

I won his daughter.

I used to win his daughter.

BRABANTIO

A maiden never bold;

She was never bold,

Of spirit so still and quiet, that her motion

But always calm and quiet, so pure that

Blush'd at herself; and she, in spite of nature,

She would blush at herself. And you are saying that she, against nature,

Of years, of country, credit, every thing,

Against difference in age, and country, and upbringing, against everything,

To fall in love with what she fear'd to look on!

Would fall in love with who she was afraid to look at!

It is a judgment maim'd and most imperfect

Only a poor and imperfect judgment

That will confess perfection so could err

Could argue that a perfect person could do something so wrong

Against all rules of nature, and must be driven

Against all rules of nature – one must be forced

To find out practises of cunning hell,

To think that it is hell itself and the tricks of the devil

Why this should be. I therefore vouch again

That would make this happen. Therefore, I again hold

That with some mixtures powerful o'er the blood,

That some sort of powerful drug to change her desires

Or with some dram conjured to this effect,

Or magical spell

He wrought upon her.

Has been given to her by him.

DUKE OF VENICE

To vouch this, is no proof,

To hold to this is not proof —

Without more wider and more overt test

One needs clear evidence, more

Than these thin habits and poor likelihoods

Than the customs and poor accusations of going against

Of modern seeming do prefer against him.

What you think is acceptable must stand against him.

First Senator

But, Othello, speak:

But tell us, Othello:

Did you by indirect and forced courses

Did you use any underhanded or manipulative means

Subdue and poison this young maid's affections?

To persuade and poison this young girl's desires?

Or came it by request and such fair question

Or did your marriage come from a simple request and a fair question,

As soul to soul affordeth?

Making it an equal decision?

OTHELLO

I do beseech you,

I beg you

Send for the lady to the Sagittary,

To bring the lady herself here to the Armory

And let her speak of me before her father:

So that she can speak plainly of me in front of her father.

If you do find me foul in her report,

If in her report you find me evil,

The trust, the office I do hold of you,

Then the position and rank you have given me

Not only take away, but let your sentence

Should be taken away, and your sentence

Even fall upon my life.

Should also cost me my life.

DUKE OF VENICE

Fetch Desdemona hither.

Bring Desdemona here.

OTHELLO

Ancient, conduct them: you best know the place.

Iago, lead them – you know where she is.

Exeunt IAGO and Attendants

And, till she come, as truly as to heaven

While we wait, as honestly

I do confess the vices of my blood,

As I confess my sins to God,

So justly to your grave ears I'll present

I will record to your serious listening

How I did thrive in this fair lady's love,

How I grew in this beautiful lady's love,

And she in mine.

And how she grew in mine.

DUKE OF VENICE

Say it, Othello.

Tell us, Othello.

OTHELLO

Her father loved me; oft invited me;

Her father has loved me and often invited me to their home

Still question'd me the story of my life,

Where he asked me to recount the story of my life,

From year to year, the battles, sieges, fortunes,

Each year, the battles and sieges and fortunes,

That I have passed.

That I have experienced.

I ran it through, even from my boyish days,

I told it all, even stories from my childhood,

To the very moment that he bade me tell it;

Everything up to the moment I was talking to him.

Wherein I spake of most disastrous chances,

I spoke of dangerous risks,

Of moving accidents by flood and field

Of adventures on sea and land,

Of hair-breadth scapes i' the imminent deadly breach,

Of escaping by a hair from imminent death,

Of being taken by the insolent foe

Of being taken by an enemy

And sold to slavery, of my redemption thence

And sold into slavery, of buying my freedom.

And portance in my travels' history:

I told him also of the travels I have had,

Wherein of antres vast and deserts idle,

Of deep caves and empty deserts,

Rough quarries, rocks and hills whose heads touch heaven

Rocky places, mountains and hills that reach up to heaven,

It was my hint to speak,--such was the process;

I spoke about everything – that was the routine –

And of the Cannibals that each other eat,

About Cannibals that eat each other

The Anthropophagi and men whose heads

Called the Anthropophagi and those whose heads

Do grow beneath their shoulders. This to hear

Grow beneath their shoulders. All the while

Would Desdemona seriously incline:

Desdemona would lean in and listen seriously,

But still the house-affairs would draw her thence:

Though soon enough she would have to leave to do chores,

Which ever as she could with haste dispatch,

Which she did quickly so she could return

She'ld come again, and with a greedy ear

And listen again, wanting to hear

Devour up my discourse: which I observing,

Everything I was saying. I observed all of this

Took once a pliant hour, and found good means

And when I was relaxing, I was able

To draw from her a prayer of earnest heart

To speak with her. She prayed earnestly

That I would all my pilgrimage dilate,

That I would tell her of everything

Whereof by parcels she had something heard,

Since she had heard some parts of the stories

But not intentively: I did consent,

But not everything. I agreed,

And often did beguile her of her tears,

And often my stories caused her to cry

When I did speak of some distressful stroke

When I spoke of some hardship

That my youth suffer'd. My story being done,

That I had suffered when I was younger. When I had finished,

She gave me for my pains a world of sighs:

She sighed at the thought of my former pains

She swore, in faith, 'twas strange, 'twas passing strange,

And told me how strange

'Twas pitiful, 'twas wondrous pitiful:

And sad, truly sad, my story was.

She wish'd she had not heard it, yet she wish'd

She said she wished that she had not heard it and yet that she wished

That heaven had made her such a man: she thank'd me,

That heaven had made a man like me for her. She thanked me

And bade me, if I had a friend that loved her,

And requested that, if I ever had a friend who loved her,

I should but teach him how to tell my story.

I would teach him how to tell a story like me,

And that would woo her. Upon this hint I spake:

And that she would fall in love with such a man. I took this hint and spoke to her.

She loved me for the dangers I had pass'd,

She loved me for the dangerous events I had experienced

And I loved her that she did pity them.

And I loved her because she felt so strongly for me from the stories.

This only is the witchcraft I have used:

This is the only magic that I used.

Here comes the lady; let her witness it.

Here comes Desdemona herself, she can support what I have said.

Enter DESDEMONA, IAGO, and Attendants

DUKE OF VENICE

I think this tale would win my daughter too.

I think such a story would win my daughter's heart, as well.

Good Brabantio,

Brabantio,

Take up this mangled matter at the best:

Try to make the most of this business.

Men do their broken weapons rather use

Using a broken weapon, even if its not what you want, is better

Than their bare hands.

Than using your empty, bare hands.

BRABANTIO

I pray you, hear her speak:

Please, here her side.

If she confess that she was half the wooer,

If she agrees and says it was mutual,

Destruction on my head, if my bad blame

Then I curse myself for allowing mistaken blame

Light on the man! Come hither, gentle mistress:

To come to someone. Come here, gentle woman:

Do you perceive in all this noble company

Do you understand in this group of noblemen

Where most you owe obedience?

To which one you owe your strongest obedience?

DESDEMONA

My noble father,

My noble father,

I do perceive here a divided duty:

I am conflicted:

To you I am bound for life and education;

I owe my life and education to you

My life and education both do learn me

And both have taught me

How to respect you; you are the lord of duty;

To respect you. You are the lord I give my duty to,

I am hitherto your daughter: but here's my husband,

And up to this point I am your daughter. But over here is my husband,

And so much duty as my mother show'd

And as my mother gave more obedience

To you, preferring you before her father,

You over her own father,

So much I challenge that I may profess

So too I wish to announce

<mark>Due to the Moor my lord.</mark>

My obedience to the Moor.

BRABANTIO

God be wi' you! I have done.

God be with you! I am done with this.

Please it your grace, on to the state-affairs:

Please, your grace, move on to the national business:

I had rather to adopt a child than get it.

I would rather adopt a child.

Come hither, Moor:

Come here, Moor:

I here do give thee that with all my heart

I hereby give you with all my heart

Which, but thou hast already, with all my heart

That which if you didn't already have it, with all my heart

I would keep from thee. For your sake, jewel,

I would keep from you. For your sake, daughter,

I am glad at soul I have no other child:

I am glad in my soul that I have no other child,

For thy escape would teach me tyranny,

For your running off would make me become tyrannous,

To hang clogs on them. I have done, my lord.

And want to tie them up at home. I am done, my lord.

DUKE OF VENICE

Let me speak like yourself, and lay a sentence,

Let me say something briefly, and give you some advice

Which, as a grise or step, may help these lovers.

Which may help you forgive these lovers.

When remedies are past, the griefs are ended

When it is too late to fix something, a sad situation often ends

By seeing the worst, which late on hopes depended.

By seeing it in the worst light since our hopes rested on fixing it.

To mourn a mischief that is past and gone

To stay sad when that situation is over

Is the next way to draw new mischief on.

Is the sure way to bring on new troubles.

What cannot be preserved when fortune takes

Luck may take something we want to keep,

Patience her injury a mockery makes.

105

But being patient through that situation mocks and injures Luck.

The robb'd that smiles steals something from the thief;

He who smiles while he is being robbed steals something from the thief,

He robs himself that spends a bootless grief.

But he who grieves robs himself of even more.

BRABANTIO

So let the Turk of Cyprus us beguile;

Then we should let the Turks take Cyprus:

We lose it not, so long as we can smile.

As long as we smile, we do not really lose it.

He bears the sentence well that nothing bears

It's easy to give advice when you do not have to feel the pain

But the free comfort which from thence he hears,

And instead can sit in your comfort and hear of others' pain.

But he bears both the sentence and the sorrow

But he who has to bear the pain and listen to such advice

That, to pay grief, must of poor patience borrow.

Might lose his patience from the weight of it all.

These sentences, to sugar, or to gall,

Your advice, both sweet and sour,

Being strong on both sides, are equivocal:

Is so extremely sweet and sour that it ends up meaning nothing.

But words are words; I never yet did hear

But words are only words and I have never heard

That the bruised heart was pierced through the ear.

Of someone's pain being comforted by hearing talk.

I humbly beseech you, proceed to the affairs of state.

Please, move on to the state affairs.

DUKE OF VENICE

The Turk with a most mighty preparation makes for

The Turk with a great fleet is heading to

Cyprus. Othello, the fortitude of the place is best

Cyprus. Othello, the strength of Cyprus is best

known to you; and though we have there a substitute

known to you and though we have an officer there

of most allowed sufficiency, yet opinion, a

who is very good, the opinion here,

sovereign mistress of effects, throws a more safer

which ultimately makes decisions, is that you are a better

voice on you: you must therefore be content to

option. Therefore, you must be ok

slubber the gloss of your new fortunes with this

with putting off the celebrations of your marriage

more stubborn and boisterous expedition.

for this expedition.

OTHELLO

The tyrant custom, most grave senators,

The military life, respected senators,

Hath made the flinty and steel couch of war

Has made the dangerous bed of war

My thrice-driven bed of down: I do agnise

As comfortable as a bed of down feathers. I have

A natural and prompt alacrity

A natural readiness

I find in hardness, and do undertake

That has come from hardness and will take on

These present wars against the Ottomites.

These battles against the Turks.

Most humbly therefore bending to your state,

I humbly obey, but also ask the state for a favor

I crave fit disposition for my wife.

Since I desire the right environment for my wife.

Due reference of place and exhibition,

Please provide her with a place to to live

With such accommodation and besort

As well as the accommodations and people

As levels with her breeding.

That match her high place in society.

DUKE OF VENICE

If you please,

If you don't mind,

Be't at her father's.

She can stay at her father's.

BRABANTIO

I'll not have it so.

I will not allow it.

OTHELLO

Nor I.

I won't either.

DESDEMONA

Nor I; I would not there reside,

Neither will I. I would not want to stay there

To put my father in impatient thoughts

And tempt my father to become upset

By being in his eye. Most gracious duke,

By being seen by him. Gracious duke,

To my unfolding lend your prosperous ear;

Please listen to my request

And let me find a charter in your voice,

And let me hear you help me

To assist my simpleness.

By allowing a simple favor.

DUKE OF VENICE

What would You, Desdemona?

What would you like, Desdemona?

DESDEMONA

That I did love the Moor to live with him,

When I decided to love the Moor, I decided to live with him,

My downright violence and storm of fortunes

As the violence and poor fortunes I now have

May trumpet to the world: my heart's subdued

Attest to everyone. My heart has become

Even to the very quality of my lord:

Similar to Othello's – I am part soldier now, too.

I saw Othello's visage in his mind,

I saw Othello truly when I saw his mind,

And to his honour and his valiant parts

And he has such honor and courage

Did I my soul and fortunes consecrate.

That I pledged my soul and life to respect these things.

So that, dear lords, if I be left behind,

So, noblemen, if I am left here

A moth of peace, and he go to the war,

In peace, and he goes off to war,

The rites for which I love him are bereft me,

Then everything I pledged to him are taken away from me,

And I a heavy interim shall support

And I must bear a heavy weight

By his dear absence. Let me go with him.

While he is gone. Let me go with him.

OTHELLO

Let her have your voices.

Please let her do this.

Vouch with me, heaven, I therefore beg it not,

Let me be clear: I do not ask you to do this

To please the palate of my appetite,

To satisfy my sexual needs

Nor to comply with heat--the young affects

Or lusting desires since these young characteristics

In me defunct--and proper satisfaction.

Are no longer in me.

But to be free and bounteous to her mind:

But I love her for her brilliant mind.

And heaven defend your good souls, that you think

And, you are wrong if you think

I will your serious and great business scant

That I will neglect the serious work you sent me to do

For she is with me: no, when light-wing'd toys

Because she is with me – this won't happen. If heady love

Of feather'd Cupid seal with wanton dullness

From Cupid ever dulls

My speculative and officed instruments,

My capabilities as a general,

That my disports corrupt and taint my business,

Or makes me obsessed with pleasure, or ruins my work,

Let housewives make a skillet of my helm,

111

Then retire me and let housewives use my helmet as a frying pan.

And all indign and base adversities

Every unworthy and awful trait

Make head against my estimation!

Should thus be accounted against my reputation!

DUKE OF VENICE

Be it as you shall privately determine,

Answer it yourselves in private,

Either for her stay or going: the affair cries haste,

But whether she stays or goes, the war won't wait

And speed must answer it.

So decide quickly.

First Senator

You must away to-night.

Othello must leave tonight.

OTHELLO

With all my heart.

I will, certainly.

DUKE OF VENICE

At nine i' the morning here we'll meet again.

We will meet here tomorrow at nine in the morning.

Othello, leave some officer behind,

Othello, leave an officer behind

And he shall our commission bring to you;

To bring your commission to you

With such things else of quality and respect

Alongside anythings else you need

As doth import you.

That you find important.

OTHELLO

So please your grace, my ancient;

If you agree to it, let me leave my flagbearer and ensign, Iago.

A man he is of honest and trust:

He is an honest and trustworthy man

To his conveyance I assign my wife,

So I will leave him responsible for bringing my wife

With what else needful your good grace shall think

Along with whatever else you think I need

To be sent after me.

To be sent along after I leave.

DUKE OF VENICE

Let it be so.

We will do that.

Good night to every one.

Goodnight, everyone.

To BRABANTIO

And, noble signior,

And, noble sir,

If virtue no delighted beauty lack,

If good character was beautiful in itself,

==Your son-in-law is far more fair than black.==

Then your new son-in-law is much more beautiful than his skin color.

First Senator

Adieu, brave Moor, use Desdemona well.

Goodbye, brave Othello. Take care of Desdemona.

BRABANTIO

Look to her, Moor, if thou hast eyes to see:

Be watchful, Moor, and be careful:

She has deceived her father, and may thee.

She tricked me: who says she won't trick you as well?

Exeunt DUKE OF VENICE, Senators, Officers, & c

OTHELLO

My life upon her faith! Honest Iago,

I will stake my life on her faithfulness! Honest Iago,

My Desdemona must I leave to thee:

I must leave Desdemona to you.

I prithee, let thy wife attend on her:

Please, let your wife wait on her

And bring them after in the best advantage.

And bring them both when you can.

Come, Desdemona: I have but an hour

Come, Desdemona, I only have an hour,

Of love, of worldly matters and direction,

before attending to my duties,

To spend with thee: we must obey the time.

To spend loving you. We must be quick.

Exeunt OTHELLO and DESDEMONA

RODERIGO

Iago,--

Iago–

IAGO

What say'st thou, noble heart?

Yes, good man?

RODERIGO

What will I do, thinkest thou?

What do you think I should do?

IAGO

Why, go to bed, and sleep.

You should go to bed and sleep.

RODERIGO

I will incontinently drown myself.

Perhaps I will drown myself.

IAGO

If thou dost, I shall never love thee after. Why,

If you do, I will never think well of you afterwards.

thou silly gentleman!

You are absurd!

RODERIGO

It is silliness to live when to live is torment; and

No, it is absurd to live life when it is so painful,

then have we a prescription to die when death is our physician.

especially when we have a prescription to end the pain through death.

IAGO

O villainous! I have looked upon the world for four

What an evil thought! I have lived for

times seven years; and since I could distinguish

28 years, and not once,

betwixt a benefit and an injury, I never found man

whether a man was lucky or unlucky, did I ever find

that knew how to love himself. Ere I would say, I

someone who could love himself. Before I would ever say something

would drown myself for the love of a guinea-hen, I

like "I would drown myself because of loving this woman whom I can't have,"

would change my humanity with a baboon.

I would give up my humanity and become a monkey instead.

RODERIGO

What should I do? I confess it is my shame to be so

So what should I do? I know it is shameful to be so

fond; but it is not in my virtue to amend it.

obsessed, but it's not in my personality to fix it.

IAGO

Virtue! a fig! 'tis in ourselves that we are thus

Personality is meaningless! We have the power to become this person

or thus. Our bodies are our gardens, to the which

or that person. Who we are is like a garden,

our wills are gardeners: so that if we will plant

and our wills are the gardeners. If we plant

nettles, or sow lettuce, set hyssop and weed up

thorns, or lettuce, or hyssop, or

thyme, supply it with one gender of herbs, or

thyme, plant only one kind of plant or

distract it with many, either to have it sterile

plant many different ones, if the garden produces nothing

with idleness, or manured with industry, why, the

because we haven't done anything to it, or if it has been worked and manured, well

power and corrigible authority of this lies in our

the power and authority for how it turns out is in our

wills. If the balance of our lives had not one

wills. If our psychologies did not include

scale of reason to poise another of sensuality, the

reason to fight against our emotional desires,

blood and baseness of our natures would conduct us

then everything we feel would lead us

to most preposterous conclusions: but we have

to absurd decisions based only on emotion. But, we have

reason to cool our raging motions, our carnal

reason to temper our desires and fleshly

stings, our unbitted lusts, whereof I take this that

impulses and lusts – and I think that what

you call love to be a sect or scion.

you call love is just another kind of impulse.

RODERIGO

It cannot be.

That's not true.

IAGO

It is merely a lust of the blood and a permission of

It's only a strong desire that you have allowed

the will. Come, be a man. Drown thyself! drown

by your will. Come on, be a man. Drown yourself, how absurd! You drown

cats and blind puppies. I have professed me thy

cats and blind puppies. I have said before that I

friend and I confess me knit to thy deserving with

am your friend, and I will stay close to you

cables of perdurable toughness; I could never

with unbreakable bonds: but never before

better stead thee than now. Put money in thy

have I been a better friend than now. Make money,

purse; follow thou the wars; defeat thy favour with

watch how the wars turn out, and fight against your feelings

an usurped beard; I say, put money in thy purse. It

like a man – and make money.

cannot be that Desdemona should long continue her

Desdemona will not continue to be

love to the Moor,-- put money in thy purse,--nor he

in love with the Moor for long – make more money – nor

his to her: it was a violent commencement, and thou

will he keep loving her. It happened quickly and you

shalt see an answerable sequestration:--put but

will see them come apart quickly as well – so

money in thy purse. These Moors are changeable in

make money. Moors change their minds

their wills: fill thy purse with money:--the food

on a whim – make more money – and what he

that to him now is as luscious as locusts, shall be

thinks now is sweet and filling will soon

to him shortly as bitter as coloquintida. She must

become as bitter as a crabapple. She will

change for youth: when she is sated with his body,

prefer a younger man when she is tired on his body,

she will find the error of her choice: she must

and will think she made a wrong decision. She must

have change, she must: therefore put money in thy

have someone different, so keep making money.

purse. If thou wilt needs damn thyself, do it a

If you want to go to hell, do it

more delicate way than drowning. Make all the money

in a better way than drowning yourself. Make as much money

thou canst: if sanctimony and a frail vow betwixt

as you can: religious vows and weak promises between

an erring barbarian and a supersubtle Venetian not

a barbarian and a tricky Venetian girl are not

too hard for my wits and all the tribe of hell, thou

too difficult for me to take advantage of. If I do well, you

shalt enjoy her; therefore make money. A pox of

will sleep with her, so make money. And stop talking

drowning thyself! it is clean out of the way: seek

of drowning! It is beside the point. Instead

thou rather to be hanged in compassing thy joy than

try to get hanged by committing wrongs in order to be with her,

to be drowned and go without her.

than to drown and be without her.

RODERIGO

Wilt thou be fast to my hopes, if I depend on

Can I trust you while I see what happens?

the issue?

IAGO

Thou art sure of me:--go, make money:--I have told

Yes. Now go, make money. I have told you

thee often, and I re-tell thee again and again, I

over and over: I

hate the Moor: my cause is hearted; thine hath no

hate the Moor. I have good reason to help you, just

less reason. Let us be conjunctive in our revenge

as you do. Let us join together to take our revenge

against him: if thou canst cuckold him, thou dost

on him and make it so you sleep with his wife,

thyself a pleasure, me a sport. There are many

which will be a great pleasure to me. Many

events in the womb of time which will be delivered.

things must happen next.

Traverse! go, provide thy money. We will have more

Now go! make more money. We will talk more

of this to-morrow. Adieu.

tomorrow. Goodbye.

RODERIGO

Where shall we meet i' the morning?

Where shall we meet tomorrow morning?

IAGO

At my lodging.

At my house.

RODERIGO

I'll be with thee betimes.

I'll be there early.

IAGO

Go to; farewell. Do you hear, Roderigo?

Good, goodbye. Oh, and Roderigo?

RODERIGO

What say you?

Yes, Iago?

IAGO

No more of drowning, do you hear?

Stop talking of drowning, alright?

RODERIGO

I am changed: I'll go sell all my land.

Yes, I have changed my mind. I will sell my land for money.

Exit

IAGO

Thus do I ever make my fool my purse:

And that is how I use fools for money.

For I mine own gain'd knowledge should profane,

If I didn't have my own gain to get out of it,

If I would time expend with such a snipe.

I would never spend time with such a fool.

But for my sport and profit. I hate the Moor:

But he helps me get money and achieve my purposes: I hate the Moor,

And it is thought abroad, that 'twixt my sheets

And there is a rumor that he has slept

He has done my office: I know not if't be true;

With my wife. I don't know if that is true,

But I, for mere suspicion in that kind,

But just because of the rumor I

Will do as if for surety. He holds me well;

Will act as if it is. He thinks highly of me,

The better shall my purpose work on him.

Which will make it easier for me to trick him.

Cassio's a proper man: let me see now:

Now then, let me see: Cassio is a good and handsome man.

To get his place and to plume up my will

How can I get his rank and hurt Othello

In double knavery--How, how? Let's see:--

At the same time? How?

After some time, to abuse Othello's ear

After a little while, I will tell Othello

That he is too familiar with his wife.

That Cassio is too close to Desdemona.

He hath a person and a smooth dispose

His personality and smooth disposition

To be suspected, framed to make women false.

Can easily be suspected, they already make him look like a seducer.

The Moor is of a free and open nature,

The Moor is a straightforward man

That thinks men honest that but seem to be so,

Who thinks other men are honest if they look honest enough,

And will as tenderly be led by the nose

And so he can be led on as easily

As asses are.

As donkeys are.

I have't. It is engender'd. Hell and night

I know what I will do. Hell and the devil

Must bring this monstrous birth to the world's light.

Will help me work out my plans.

Exit

Act II

Scene I. A Sea-port in Cyprus. An open place near the quay.

Enter MONTANO and two Gentlemen

MONTANO

What from the cape can you discern at sea?

What do you see out in the ocean?

First Gentleman

Nothing at all: it is a highwrought flood;

Nothing. The water is so rough

I cannot, 'twixt the heaven and the main,

That I cannot see between the ocean and heaven

Descry a sail.

A single sail.

MONTANO

Methinks the wind hath spoke aloud at land;

It is windy here on the land as well.

A fuller blast ne'er shook our battlements:

A gust shook our fortifications:

If it hath ruffian'd so upon the sea,

If it is so strong out on the sea,

What ribs of oak, when mountains melt on them,

Why wooden whip, when mountains of water fall on them,

Can hold the mortise? What shall we hear of this?

Can stay together? What is going to happen?

Second Gentleman

A segregation of the Turkish fleet:

The Turkish fleet will be broken up.

For do but stand upon the foaming shore,

Standing here on the shore,

The chidden billow seems to pelt the clouds;

The waves look like they will hit the clouds.

The wind-shaked surge, with high and monstrous mane,

The surge of water powered by the winds, rising high,

Seems to cast water on the burning bear,

Seems to throw water to the constellations

And quench the guards of the ever-fixed pole:

And drench the polestars.

I never did like molestation view

I have never seen such a storm

On the enchafed flood.

Out on the sea.

MONTANO

If that the Turkish fleet

If the Turkish ships

Be not enshelter'd and embay'd, they are drown'd:

Do not find shelter and rest, they will be sunk.

It is impossible they bear it out.

It is impossible for them to withstand this.

Enter a third Gentleman

Third Gentleman

News, lads! our wars are done.

I have news! The fighting is done.

The desperate tempest hath so bang'd the Turks,

The storm has injured the Turks so much

That their designment halts: a noble ship of Venice

That they have stopped their plans. A ship from Venice

Hath seen a grievous wreck and sufferance

Has seen an awful wreck of theirs and the sufferings

On most part of their fleet.

Of most of their fleet.

MONTANO

How! is this true?

What! Is this true!

Third Gentleman

The ship is here put in,

The ship has just landed,

A Veronesa; Michael Cassio,

From Verona. Michael Cassio,

Lieutenant to the warlike Moor Othello,

Lieutenant to the Moor general Othello,

Is come on shore: the Moor himself at sea,

Is on the shore. The Moor himself is at sea

And is in full commission here for Cyprus.

And is coming with full commission to Cyprus.

MONTANO

I am glad on't; 'tis a worthy governor.

I am glad, he is a worthy leader.

Third Gentleman

But this same Cassio, though he speak of comfort

But this Cassio fellow, though he has good news

Touching the Turkish loss, yet he looks sadly,

About the Turkish losses, is sad

And prays the Moor be safe; for they were parted

And prays for the Moor's safety. They were separated

With foul and violent tempest.

In the storm.

MONTANO

Pray heavens he be;

Yes, I pray he is safe.

For I have served him, and the man commands

I have served under him and he leads

Like a full soldier. Let's to the seaside, ho!

Like a great soldier. Let us go to the shore.

As well to see the vessel that's come in

See to the vessel that has arrived and

As to throw out our eyes for brave Othello,

Look for brave Othello

Even till we make the main and the aerial blue

Until the sea and sky blur together

An indistinct regard.

And are indistinguishable.

Third Gentleman

Come, let's do so:

Come, let's go.

For every minute is expectancy

Every minute we can expect

Of more arrivance.

Their arrival.

Enter CASSIO

CASSIO

Thanks, you the valiant of this warlike isle,

Thank you, you brave men who defend the island

That so approve the Moor! O, let the heavens

And respect the Moor! O, I pray that the heavens

Give him defence against the elements,

Defend him against the storm,

For I have lost us him on a dangerous sea.

For we were separated on the dangerous sea.

MONTANO

Is he well shipp'd?

Is his ship strong?

CASSIO

His bark is stoutly timber'd, his pilot

The wood is good and strong, and his pilot

Of very expert and approved allowance;

Is experienced – a true expert.

Therefore my hopes, not surfeited to death,

Therefore, I hope for his safety, though

Stand in bold cure.

They are not without their fears.

A cry within 'A sail, a sail, a sail!'
Enter a fourth Gentleman

CASSIO

What noise?

What is that sound?

Fourth Gentleman

The town is empty; on the brow o' the sea

The whole town is at the shore

Stand ranks of people, and they cry 'A sail!'

Standing in lines and shouting that they see a sail!

CASSIO

My hopes do shape him for the governor.

I hope it is Othello.

Guns heard

Second Gentlemen

They do discharge their shot of courtesy:

They have fired a friendly shot,

Our friends at least.

So they are at least our allies.

CASSIO

I pray you, sir, go forth,

Please, sir, go

And give us truth who 'tis that is arrived.

And tell us who it is who is arriving.

Second Gentleman

I shall.

I will.

Exit

MONTANO

But, good lieutenant, is your general wived?

Good lieutenant, does the general have a wife?

CASSIO

Most fortunately: he hath achieved a maid

Yes, and he is very lucky. His wife's virtues

That paragons description and wild fame;

Cannot be described or become famous enough to match them.

One that excels the quirks of blazoning pens,

She is no match for a writer who,

And in the essential vesture of creation

In trying to capture her, God's special creation,

Does tire the ingener.

Will become tired.

Re-enter second Gentleman

How now! who has put in?

Hello, who is it that has arrive?

Second Gentleman

'Tis one Iago, ancient to the general.

It is one named Iago, ensign to the general.

CASSIO

Has had most favourable and happy speed:

He has come very quickly.

Tempests themselves, high seas, and howling winds,

Storms and high seas and howling winds,

The gutter'd rocks and congregated sands--

And the dangerous rocks and swirling sands –

Traitors ensteep'd to clog the guiltless keel,--

Everything that will slow and stop a ship –

As having sense of beauty, do omit

Must have a sense of beauty, for they

Their mortal natures, letting go safely by

Have acted against their natures and allowed

The divine Desdemona.

The beautiful Desdemona to travel safely.

MONTANO

What is she?

Who is Desdemona?

CASSIO

She that I spake of, our great captain's captain,

She is whom I spoke of, the wife of Othello,

Left in the conduct of the bold Iago,

Given to brave Iago's care,

Whose footing here anticipates our thoughts

And he has arrive here

A se'nnight's speed. Great Jove, Othello guard,

A week earlier than expected. Dear God, protect Othello

And swell his sail with thine own powerful breath,

And make his ship sail faster with your breath pushing it

That he may bless this bay with his tall ship,

That he might arrive here in his great ship,

Make love's quick pants in Desdemona's arms,

Be joined in love with Desdemona,

Give renew'd fire to our extincted spirits

Replenish the fire of our spirits,

And bring all Cyprus comfort!

And bring all of Cyprus comfort!

Enter DESDEMONA, EMILIA, IAGO, RODERIGO, and Attendants

O, behold,

Behold,

The riches of the ship is come on shore!

The riches from the ship have come onto the shore!

Ye men of Cyprus, let her have your knees.

Men of Cyprus, bow to her.

Hail to thee, lady! and the grace of heaven,

Hello, lady! May the grace of heaven

Before, behind thee, and on every hand,

Be before you, behind you, on each side,

Enwheel thee round!

All around you!

DESDEMONA

I thank you, valiant Cassio.

Thank you, brave Cassio.

What tidings can you tell me of my lord?

How is Othello doing?

135

CASSIO

He is not yet arrived: nor know I aught

He has not arrived yet, so I don't know anything

But that he's well and will be shortly here.

Except that he is fine and will soon be here.

DESDEMONA

O, but I fear--How lost you company?

O, but I am scared. How did you get separated?

CASSIO

The great contention of the sea and skies

The great storm of the sea and skies

Parted our fellowship--But, hark! a sail.

Parted us. But wait! a sail.

Within 'A sail, a sail!' Guns heard

Second Gentleman

They give their greeting to the citadel;

Another greeting shot to the city:

This likewise is a friend.

This is also an ally.

CASSIO

See for the news.

See who it is.

Exit Gentleman

Good ancient, you are welcome.

Good ensign, you are welcome here.

To EMILIA

Welcome, mistress.

And mistress, welcome.

Let it not gall your patience, good Iago,

I hope this does not offend you, good Iago,

That I extend my manners; 'tis my breeding

That I greet your wife like this. I have been raised

That gives me this bold show of courtesy.

To give such a bold custom of greeting.

Kissing her

IAGO

Sir, would she give you so much of her lips

Sir, if she gives you as much of her lips

As of her tongue she oft bestows on me,

As she gives me by berating me,

You'll have enough.

You'll be sick of her.

DESDEMONA

Alas, she has no speech.

137

No, she seems to say nothing.

IAGO

In faith, too much;

Truly, she says too much,

I find it still, when I have list to sleep:

Even when I am trying to sleep.

Marry, before your ladyship, I grant,

Yes, in front of you, I agree

She puts her tongue a little in her heart,

She says very little, but in her heart

And chides with thinking.

She is speaking scornfully to me.

EMILIA

You have little cause to say so.

You have no reason to say that.

IAGO

Come on, come on; you are pictures out of doors,

Come on now. Out in public you women are pretty as a picture,

Bells in your parlors, wild-cats in your kitchens,

But you are loud bells at home, wildcats in the kitchen,

Saints in your injuries, devils being offended,

Saints when injured, devils when offended,

Players in your housewifery, and housewives' in your beds.

Idle actresses in your housewife duties, and hussies in your bed.

DESDEMONA

O, fie upon thee, slanderer!

O, a curse on you, you slanderer.

IAGO

Nay, it is true, or else I am a Turk:

No, I would be a Turk if what I say is not true.

You rise to play and go to bed to work.

You get up in order to enjoy yourselves, and you go to bed in order to work.

EMILIA

You shall not write my praise.

You will not say anything good about me.

IAGO

No, let me not.

No, I won't.

DESDEMONA

What wouldst thou write of me, if thou shouldst

What verse would you write of me if you had to say

praise me?

something nice?

IAGO

O gentle lady, do not put me to't;

Gentle lady, do not make me do that.

For I am nothing, if not critical.

I am a critical person by nature.

DESDEMONA

Come on assay. There's one gone to the harbour?

Come on, try. And has someone gone to the harbor?

IAGO

Ay, madam.

Yes, madam.

DESDEMONA

I am not merry; but I do beguile

I am not really this playful, but I don't want to show

The thing I am, by seeming otherwise.

How I really am by seeming other than playful.

Come, how wouldst thou praise me?

Come on, how would you praise me?

IAGO

I am about it; but indeed my invention

I am thinking, but creative verse

Comes from my pate as birdlime does from frize;

Comes from my head as difficultly as sticky birdlime comes out of wool cloth.

It plucks out brains and all: but my Muse labours,

It takes all of my brains. But my Muse has worked at it,

And thus she is deliver'd.

And I have something:

If she be fair and wise, fairness and wit,

"If a woman has beauty and intelligence,

The one's for use, the other useth it.

She uses her beauty to get what she wants, and uses it as a tool of her intelligence."

DESDEMONA

Well praised! How if she be black and witty?

Well said! But what if she is ugly and smart?

IAGO

If she be black, and thereto have a wit,

"If she is ugly, but still have brains,

She'll find a white that shall her blackness fit.

She will trick some handsome man to love her ugliness."

DESDEMONA

Worse and worse.

This is getting even worse.

EMILIA

How if fair and foolish?

What if she is beautiful and dumb?

IAGO

She never yet was foolish that was fair;

"No beautiful woman was ever dumb,

For even her folly help'd her to an heir.

Because even her foolishness makes her seem attractive."

DESDEMONA

These are old fond paradoxes to make fools laugh i'

These are old jokes intended for laughs in

the alehouse. What miserable praise hast thou for

the tavern. What awful things do you have to say

her that's foul and foolish?

About the woman who is ugly and dumb?

IAGO

There's none so foul and foolish thereunto,

"No matter how dumb and ugly a woman is,

But does foul pranks which fair and wise ones do.

She tricks men just like the beautiful and smart ones do."

DESDEMONA

O heavy ignorance! thou praisest the worst best.

O you are so ignorant! You praise the worst combination most!

But what praise couldst thou bestow on a deserving

But what would you say about a very good woman,

woman indeed, one that, in the authority of her

one that, based on her own

merit, did justly put on the vouch of very malice itself?

good merit, can have nothing bad said of her?

IAGO

She that was ever fair and never proud,

"She who was beautiful but never proud,

Had tongue at will and yet was never loud,

Could speak well but was never loud,

Never lack'd gold and yet went never gay,

Always looked good, but not ostentatious,

Fled from her wish and yet said 'Now I may,'

Who could get what she wanted, but chose against it,

She that being anger'd, her revenge being nigh,

Who when angry was not revengeful,

Bade her wrong stay and her displeasure fly,

And overlooked it when people wronged her,

She that in wisdom never was so frail

She whose wisdom is not so weak that she would

To change the cod's head for the salmon's tail;

Mix up the head of a codfish with the tail of a salmon,

She that could think and ne'er disclose her mind,

She who can think but doesnt need to reveal her thoughts,

See suitors following and not look behind,

143

Who sees suitors following after her but does not look behind at them,

She was a wight, if ever such wight were,--

She is a woman, if ever such a woman existed–

DESDEMONA

To do what?

And what would she do?

IAGO

To suckle fools and chronicle small beer.

She would raise children, and keep track of trifles.

DESDEMONA

O most lame and impotent conclusion! Do not learn

O what a pathetic ending! Do not listen

of him, Emilia, though he be thy husband. How say

to him, Emilia, even if he is your husband. What do

you, Cassio? is he not a most profane and liberal

you think, Cassio? Isn't he the rudest

counsellor?

teacher?

CASSIO

He speaks home, madam: You may relish him more in

He speaks commonly, madam. You will find more worth in him

the soldier than in the scholar.

144

as a soldier than as a scholar.

IAGO

[Aside] He takes her by the palm: ay, well said,

He holds her hand. Yes, good,

whisper: with as little a web as this will I

whisper together. This itself is enough

ensnare as great a fly as Cassio. Ay, smile upon

for me to use Cassio for my plans. Good, smile

her, do; I will gyve thee in thine own courtship.

at her. Your manners will help me bind you.

You say true; 'tis so, indeed: if such tricks as

You speak truly of your manners: if they

these strip you out of your lieutenantry, it had

will be used to take your rank away from you, maybe you should

been better you had not kissed your three fingers so

not have done such polite mannerisms so

oft, which now again you are most apt to play the

often, which you are very good at

sir in. Very good; well kissed! an excellent

doing. Very good, kiss her! A wonderful

courtesy! 'tis so, indeed. Yet again your fingers

gesture indeed. And again you place your fingers

to your lips? would they were clyster-pipes for your sake!

to your lips? If only they were enema tubes to clean out your crap!

Trumpet within

145

The Moor! I know his trumpet.

That's the Moor; I recognize his trumpet!

CASSIO

'Tis truly so.

It's true.

DESDEMONA

Let's meet him and receive him.

Let's go meet him.

CASSIO

Lo, where he comes!

There he is, coming to us.

Enter OTHELLO and Attendants

OTHELLO

O my fair warrior!

O my beautiful warrior!

DESDEMONA

My dear Othello!

My dear Othello!

OTHELLO

It gives me wonder great as my content

I am amazed as well as happy

To see you here before me. O my soul's joy!

To see you here before I arrived. O joy!

If after every tempest come such calms,

If every storm had after it such calms,

May the winds blow till they have waken'd death!

Then the winds should blow so hard that they wake the dead!

And let the labouring bark climb hills of seas

Let the ships ride the high waves,

Olympus-high and duck again as low

As high as Mt. Olympus, and duck low again,

As hell's from heaven! If it were now to die,

As far as hell is from heaven! If I died now,

'Twere now to be most happy; for, I fear,

I would die most happy, for I fear

My soul hath her content so absolute

That since I am so completely content,

That not another comfort like to this

No comfort will come close to this

Succeeds in unknown fate.

In my lifetime.

DESDEMONA

The heavens forbid

I pray to God

But that our loves and comforts should increase,

147

That our love and comfort increases

Even as our days do grow!

As we grow older!

OTHELLO

Amen to that, sweet powers!

Amen to that!

I cannot speak enough of this content;

I cannot say anything more about my happiness,

It stops me here; it is too much of joy:

It forces me to stop speaking because it is too much to comprehend.

And this, and this, the greatest discords be

And I hope this kiss is the greatest fight

Kissing her

That e'er our hearts shall make!

That we ever face!

IAGO

[Aside] O, you are well tuned now!

O, you are in good spirits now!

But I'll set down the pegs that make this music,

I'll bring you down from this height,

As honest as I am.

Since I am the honest man.

OTHELLO

Come, let us to the castle.

Come, let's go to the castle.

News, friends; our wars are done, the Turks are drown'd.

Friends, our fighting is over; the Turks have drowned.

How does my old acquaintance of this isle?

How are my old friends on the island?

Honey, you shall be well desired in Cyprus;

Honey, you will be loved here in Cyprus;

I have found great love amongst them. O my sweet,

I myself have been treated well here. O my sweet,

I prattle out of fashion, and I dote

I am talking nonsense and I am obsessing

In mine own comforts. I prithee, good Iago,

Over my happiness. Please, good Iago,

Go to the bay and disembark my coffers:

Go to the bay and get me things,

Bring thou the master to the citadel;

And bring the captain of the ship to the castle.

He is a good one, and his worthiness

He is a good soldier, and his worth

Does challenge much respect. Come, Desdemona,

Makes me respect him greatly. Come, Desdemona,

Once more, well met at Cyprus.

I'll say it again, I am happy to see you at Cyprus!

Exeunt OTHELLO, DESDEMONA, and Attendants

IAGO

Do thou meet me presently at the harbour. Come

Meet me at the harbor now. Come

hither. If thou be'st valiant,-- as, they say, base

on. If you are brave – as they say, evil

men being in love have then a nobility in their

men in love have a nobility and braveness

natures more than is native to them--list me. The

that is not naturally in them – listen to me.

lieutenant tonight watches on the court of

Cassio is tasked tonight with

guard:--first, I must tell thee this--Desdemona is

guard duty, and I must tell you: Desdemona is

directly in love with him.

in love with him.

RODERIGO

With him! why, 'tis not possible.

With him! That's not possible.

IAGO

Lay thy finger thus, and let thy soul be instructed.

Be quiet and listen to what I will tell you.

Mark me with what violence she first loved the Moor,

Look at how quickly and impulsively she fell in love for the Moor,

but for bragging and telling her fantastical lies:

from his bragging and tall tales,

and will she love him still for prating? let not

do you think she will keep loving him as he speaks nonsense? Don't

thy discreet heart think it. Her eye must be fed;

be stupid enough to think so. She needs someone handsome

and what delight shall she have to look on the

and how could she possibly enjoy looking at that

devil? When the blood is made dull with the act of

devil? In time, the heat of romance goes away,

sport, there should be, again to inflame it and to

and one needs certain things to reignite it and

give satiety a fresh appetite, loveliness in favour,

recreate sexual appetite, like handsomeness and

sympathy in years, manners and beauties; all which

similarity in age, customs, and appearance.

the Moor is defective in: now, for want of these

The Moor has none of these. Since she has none

required conveniences, her delicate tenderness will

of these necessary qualities in her partner, she will feel

find itself abused, begin to heave the gorge,

sick of him, to the point of puking,

disrelish and abhor the Moor; very nature will

and will disgust the Moor. Her nature will

instruct her in it and compel her to some second

cause this disgust and then turn her to look for a second

choice. Now, sir, this granted,--as it is a most

option. Now since this is true – it's a very

pregnant and unforced position--who stands so

natural string of events – who would be

eminent in the degree of this fortune as Cassio

a better second option for her than Cassio?

does? a knave very voluble; no further

After all, he is a very smooth speaker,

conscionable than in putting on the mere form of

a trait that makes him seem conscientious, as if he is

civil and humane seeming, for the better compassing

polite and civil, but in reality it hides

of his salt and most hidden loose affection? why,

his inner, strong lustfulness.

none; why, none: a slipper and subtle knave, a

No one stands in a better position, and no one is trickier than he is,

finder of occasions, that has an eye can stamp and

a man who finds the right time for his moves, who sees

counterfeit advantages, though true advantage never

and creates his own advantageous situations even if a real advantage

present itself; a devilish knave. Besides, the

is never there – he is a devilish trickster. Besides,

knave is handsome, young, and hath all those

he is handsome and young, with all of the

requisites in him that folly and green minds look

qualities that naive youths look for.

after: a pestilent complete knave; and the woman

He is an awful man, but seems the perfect one, and Desdemona

hath found him already.

has already fallen for him.

RODERIGO

I cannot believe that in her; she's full of

I do not believe it. She is a very

most blessed condition.

moral and trustworthy woman.

IAGO

Blessed fig's-end! the wine she drinks is made of

Nonsense! She drinks the same wine we do,

grapes: if she had been blessed, she would never

made of grapes – she has the same desires we do. If she was blessedly moral, she never

have loved the Moor. Blessed pudding! Didst thou

would have loved the Moor. Didn't you

not see her paddle with the palm of his hand? didst

see her fondle Cassio's hands? Didn't you

not mark that?

notice?

RODERIGO

Yes, that I did; but that was but courtesy.

Yes, but that was just politeness.

IAGO

Lechery, by this hand; an index and obscure prologue

It was lust, and it foreshadows

to the history of lust and foul thoughts. They met

a future of lust and impure thoughts between them. They came

so near with their lips that their breaths embraced

so close to each others lips that their breaths hugged.

together. Villanous thoughts, Roderigo! when these

Evil thoughts, Roderigo! When two

mutualities so marshal the way, hard at hand comes

people mutually act like this, quickly will come

the master and main exercise, the incorporate

the main goal of their actions, the obvious

conclusion, Pish! But, sir, be you ruled by me: I

conclusion, which is sex. But, Roderigo, listen to me: I

have brought you from Venice. Watch you to-night;

brought you here from Venice. Keep watch tonight

for the command, I'll lay't upon you. Cassio knows

and I will give you the sign to act. Cassio doesn't know

you not. I'll not be far from you: do you find

you. I will be nearby: you must find

some occasion to anger Cassio, either by speaking

some way to make Cassio angry, either by speaking

too loud, or tainting his discipline; or from what

obnoxiously, or insulting him, or however

other course you please, which the time shall more

you want according to the situation.

favourably minister.

RODERIGO

Well.

Fine.

IAGO

Sir, he is rash and very sudden in choler, and haply

Sir, he has a poor temper and angers easily, he

may strike at you: provoke him, that he may; for

may try to hit you. Try to get him to do that

even out of that will I cause these of Cyprus to

and from that simple action I will cause Cyprus to

mutiny; whose qualification shall come into no true

mutiny against him so that they will not become

taste again but by the displanting of Cassio. So

peaceful until Cassio is removed from his post. Thus,

shall you have a shorter journey to your desires by

you will have an easier path to your desire for Desdemona by

the means I shall then have to prefer them; and the

these means which will

impediment most profitably removed, without the

remove your biggest obstacle. If it is not removed,

which there were no expectation of our prosperity.

then there is no hope of succeeding.

RODERIGO

I will do this, if I can bring it to any

I will do this as long as it gives

opportunity.

me a chance.

IAGO

I warrant thee. Meet me by and by at the citadel:

I promise you. Meet me soon at the castle;

I must fetch his necessaries ashore. Farewell.

I must get Othello's things from the ship. Goodbye.

RODERIGO

Adieu.

Goodbye.

Exit

IAGO

That Cassio loves her, I do well believe it;

I actually think Cassio does love her,

That she loves him, 'tis apt and of great credit:

And it makes sense that she would love him as well.

The Moor, howbeit that I endure him not,

The Moor whom I can't stand

Is of a constant, loving, noble nature,

Is such an honest, loving, noble man

And I dare think he'll prove to Desdemona

And I think he will be to Desdemona

A most dear husband. Now, I do love her too;

A very good husband. I love Desdemona as well,

Not out of absolute lust, though peradventure

Though not from lust as much as from

I stand accountant for as great a sin,

Needing to get even with the Moor.

But partly led to diet my revenge,

I want to get revenge

For that I do suspect the lusty Moor

Since I think that the lustful Moor

Hath leap'd into my seat; the thought whereof

Slept with my wife – this thought,

Doth, like a poisonous mineral, gnaw my inwards;

Like a poison, eats at me inside.

And nothing can or shall content my soul

Nothing can or will make me feel better

Till I am even'd with him, wife for wife,

Until I am even with him, wife for wife,

Or failing so, yet that I put the Moor

Or, if I fail to do that, I will at least make the Moor

At least into a jealousy so strong

So extremely jealous

That judgment cannot cure. Which thing to do,

That he won't be able to think properly.

If this poor trash of Venice, whom I trash

If I can make Roderigo, that Venetian trash,

For his quick hunting, stand the putting on,

Do whatever I need him to do,

I'll have our Michael Cassio on the hip,

I will have control over Cassio

Abuse him to the Moor in the rank garb--

And will defame him to the Moor –

For I fear Cassio with my night-cap too--

After all, I am afraid Cassio might have slept with my wife as well –

Make the Moor thank me, love me and reward me

And by doing this the Moor will thank me, love me, and reward me,

For making him egregiously an ass

All for making a fool of him

And practising upon his peace and quiet

And removing his peace and quietness,

Even to madness. 'Tis here, but yet confused:

Replacing it with madness. Everything is here that I need, just not perfectly planned yet.

Knavery's plain face is never seen till used.

I never fully know a trick until the moment when it is put into action.

Exit

Scene II. A street.

Enter a Herald with a proclamation; People following

Herald

It is Othello's pleasure, our noble and valiant

It is the order of Othelle, the brave and noble

general, that, upon certain tidings now arrived,

general, that since we now have new

importing the mere perdition of the Turkish fleet,

of the destruction of the Turkish fleet,

every man put himself into triumph; some to dance,

everyone should celebrate, and dance,

some to make bonfires, each man to what sport and

and make bonfires, each person to whatever fun

revels his addiction leads him: for, besides these

and partying he wants. On top of this

beneficial news, it is the celebration of his

great news, we will celebrate Othello's

nuptial. So much was his pleasure should be

wedding. That was the entirety of his

proclaimed. All offices are open, and there is full

announcement. There will be a full

liberty of feasting from this present hour of five

feast from now, five o'clock,

till the bell have told eleven. Heaven bless the

until the bell tolls eleven. God bless the

isle of Cyprus and our noble general Othello!

island of Cyprus and our brave general Othello!

Exeunt

Scene III. A hall in the castle.

Enter OTHELLO, DESDEMONA, CASSIO, and Attendants

OTHELLO

Good Michael, look you to the guard to-night:

Good Michael Cassio, keep the guard tonight

Let's teach ourselves that honourable stop,

And help the festivities show restraint,

Not to outsport discretion.

And not get out of control.

CASSIO

Iago hath direction what to do;

Iago has instructions on what to do.

But, notwithstanding, with my personal eye

But, regardless, I will personally

Will I look to't.

Look after it.

OTHELLO

Iago is most honest.

Iago is very honest.

Michael, good night: to-morrow with your earliest

Michael, goodnight. Early tomorrow

Let me have speech with you.

I would like to talk with you.

To DESDEMONA

Come, my dear love,

Come, my love,

The purchase made, the fruits are to ensue;

The purchase of marrying you has been made, the fruits of sex are to come next.

That profit's yet to come 'tween me and you.

That pleasure hasn't happened yet, but is next for us.

Good night.

Goodnight.

Exeunt OTHELLO, DESDEMONA, and Attendants

Enter IAGO

CASSIO

Welcome, Iago; we must to the watch.

Welcome, Iago, let's go to keep watch.

IAGO

Not this hour, lieutenant; 'tis not yet ten o' the

Not yet, lieutenant. It's not yet ten o' clock.

clock. Our general cast us thus early for the love

Our general mades us leave early because of his love

of his Desdemona; who let us not therefore blame:

for Desdemona. We can't blame him though:

he hath not yet made wanton the night with her; and

he hasn't yet slept with her, and

she is sport for Jove.

she is beautiful enough for Jove to love her.

CASSIO

She's a most exquisite lady.

She is a beautiful lady.

IAGO

And, I'll warrant her, fun of game.

And, I'll bet, very good in bed.

CASSIO

Indeed, she's a most fresh and delicate creature.

Yes, she's very young and delicate.

IAGO

What an eye she has! methinks it sounds a parley of

And what beautiful eyes! They are almost

provocation.

provocatively inviting.

CASSIO

An inviting eye; and yet methinks right modest.

Inviting, yes, but I think she is still appropriately modest.

IAGO

And when she speaks, is it not an alarum to love?

And isn't her voice a beautiful bell?

CASSIO

She is indeed perfection.

She is quite perfect.

IAGO

Well, happiness to their sheets! Come, lieutenant, I

Well, I wish their marriage bed happiness! Come, lieutenant, I

have a stoup of wine; and here without are a brace

have a bottle of wine, and here is a group

of Cyprus gallants that would fain have a measure to

of Cyprus gentlemen who would love to drink to

the health of black Othello.

black Othello's health.

CASSIO

Not to-night, good Iago: I have very poor and

Not tonight, good Iago: I have very poor

unhappy brains for drinking: I could well wish

tolerance for alcohol. I wish

courtesy would invent some other custom of

that society would invent some other way

entertainment.

to celebrate.

IAGO

O, they are our friends; but one cup: I'll drink for
you.

*But these are friends. Drink one cup, I'll drink the rest
for you.*

CASSIO

I have drunk but one cup to-night, and that was
craftily qualified too, and, behold, what innovation
it makes here: I am unfortunate in the infirmity,
and dare not task my weakness with any more.

*I have already had a cup tonight, and even that
was watered down, and yet look at how drunk
it has made me. I have an unfortunately weak tolerance,
and wouldn't want to test my weakness by drinking more.*

IAGO

What, man! 'tis a night of revels: the gallants
desire it.

*You can't be serious! Tonight is a night of partying, and the gentlemen
want you to drink.*

CASSIO

Where are they?

Where are they?

IAGO

Here at the door; I pray you, call them in.

Just outside the door. Please, ask them to come in.

CASSIO

I'll do't; but it dislikes me.

I'll do it, but I don't want to.

Exit

IAGO

If I can fasten but one cup upon him,

If I can make him drink only one cup more

With that which he hath drunk to-night already,

On top of what he has already drunk tonight,

He'll be as full of quarrel and offence

Then he will be as aggressive and ready to fight

As my young mistress' dog. Now, my sick fool Roderigo,

As my mistress's dog. Now, my lovesick fool Roderigo,

Whom love hath turn'd almost the wrong side out,

Whom love has twisted up and confused,

To Desdemona hath to-night caroused

Has drunk tonight to Desdemona

Potations pottle-deep; and he's to watch:

In a number of toasts, and he's on guard duty as well.

Three lads of Cyprus, noble swelling spirits,

Three Cyprus men, brave spirits

That hold their honours in a wary distance,

That have a good notion of their honor

The very elements of this warlike isle,

Like everyone on this warring island,

Have I to-night fluster'd with flowing cups,

I have also gotten drunk,

And they watch too. Now, 'mongst this flock of drunkards,

And they are on duty as well. Now, with this group of drunkards –

Am I to put our Cassio in some action

I need to get Cassio to do something

That may offend the isle.--But here they come:

To offend their island. Here they come:

If consequence do but approve my dream,

If I can engineer this situation to match my plans,

My boat sails freely, both with wind and stream.

Then I will get what I want.

Re-enter CASSIO; with him MONTANO and Gentlemen; servants following with wine

CASSIO

'Fore God, they have given me a rouse already.

By God, they have already given me quite a lot to drink.

MONTANO

Good faith, a little one; not past a pint, as I am

Truly, only a small cup. It wasn't even a pint, I promise

a soldier.

as a soldier.

IAGO

Some wine, ho!

More wine!

Sings

And let me the canakin clink, clink;

And clink your glasses together

And let me the canakin clink

And clink your glasses together

A soldier's a man;

A soldier is a man,

A life's but a span;

And a life is only so long,

Why, then, let a soldier drink.

So let the soldier drink!

Some wine, boys!

More wine, boys!

CASSIO

'Fore God, an excellent song.

By God, a great song.

IAGO

I learned it in England, where, indeed, they are

I learned it in England, where they are

most potent in potting: your Dane, your German, and

very good at drinking. The Dane, or German, or

your swag-bellied Hollander--Drink, ho!--are nothing

fat Dutchman – Drink! – they are no match

to your English.

to the English.

CASSIO

Is your Englishman so expert in his drinking?

Is the Englishman truly an expert at drinking?

IAGO

Why, he drinks you, with facility, your Dane dead

Why, he will easily drink a Dane into a stupor,

drunk; he sweats not to overthrow your Almain; he

he has no problem outdrinking the German, and he

gives your Hollander a vomit, ere the next pottle

will make a Dutchman pute before the next glass

can be filled.

can be filled.

CASSIO

To the health of our general!

To the health of Othello!

MONTANO

I am for it, lieutenant; and I'll do you justice.

I will drink to that, lieutenant, as much as you will.

IAGO

O sweet England!

O sweet England!

King Stephen was a worthy peer,

King Stephen was a good king,

His breeches cost him but a crown;

And his pants were very cheap.

He held them sixpence all too dear,

He thought he spent sixpence too much

With that he call'd the tailor lown.

And called his tailor a rascal.

He was a wight of high renown,

He was a man of great reputation,

And thou art but of low degree:

And you are a man of low rank:

'Tis pride that pulls the country down;

It's pride that destroys the country,

Then take thine auld cloak about thee.

So be happy with your old cloak

Some wine, ho!

More wine!

CASSIO

Why, this is a more exquisite song than the other.

Why, that is an even better song than the last one.

IAGO

Will you hear't again?

Would you like me to sing it again?

CASSIO

No; for I hold him to be unworthy of his place that

No, I don't think it is right for us to be

does those things. Well, God's above all; and there

doing those things. Well, God's in charge, and there

be souls must be saved, and there be souls must not be saved.

must be some souls that get saved, and some that don't

IAGO

It's true, good lieutenant.

Very true, lieutenant.

CASSIO

For mine own part,--no offence to the general, nor

For me – and no offense to the general or

any man of quality,--I hope to be saved.

anyone else – I hope I am saved.

IAGO

And so do I too, lieutenant.

As do I, lieutenant.

CASSIO

Ay, but, by your leave, not before me; the

Yes, but please, not before me. The

lieutenant is to be saved before the ancient. Let's

lieutenant must be saved before the ensign. But

have no more of this; let's to our affairs.--Forgive

no more of this, let's go to the watch. Forgive

us our sins!--Gentlemen, let's look to our business.

us our sins! Gentlemen, let's do our work.

Do not think, gentlemen, I am drunk: this is my

Do not think, men, that I am drunk. Look: this is my

ancient; this is my right hand, and this is my left:

ensign, this is my right hand, this is my left hand –

I am not drunk now; I can stand well enough, and

you can see I am not drunk. I can stand and

speak well enough.

speak well enough.

All

Excellent well.

Yes, very well.

CASSIO

Why, very well then; you must not think then that I am drunk.

Yes, very well. You must not think I am drunk.

Exit

MONTANO

To the platform, masters; come, let's set the watch.

Let's go to the platform, everyone, and get to the watch.

IAGO

You see this fellow that is gone before;

You see that man who just left?

He is a soldier fit to stand by Caesar

He is a good enough soldier to stand next to Caesar

And give direction: and do but see his vice;

And give orders, but you see his vice,

'Tis to his virtue a just equinox,

Which is an extreme opposite to his virtue.

The one as long as the other: 'tis pity of him.

The one is as great as the other, it's too bad.

I fear the trust Othello puts him in

I am afraid that Othello trusts him too much

On some odd time of his infirmity,

And that at some time this weakness

Will shake this island.

Will be bad for the island.

MONTANO

But is he often thus?

Is he often this drunk?

IAGO

'Tis evermore the prologue to his sleep:

It's usually what he does before going to bed.

He'll watch the horologe a double set,

He would stay awake for a full day

If drink rock not his cradle.

If he does not have a drink to put him to sleep.

MONTANO

It were well

It would be good

The general were put in mind of it.

If the general knew about this.

Perhaps he sees it not; or his good nature

Perhaps he doesn't see it, or his trusting

Prizes the virtue that appears in Cassio,

Sees only Cassio's virtues,

And looks not on his evils: is not this true?

And not his evils. Doesn't that make sense?

Enter RODERIGO

IAGO

[Aside to him] How now, Roderigo!

What is it, Roderigo!

I pray you, after the lieutenant; go.

Please, go after the lieutenant, now.

Exit RODERIGO

MONTANO

And 'tis great pity that the noble Moor

It's too bad that the good Moor

Should hazard such a place as his own second

Should be so risky with his second-in-command by appointing

With one of an ingraft infirmity:

Someone with such a vice.

It were an honest action to say

It would be honest to tell this

So to the Moor.

To the Moor.

IAGO

Not I, for this fair island:

I won't tell him, not if you have me the whole island.

I do love Cassio well; and would do much

I love Cassio and would rather do what I can

To cure him of this evil--But, hark! what noise?

To cure him instead of ruining him. But wait, what is that sound?

Cry within: 'Help! help!'

Re-enter CASSIO, driving in RODERIGO

CASSIO

You rogue! you rascal!

You villain and rascal!

MONTANO

What's the matter, lieutenant?

What is the matter, lieutenant?

CASSIO

A knave teach me my duty!

You fool, trying to teach me my duty!

I'll beat the knave into a twiggen bottle.

I will beat you until you are criss-crossed like a straw covered bottle.

RODERIGO

Beat me!

Beat me!?

CASSIO

Dost thou prate, rogue?

Are you talking, you villain?

Striking RODERIGO

MONTANO

Nay, good lieutenant;

Stop, good lieutenant.

Staying him

I pray you, sir, hold your hand.

Please, sir, hold yourself back.

CASSIO

Let me go, sir,

Let me go

Or I'll knock you o'er the mazzard.

Or I will knock on the head.

MONTANO

Come, come,

Now, now, come on,

you're drunk.

you are drunk.

CASSIO

Drunk!

Drunk!

They fight

IAGO

[Aside to RODERIGO] Away, I say; go out, and cry a mutiny.

Now go and cry out that there is a fight.

Exit RODERIGO

Nay, good lieutenant,--alas, gentlemen;--

No, lieutenant, stop – oh, gentlemen –

Help, ho!--Lieutenant,--sir,--Montano,--sir;

Help! – Lieutenant – sir – Montano – sir –

Help, masters!--Here's a goodly watch indeed!

Help, someone! – Fine way to guard the night!

Bell rings

Who's that which rings the bell?--Diablo, ho!

Who is ringing the bell? – Oh, damn!

The town will rise: God's will, lieutenant, hold!

The whole town will come out. By God, lieutenant, stop!

You will be shamed for ever.

You will be ruined forever.

Re-enter OTHELLO and Attendants

OTHELLO

What is the matter here?

What is the matter here.

MONTANO

'Zounds, I bleed still; I am hurt to the death.

Oh I am bleeding! I am hurt to death.

Faints

OTHELLO

Hold, for your lives!

Stop, or your lives will be at stake!

IAGO

Hold, ho! Lieutenant,--sir--Montano,--gentlemen,--

Stop! – Lieutenant – sir – Montano – men –

Have you forgot all sense of place and duty?

Have you all forgotten your sense of duty and honor?

Hold! the general speaks to you; hold, hold, for shame!

Stop! The general is speaking to you! Stop, how shameful!

OTHELLO

Why, how now, ho! from whence ariseth this?

Why, how! How did this happen?

Are we turn'd Turks, and to ourselves do that

Have we become the Turks ourselves, and thus

Which heaven hath forbid the Ottomites?

Do what heaven stopped the Turks from doing to us?

For Christian shame, put by this barbarous brawl:

For the sake of Christianity stop this fighting:

He that stirs next to carve for his own rage

Whoever moves next to unleash his anger

Holds his soul light; he dies upon his motion.

Is risking his own life: he will die once he moves.

Silence that dreadful bell: it frights the isle

Someone stop that awful bell, it is frightening

From her propriety. What is the matter, masters?

The islanders. What happened here, sirs?

Honest Iago, that look'st dead with grieving,

Good Iago, you look exhausted and upset.

Speak, who began this? on thy love, I charge thee.

Speak up, who started this? I'm asking you out of love.

IAGO

I do not know: friends all but now, even now,

I don't know. We were all friends until now,

In quarter, and in terms like bride and groom

We were like bride and groom

Devesting them for bed; and then, but now--

Undressing for bed, and then, just now –

As if some planet had unwitted men--

As if the alignment of the planets had made them crazy –

Swords out, and tilting one at other's breast,

Swords came out, pointed at each other's chest

In opposition bloody. I cannot speak

In order to fight. I can't speak

Any beginning to this peevish odds;

To how this all began,

And would in action glorious I had lost

And I wish that in previous battles I had lost

Those legs that brought me to a part of it!

My legs so I wouldn't have come to see this!

OTHELLO

How comes it, Michael, you are thus forgot?

What happened, Michael, that you lost yourself?

CASSIO

I pray you, pardon me; I cannot speak.

Please, forgive me. I cannot speak.

OTHELLO

Worthy Montano, you were wont be civil;

Worthy Montano, you have been so polite.

The gravity and stillness of your youth

As a young man, your seriousness and calmness

The world hath noted, and your name is great

Was noted by the world, and your name is mentioned

In mouths of wisest censure: what's the matter,

By the wisest men. What happened

That you unlace your reputation thus

That you ruin your reputation like this

And spend your rich opinion for the name

And destroy these good estimations to become

Of a night-brawler? give me answer to it.

181

Someone who fights at night? Give me an answer.

MONTANO

Worthy Othello, I am hurt to danger:

Worthy Othello, I am badly injured.

Your officer, Iago, can inform you,--

Your officer, Iago, can tell you –

While I spare speech, which something now offends me,--

I should save my breath, it hurts me to talk –

Of all that I do know: nor know I aught

He can tell you everything I know. I have done

By me that's said or done amiss this night;

Nothing wrong tonight,

Unless self-charity be sometimes a vice,

Unless it is wrong to look out for ourselves

And to defend ourselves it be a sin

And a sin to defend ourselves

When violence assails us.

Against attack.

OTHELLO

Now, by heaven,

As God is my witness,

My blood begins my safer guides to rule;

I am beginning to lose my temper.

And passion, having my best judgment collied,

182

Passion is dirtying my sound judgment

Assays to lead the way: if I once stir,

And wants to be in charge of my decision making. If I move

Or do but lift this arm, the best of you

Or lift this arm, everyone

Shall sink in my rebuke. Give me to know

Will suffer at my hands. Tell me

How this foul rout began, who set it on;

How this fighting started, and who began it.

And he that is approved in this offence,

Whoever is proved the offender,

Though he had twinn'd with me, both at a birth,

Even if he were my twin at birth,

Shall lose me. What! in a town of war,

Shall lose my respect. Really! In a town already avoiding a war,

Yet wild, the people's hearts brimful of fear,

Where the people's hearts are already scared,

To manage private and domestic quarrel,

You have created this private fight

In night, and on the court and guard of safety!

At night, when you were supposed to be on guard!

'Tis monstrous. Iago, who began't?

This is awful. Iago, who started it.

MONTANO

If partially affined, or leagued in office,

If you speak from partiality or are in league with the offender

Thou dost deliver more or less than truth,

And thus do not speak the real truth,

Thou art no soldier.

You are no soldier.

IAGO

Touch me not so near:

Do not say such things to me.

I had rather have this tongue cut from my mouth

I would rather cut my tongue out of my mouth

Than it should do offence to Michael Cassio;

Than speak ill of Michael Cassio.

Yet, I persuade myself, to speak the truth

Yes, I believe that by telling the truth

Shall nothing wrong him. Thus it is, general.

I do not do anything wrong to him. So here it is, general.

Montano and myself being in speech,

Montano and I were talking,

There comes a fellow crying out for help:

And a fellow came crying out for help.

And Cassio following him with determined sword,

Cassio was following him with a sword,

To execute upon him. Sir, this gentleman

Intent on executing him. Sir, this gentelman Montano

Steps in to Cassio, and entreats his pause:

Stepped in to stop Cassio,

Myself the crying fellow did pursue,

And I followed after the man crying out for help,

Lest by his clamour--as it so fell out--

So that his awful shouting

The town might fall in fright: he, swift of foot,

Would not terrify the town. He, being very fast,

Outran my purpose; and I return'd the rather

Outran me, and I came back

For that I heard the clink and fall of swords,

Hearing the sound of swordfighting

And Cassio high in oath; which till to-night

And Cassio swearing, which until tonight

I ne'er might say before. When I came back--

I have never heard before. When I returned –

For this was brief--I found them close together,

This was quick – I found them together

At blow and thrust; even as again they were

Fighting, just as they were

When you yourself did part them.

When you separated them.

More of this matter cannot I report: *I have nothing more to say*

But men are men; the best sometimes forget:

Except that men are men, we forget this sometimes,

Though Cassio did some little wrong to him,

And though Cassio injured Montano,

As men in rage strike those that wish them best,

Striking out of rage at whoever is close no matter who they are or their intentions are,

Yet surely Cassio, I believe, received

I am also certain that Cassio received

From him that fled some strange indignity,

A cruel insult from the man who fled

Which patience could not pass.

Which even patience could not let pass.

OTHELLO

I know, Iago,

I know, Iago,

Thy honesty and love doth mince this matter,

That your honest and love affect your judgment

Making it light to Cassio. Cassio, I love thee

And seek to lighten Cassio's sin. Cassio, I love you,

But never more be officer of mine.

But you are no longer my officer.

Re-enter DESDEMONA, attended

Look, if my gentle love be not raised up!

Look, you have woken my gentle love!

I'll make thee an example.

I will make an example out of you.

DESDEMONA

What's the matter?

What happened?

OTHELLO

All's well now, sweeting; come away to bed.

All is well, sweetheart. Come back to bed.

Sir, for your hurts, myself will be your surgeon:

Sir, for your injuries, I will make sure you are treated.

Lead him off.

Lead him away.

To MONTANO, who is led off

Iago, look with care about the town,

Iago, go care for the townspeople

And silence those whom this vile brawl distracted.

And calm them whom were woken by this fight.

Come, Desdemona: 'tis the soldiers' life

Come Desdemona: it's the soldier's life

To have their balmy slumbers waked with strife.

To have their sleep interrupted by fighting.

Exeunt all but IAGO and CASSIO

IAGO

What, are you hurt, lieutenant?

Are you hurt, lieutenant?

CASSIO

Ay, past all surgery.

Yes, past all recovery.

IAGO

Marry, heaven forbid!

No, I hope not!

CASSIO

Reputation, reputation, reputation! O, I have lost

Reputation, reputation, reputation! O, I have lose

my reputation! I have lost the immortal part of

my reputation! I have lost the eternal part of

myself, and what remains is bestial. My reputation,

myself and only this animal side remains. My reputation,

Iago, my reputation!

Iago, my reputation!

IAGO

As I am an honest man, I thought you had received

I honestly thought that you had received

some bodily wound; there is more sense in that than

a physical injury – that means much more than

in reputation. Reputation is an idle and most false

your reputation. Reputation is a lazy and fake quality

imposition: oft got without merit, and lost without

that others impose. Often it has no merit, and it can be lost without

deserving: you have lost no reputation at all,

warrant. You have lost no reputation

unless you repute yourself such a loser. What, man!

unless you think you have. What!

there are ways to recover the general again: you

There are many ways to get back on the general's good side, right now

are but now cast in his mood, a punishment more in

you are dealing with a mood of his, but the punishment came from

policy than in malice, even so as one would beat his

policy, not from ill-will, just as someone would beat

offenceless dog to affright an imperious lion: sue

his dog to frighten off a lion. Go to him and ask,

to him again, and he's yours.

and he will change his mind.

CASSIO

I will rather sue to be despised than to deceive so

I would rather ask him to hate me than to trick

good a commander with so slight, so drunken, and so

a good commander to allow a worthless, drunken,

indiscreet an officer. Drunk? and speak parrot?

stupid officer back. Drunk? Speaking nonsense?

and squabble? swagger? swear? and discourse

And swearing? Raving

fustian with one's own shadow? O thou invisible

At one's own shadow? O invisible

spirit of wine, if thou hast no name to be known by,

demon of wine, if you have no other name,

let us call thee devil!

i will call you devil!

IAGO

What was he that you followed with your sword? What

Who was he whom you were chasing with your sword? What

had he done to you?

did he say to you?

CASSIO

I know not.

I don't know.

IAGO

Is't possible?

Is that possible?

CASSIO

I remember a mass of things, but nothing distinctly;

I remember a number of things, but nothing distinctly:

a quarrel, but nothing wherefore. O God, that men

a fight, but nothing else. O God, how awful that men

should put an enemy in their mouths to steal away

would put an enemy into their mouths through wine that steals

their brains! that we should, with joy, pleasance

their minds! How horrible that we should joyfully

revel and applause, transform ourselves into beasts!

party and thus transform ourselves into animals!

IAGO

Why, but you are now well enough: how came you thus

You seem very sober now, how did you

recovered?

recover so quickly?

CASSIO

It hath pleased the devil drunkenness to give place

The devil called drunkenness went away and gave his spot

to the devil wrath; one unperfectness shows me

to the devil called wrath. One vice opens up to

another, to make me frankly despise myself.

another, and makes me hate myself.

IAGO

Come, you are too severe a moraler: as the time,

You are much to hard on yourself. Given the time.

the place, and the condition of this country

and your rank, and the condition of the island,

stands, I could heartily wish this had not befallen;

I of course wish this had not happened –

but, since it is as it is, mend it for your own good.

but since it has, try to work it for your own good.

CASSIO

I will ask him for my place again; he shall tell me

If I ask him for my rank again he shall tell me

I am a drunkard! Had I as many mouths as Hydra,

that I am an alcoholic! Even if I had as many mouths as the Hydra of myth,

such an answer would stop them all. To be now a

an answer like that would quiet them all. First I was a

sensible man, by and by a fool, and presently a

reasonable person, and then I was a fool, and now I am

beast! O strange! Every inordinate cup is

an animal! How strange! Every cup of wine

unblessed and the ingredient is a devil.

is an evil curse of the devil.

IAGO

Come, come, good wine is a good familiar creature,

Come now, wine is a good substance

if it be well used: exclaim no more against it.

if it is used appropriately. Stop speaking against it,

And, good lieutenant, I think you think I love you.

And, good lieutenant, I think you know that I am your friend.

CASSIO

I have well approved it, sir. I drunk!

I know that well, sir. Me! A drunkard!

IAGO

You or any man living may be drunk! at a time, man.

You or any man might become drunk at any time, my man.

I'll tell you what you shall do. Our general's wife

This is what you shall now do: Othello's wife

is now the general: may say so in this respect, for

is his general, which I say because

that he hath devoted and given up himself to the

he has so devoted himself to her and given himself away

contemplation, mark, and denotement of her parts and

to thinking about and noting her bodyparts and

graces: confess yourself freely to her; importune

qualities. Tell your story to her and beg

her help to put you in your place again: she is of

her to help you regain your rank. She is

so free, so kind, so apt, so blessed a disposition,

so kind and has such a gracious nature

she holds it a vice in her goodness not to do more

that she considers it wrongdoing to not help someone

than she is requested: this broken joint between

as much as they ask. The brokenness between

you and her husband entreat her to splinter; and, my

you and Othello can be mended by her, and I

fortunes against any lay worth naming, this

193

would bet that

crack of your love shall grow stronger than it was before.

the love between you two will grow to be even stronger than it was before.

CASSIO

You advise me well.

You have good advice.

IAGO

I protest, in the sincerity of love and honest kindness.

No, only the sincerity of my love and kindness for you.

CASSIO

I think it freely; and betimes in the morning I will

I believe you. Early tomorrow morning I will

beseech the virtuous Desdemona to undertake for me:

go to good Desdemona and plead my case.

I am desperate of my fortunes if they cheque me here.

I am desperate to turn my fortunes around.

IAGO

You are in the right. Good night, lieutenant; I

That's the right thing to do. Goodnight lieutenant. I

must to the watch.

must go to keep the watch.

CASSIO

Good night, honest Iago.

Goodnight, honest Iago.

Exit

IAGO

And what's he then that says I play the villain?

And who says I am the villain?

When this advice is free I give and honest,

My advice is so good and honest,

Probal to thinking and indeed the course

And it probably is the best course

To win the Moor again? For 'tis most easy

To get back in the Moor's good favor. It is very easy

The inclining Desdemona to subdue

To convince the willing Desdemona to help

In any honest suit: she's framed as fruitful

Any case since she has the best wishes for others.

As the free elements. And then for her

And then, for her

To win the Moor--were't to renounce his baptism,

To convince the Moor – it could be as serious as renouncing his baptism

All seals and symbols of redeemed sin,

And all the other marks of his salvation,

His soul is so enfetter'd to her love,

But he is so completely in love with her

That she may make, unmake, do what she list,

That she can do whatever she wants

Even as her appetite shall play the god

And through her desires have as much control as God

With his weak function. How am I then a villain

Compared to his weak resistance. So how am I a villain

To counsel Cassio to this parallel course,

To suggest to Cassio to take this course,

Directly to his good? Divinity of hell!

Which is for his benefit? I am like Satan himself!

When devils will the blackest sins put on,

When devils are looking to do the most evil sins they can,

They do suggest at first with heavenly shows,

They first take on a heavenly appearance

As I do now: for whiles this honest fool

Just as I am doing. While this honest fool

Plies Desdemona to repair his fortunes

Seeks to get Desdemona to help him

And she for him pleads strongly to the Moor,

And she pleads his case to the Moor,

I'll pour this pestilence into his ear,

I will poison his ear

That she repeals him for her body's lust;

With talk of her being disgusted at his appearance

And by how much she strives to do him good,

And so the stronger she strives to help Cassio,

She shall undo her credit with the Moor.

The more she will become suspicious to the Moor.

So will I turn her virtue into pitch,

So I will turn her goodness into evil,

And out of her own goodness make the net

And out of it create a net

That shall enmesh them all.

To trap them all.

Re-enter RODERIGO

How now, Roderigo!

How are you, Roderigo?

RODERIGO

I do follow here in the chase, not like a hound that

I am spent from the chase, not like the hound

hunts, but one that fills up the cry. My money is

hunting, but like the hunted. My money is

almost spent; I have been to-night exceedingly well

nearly gone and tonight I have been very brutally

cudgelled; and I think the issue will be, I shall

beaten. I think that in return I have

have so much experience for my pains, and so, with

gained more experience for my sufferings, so with

no money at all and a little more wit, return again to Venice.

no money, and a little more wisdom, I am going back to Venice.

IAGO

How poor are they that have not patience!

How pathetic they are who do not have patience!

What wound did ever heal but by degrees?

Don't wounds heal slowly, not all at once?

Thou know'st we work by wit, and not by witchcraft;

You know that we are working through trickery, not magic,

And wit depends on dilatory time.

And such tricks require time.

Does't not go well? Cassio hath beaten thee.

Aren't you alright? Cassio beat you,

And thou, by that small hurt, hast cashier'd Cassio:

But because of that small injury, you have gotten Cassio discounted!

Though other things grow fair against the sun,

Our work is making the right things grow under the sun,

Yet fruits that blossom first will first be ripe:

And the fruits of this work will soon be ripe,

Content thyself awhile. By the mass, 'tis morning;

So be patient. My God, it's already morning:

Pleasure and action make the hours seem short.

Partying and action made time fly.

Retire thee; go where thou art billeted:

Go to sleep back where you are staying.

Away, I say; thou shalt know more hereafter:

Go now, you will know more later.

Nay, get thee gone.

No, get going.

Exit RODERIGO

Two things are to be done:

Two things still must be done:

My wife must move for Cassio to her mistress;

My wife must plead Cassio's case to Desdemona.

I'll set her on;

Which I can convince her to do.

Myself the while to draw the Moor apart,

Meanwhile I must go to the Moor

And bring him jump when he may Cassio find

And make sure he sees Cassio

Soliciting his wife: ay, that's the way

Pleading to his wife. Yes, thats what needs to happen,

Dull not device by coldness and delay.

And I must not ruin the plan through stupidity or slowness.

Exit

Act III

Scene I. Before the castle.

Enter CASSIO and some Musicians

CASSIO

Masters, play here; I will content your pains;

Masters, play now – I will pay you.

Something that's brief; and bid 'Good morrow, general.'

Play something brief, but happy, and remember to say, "Good morning, general."

Music

Enter Clown

Clown

Why masters, have your instruments been in Naples,

Why masters, have your instruments been to Naples?

that they speak i' the nose thus?

Is that why they have a nasal sound?

First Musician

How, sir, how!

What!

Clown

Are these, I pray you, wind-instruments?

Please tell me, are these wind instruments?

First Musician

Ay, marry, are they, sir.

They are, sir, yes.

Clown

O, thereby hangs a tail.

There's the problem.

First Musician

Whereby hangs a tale, sir?

What is the problem, sir?

Clown

Marry, sir, by many a wind-instrument that I know.

Well, sir, I know many people who are all wind.

But, masters, here's money for you: and the general

But, masters, here's some money. The general

so likes your music, that he desires you, for love's

likes your music so much that he desires, out of love,

sake, to make no more noise with it.

that you stop making noise out of it.

First Musician

Well, sir, we will not.

Well then we will stop.

Clown

If you have any music that may not be heard, to't

If you have any music that makes no sound, do play it

again: but, as they say to hear music the general

again. But as I said, with music that can be heard, the general

does not greatly care.

does not care for that.

First Musician

We have none such, sir.

We have no music like that, sir.

Clown

Then put up your pipes in your bag, for I'll away:

Then put your instruments away,

go; vanish into air; away!

go, leave into the air, goodbye!

Exeunt Musicians

CASSIO

Dost thou hear, my honest friend?

Do you hear, my honest friend?

Clown

No, I hear not your honest friend; I hear you.

No, I don't hear your honest friend, but I hear you.

CASSIO

Prithee, keep up thy quillets. There's a poor piece

Please, keep your jokes to yourself. Here's a bit

of gold for thee: if the gentlewoman that attends

of money. If the woman who is attending to

the general's wife be stirring, tell her there's

the general's wife is up, tell her

one Cassio entreats her a little favour of speech:

Cassio would like to speak with her –

wilt thou do this?

will you do this?

Clown

She is stirring, sir: if she will stir hither, I

She is up, sir, and if she comes this way, I

shall seem to notify unto her.

will tell her.

CASSIO

Do, my good friend.

Do, my friend.

Exit Clown

Enter IAGO

In happy time, Iago.

Good to see you, Iago.

IAGO

You have not been a-bed, then?

Have you not slept yet?

CASSIO

Why, no; the day had broke

No, the morning came

Before we parted. I have made bold, Iago,

Before we parted. I decided, Iago,

To send in to your wife: my suit to her

To send after your wife and talk to her

Is, that she will to virtuous Desdemona

In order to ask that she will go to virtuous Desdemona

Procure me some access.

And find me access to talk to Desdemona.

IAGO

I'll send her to you presently;

I will send her to you now

And I'll devise a mean to draw the Moor

And will devise a scheme to keep the Moor

Out of the way, that your converse and business

Out of the way so that your conversation

May be more free.

Can be without interruption.

CASSIO

I humbly thank you for't.

Thank you.

Exit IAGO

I never knew

I never knew

A Florentine more kind and honest.

A more kind and honest man from Florence.

Enter EMILIA

EMILIA

Good morrow, good Lieutenant: I am sorry

Good morning, good lieutenant. I am sorry

For your displeasure; but all will sure be well.

For your misfortunes, but I hope all will soon be fixed.

The general and his wife are talking of it;

The general and his wife are talking about it

And she speaks for you stoutly: the Moor replies,

And she defends you very strongly. Then the Moor replies

That he you hurt is of great fame in Cyprus,

That you hurt a very famous man in Cyprus,

And great affinity, and that in wholesome wisdom

One who is well liked, and that in the wisdom of the situation

He might not but refuse you; but he protests he loves you

He has no choice but to refuse you. Still, he says that he loves you

And needs no other suitor but his likings

And that he needs no one to convince him, that by his own preference

To take the safest occasion by the front

He is looking for a safe time to

To bring you in again.

Reinstate you.

CASSIO

Yet, I beseech you,

Still, I beg you,

If you think fit, or that it may be done,

If you think it is appropriate or possible,

Give me advantage of some brief discourse

Let me have some brief conversation

With Desdemona alone.

With Desdemona herself.

EMILIA

Pray you, come in;

Yes, come in.

I will bestow you where you shall have time

I will take you to where you will be able

To speak your bosom freely.

To speak freely with her.

CASSIO

I am much bound to you.

I am indebted to you.

Exeunt

Scene II. A room in the castle.

Enter OTHELLO, IAGO, and Gentlemen

OTHELLO

These letters give, Iago, to the pilot;

Iago, give these letters to the pilot

And by him do my duties to the senate:

And ask him to pay my respects to the Senate.

That done, I will be walking on the works;

With that done, I will be walking along the walls;

Repair there to me.

Find me there when you are done.

IAGO

Well, my good lord, I'll do't.

Very well, my lord. I will do it.

OTHELLO

This fortification, gentlemen, shall we see't?

Gentlemen, shall you show me around the fortifications?

Gentleman

We'll wait upon your lordship.

Whatever you would like, my lord.

Exeunt

Scene III. The garden of the castle.

Enter DESDEMONA, CASSIO, and EMILIA

DESDEMONA

Be thou assured, good Cassio, I will do

Be certain, Cassio, that I will do

All my abilities in thy behalf.

Everything I can.

EMILIA

Good madam, do: I warrant it grieves my husband,

Please do, madam. I believe it upsets my husband so much

As if the case were his.

That it seems like it is his case.

DESDEMONA

O, that's an honest fellow. Do not doubt, Cassio,

O, well he is a good man. Do not doubt, Cassio,

But I will have my lord and you again

That I will make sure that you and my husband

As friendly as you were.

Become as friendly as you ever were.

CASSIO

Bounteous madam,

Good lady,

Whatever shall become of Michael Cassio,

Whatever happens to me,

He's never any thing but your true servant.

I will always be your devoted servant.

DESDEMONA

I know't; I thank you. You do love my lord:

I know, thank you. You do love Othello,

You have known him long; and be you well assured

And you have known him a long time. Be assured:

He shall in strangeness stand no further off

He only stands away from you

Than in a polite distance.

From a political need.

CASSIO

Ay, but, lady,

Yes, but lady,

That policy may either last so long,

That political need may go on for too long,

Or feed upon such nice and waterish diet,

Or may create a such a diet and daily that I am not missed,

Or breed itself so out of circumstance,

Or may continue on unquestioned,

That, I being absent and my place supplied,

That, since I am gone and my position taken,

My general will forget my love and service.

Othello will forget about my love and my service to him.

DESDEMONA

Do not doubt that; before Emilia here

Do not think about that. Before Emilia as my witness,

I give thee warrant of thy place: assure thee,

I promise you your position. Rest assured,

If I do vow a friendship, I'll perform it

If I vow someone my friendship, I act on it

To the last article: my lord shall never rest;

To my fullest. Othello shall never gain rest

I'll watch him tame and talk him out of patience;

Since I will watch him and talk to him until his patience is gone,

His bed shall seem a school, his board a shrift;

And his bed and dinner table will seem like a school for all of my talking.

I'll intermingle every thing he does

I will mix everything he does

With Cassio's suit: therefore be merry, Cassio;

With your case, so be happy, Cassio.

For thy solicitor shall rather die

I, your attorney, would rather die

Than give thy cause away.

Than forget your cause.

212

EMILIA

Madam, here comes my lord.

Madam, here comes Othello.

CASSIO

Madam, I'll take my leave.

I will take my leave, madam.

DESDEMONA

Why, stay, and hear me speak.

No, stay, and hear what I will say.

CASSIO

Madam, not now: I am very ill at ease,

Madam, not now. I do not feel comfortable

Unfit for mine own purposes.

And that will not help my case.

DESDEMONA

Well, do your discretion.

As you will.

Exit CASSIO

Enter OTHELLO and IAGO

IAGO

Ha! I like not that.

Well! I don't like that.

OTHELLO

What dost thou say?

What is it?

IAGO

Nothing, my lord: or if--I know not what.

Nothing, my lord – or it – I don't know.

OTHELLO

Was not that Cassio parted from my wife?

Was that Cassio leaving my wife?

IAGO

Cassio, my lord! No, sure, I cannot think it,

Cassio! No, I don't think so.

That he would steal away so guilty-like,

He would not leave looking so guilty

Seeing you coming.

From seeing you coming.

OTHELLO

I do believe 'twas he.

I think it was him.

DESDEMONA

How now, my lord!

Hello, my lord!

I have been talking with a suitor here,

I have been talking with a man with a suit

A man that languishes in your displeasure.

Who suffers from your anger at him.

OTHELLO

Who is't you mean?

Who are you talking about?

DESDEMONA

Why, your lieutenant, Cassio. Good my lord,

Why, Cassio, your lieutenant. Good lord,

If I have any grace or power to move you,

If I have power to influence you,

His present reconciliation take;

Please accept his desire to reconcile.

For if he be not one that truly loves you,

He is someone who truly loves you

That errs in ignorance and not in cunning,

And his mistakes come from ignorance, not from deviousness –

I have no judgment in an honest face:

If I am wrong, I am an awful judge of character.

I prithee, call him back.

Please, call him back.

OTHELLO

Went he hence now?

Did he leave just now?

DESDEMONA

Ay, sooth; so humbled

Yes, he went away humbled

That he hath left part of his grief with me,

And left some of his sadness with me

To suffer with him. Good love, call him back.

So that I suffer with him. My love, call him back.

OTHELLO

Not now, sweet Desdemona; some other time.

Not yet, sweet Desdemona. Another time.

DESDEMONA

But shall't be shortly?

But will it be shortly?

OTHELLO

The sooner, sweet, for you.

Sooner than later, because you ask, sweetheart.

DESDEMONA

Shall't be to-night at supper?

Perhaps tonight at dinner?

OTHELLO

No, not to-night.

No, not tonight.

DESDEMONA

To-morrow dinner, then?

Tomorrow at dinner, then?

OTHELLO

I shall not dine at home;

I will not be eating at home,

I meet the captains at the citadel.

But meeting with the captains at the castle.

DESDEMONA

Why, then, to-morrow night; or Tuesday morn;

Then tomorrow night, or Tuesday morning,

On Tuesday noon, or night; on Wednesday morn:

Or Tuesday at noon, or night, or on Wednesday morning,

I prithee, name the time, but let it not

But please name the time, and do not let it

Exceed three days: in faith, he's penitent;

217

Go past three days because, truly, he is remorseful.

And yet his trespass, in our common reason--

And anyway, his offense, in all reason –

Save that, they say, the wars must make examples

Though, of course in wartime examples must be made

Out of their best--is not almost a fault

Out of the best of men – is not a fault

To incur a private cheque. When shall he come?

So great that it deserves such punishment. When should he come?

Tell me, Othello: I wonder in my soul,

Tell me, Othello. I wonder:

What you would ask me, that I should deny,

Is there anything you could ask me that I would deny you

Or stand so mammering on. What! Michael Cassio,

Or stand muttering about? This is Michael Cassio,

That came a-wooing with you, and so many a time,

He who came with you to woo me so many times,

When I have spoke of you dispraisingly,

Who, when I criticized you to him,

Hath ta'en your part; to have so much to do

Took your side and defended you, and now I have to make so much noise

To bring him in! Trust me, I could do much,--

just so you will bring him back! Trust me, I can do much more –

OTHELLO

Prithee, no more: let him come when he will;

Please, no more. He can come back when he wants,

I will deny thee nothing.

I will deny you nothing.

DESDEMONA

Why, this is not a boon;

It's not like you are doing me a favor:

'Tis as I should entreat you wear your gloves,

It's just like if I were to tell you to wear gloves in the cold

Or feed on nourishing dishes, or keep you warm,

Or eat healthy food, or stay warm

Or sue to you to do a peculiar profit

Or request you to do anything that will profit

To your own person: nay, when I have a suit

yourself. No, when I have a request

Wherein I mean to touch your love indeed,

Where I need to appeal to your love for me,

It shall be full of poise and difficult weight

It will be one that is very difficult

And fearful to be granted.

And terrible to be granted.

OTHELLO

I will deny thee nothing:

I will deny you nothing,

Whereon, I do beseech thee, grant me this,

But please, grant me one thing:

To leave me but a little to myself.

Leave me alone for a little while.

DESDEMONA

Shall I deny you? no: farewell, my lord.

Would I deny you? No. Goodbye, my lord.

OTHELLO

Farewell, my Desdemona: I'll come to thee straight.

Goodbye, my Desdemona. I will come to you soon.

DESDEMONA

Emilia, come. Be as your fancies teach you;

Emilia, come. Othello, do what you feel like,

Whate'er you be, I am obedient.

Whatever you do, I will obey you.

Exeunt DESDEMONA and EMILIA

OTHELLO

Excellent wretch! Perdition catch my soul,

Wonderful woman! Heaven help me,

But I do love thee! and when I love thee not,

But I love you! And if I stop loving you,

Chaos is come again.

May the universe return to Chaos, as it was before the world was made.

IAGO

My noble lord--

My noble lord–

OTHELLO

What dost thou say, Iago?

What is it, Iago?

IAGO

Did Michael Cassio, when you woo'd my lady,

Did Michael Cassio, when you courted Desdemona,

Know of your love?

Know about your love for her?

OTHELLO

He did, from first to last: why dost thou ask?

He did, right from the beginning, why?

IAGO

But for a satisfaction of my thought;

Just for my own curiosity,

No further harm.

No other reason.

OTHELLO

Why of thy thought, Iago?

What are you curious about, Iago?

IAGO

I did not think he had been acquainted with her.

I did not know that he knew her.

OTHELLO

O, yes; and went between us very oft.

O yes, and he talked to her for me often.

IAGO

Indeed!

Really!

OTHELLO

Indeed! ay, indeed: discern'st thou aught in that?

Yes, really: is there something wrong with that?

Is he not honest?

Don't you think he is honest?

IAGO

Honest, my lord!

Honest, my lord!

OTHELLO

Honest! ay, honest.

Honest! yes, honest.

IAGO

My lord, for aught I know.

For all I know, my lord.

OTHELLO

What dost thou think?

And what do you think?

IAGO

Think, my lord!

What do I think, my lord?

OTHELLO

Think, my lord!

What do I think, my lord?

By heaven, he echoes me,

By God, he repeats what I say

As if there were some monster in his thought

As if he is thinking something so monstrous

Too hideous to be shown. Thou dost mean something:

That he must hide hit. You must mean something that you won't tell me:

I heard thee say even now, thou likedst not that,

I heard you comment as if you did not like it

When Cassio left my wife: what didst not like?

When you saw Cassio leave my wife. Why did you not like it?

And when I told thee he was of my counsel

And when I told you he helped me

In my whole course of wooing, thou criedst 'Indeed!'

When I was courting Desdemona you cried out, "Really!"

And didst contract and purse thy brow together,

While you wrinkled your brow

As if thou then hadst shut up in thy brain

As if you had thought of some

Some horrible conceit: if thou dost love me,

Awful imagination. If you love me,

Show me thy thought.

Tell me what you thought.

IAGO

My lord, you know I love you.

My lord, you know I love you.

OTHELLO

I think thou dost;

I think you do,

And, for I know thou'rt full of love and honesty,

And I know that you are loving and honest,

And weigh'st thy words before thou givest them breath,

That you weigh your words carefully before you speak,

Therefore these stops of thine fright me the more:

So your pauses even more frighten me.

For such things in a false disloyal knave

In a disloyal liar,

Are tricks of custom, but in a man that's just

These are common tricks, but in a man who is just

They are close delations, working from the heart

They are indictments that work in the heart

That passion cannot rule.

And even passion cannot stop them.

IAGO

For Michael Cassio,

As for Michael Cassio,

I dare be sworn I think that he is honest.

I swear that I think he is honest.

OTHELLO

I think so too.

I agree.

IAGO

Men should be what they seem;

Men should be what they look like they are,

Or those that be not, would they might seem none!

And those that are not honest should not seem honest!

OTHELLO

Certain, men should be what they seem.

Agreed, men should be in reality what they look like they are.

IAGO

Why, then, I think Cassio's an honest man.

Then I think Cassio is in reality an honest man.

OTHELLO

Nay, yet there's more in this:

No, there's more to it than this.

I prithee, speak to me as to thy thinkings,

Please, tell me what you are thinking,

As thou dost ruminate, and give thy worst of thoughts

Whatever you are pondering, and say even your worst fears

The worst of words.

Clearly, in their awful content.

IAGO

Good my lord, pardon me:

My lord, please excuse me:

Though I am bound to every act of duty,

Though I will obey everything you ask,

I am not bound to that all slaves are free to.

I do not need to obey that which even slaves are not forced to do.

Utter my thoughts? Why, say they are vile and false;

Tell you my thoughts? What if they are awful and wrong,

As where's that palace whereinto foul things

Since there is no place where awful things

Sometimes intrude not? who has a breast so pure,

Might enter into, and similarly no one has a mind so pure

But some uncleanly apprehensions

That no unclean, dirty thoughts

Keep leets and law-days and in session sit

Sometimes come into it and mingle

With meditations lawful?

With their pure thoughts and meditaitons.

OTHELLO

Thou dost conspire against thy friend, Iago,

You are working against your own friend, Iago,

If thou but think'st him wrong'd and makest his ear

If you think he has been wronged and yet keep him

A stranger to thy thoughts.

Away from your thoughts.

IAGO

I do beseech you--

I beg you –

Though I perchance am vicious in my guess,

Since I am often too suspicious

As, I confess, it is my nature's plague

And, truly, it is a curse of my character

To spy into abuses, and oft my jealousy

That I imagine problems and often my imaginations

Shapes faults that are not--that your wisdom yet,

Create faults where there are none – that your mind,

From one that so imperfectly conceits,

From someone who inaccurately imagines,

Would take no notice, nor build yourself a trouble

Will not be troubled by me or

Out of his scattering and unsure observance.

What I have uncertainly and haphazardly observed.

It were not for your quiet nor your good,

It would harm your peace and your goodness,

Nor for my manhood, honesty, or wisdom,

And I would sooner give up my manhood, honesty, or intelligence

To let you know my thoughts.

Than tell you what I think.

OTHELLO

What dost thou mean?

What do you mean?

IAGO

Good name in man and woman, dear my lord,

A man and a woman's reputation, my lord,

Is the immediate jewel of their souls:

Is the most worthy part of who they are:

Who steals my purse steals trash; 'tis something, nothing;

If someone steals my money, they steal trash. It is something, and then nothing,

'Twas mine, 'tis his, and has been slave to thousands:

It was mine and now it is his, and it has been owned by thousands before.

But he that filches from me my good name

But whoever steals my reputation

Robs me of that which not enriches him

Takes away something that does not help him

And makes me poor indeed.

But all the while truly hurts me.

OTHELLO

By heaven, I'll know thy thoughts.

By God, tell me what you think.

IAGO

You cannot, if my heart were in your hand;

You cannot know, not even if you held my heart,

Nor shall not, whilst 'tis in my custody.

Which you can't since it is still in my body.

OTHELLO

Ha!

Ha!

IAGO

O, beware, my lord, of jealousy;

My lord, be careful not to fall into jealousy.

It is the green-eyed monster which doth mock

It is a green eyed monster who taunts

The meat it feeds on; that cuckold lives in bliss

Its victim. The man who is cheated on is happy

Who, certain of his fate, loves not his wronger;

If he knows he is being cheated on and does not love the other man.

But, O, what damned minutes tells he o'er

But O how horrible for the man

Who dotes, yet doubts, suspects, yet strongly loves!

Who loves, yet doubts his beloved and is suspicious, yet still loves!

OTHELLO

O misery!

What misery!

IAGO

Poor and content is rich and rich enough,

Being poor and happy is rich enough,

But riches fineless is as poor as winter

But he who is rich without measure is as poor as winter is

To him that ever fears he shall be poor.

If he fears that he will someday be poor.

Good heaven, the souls of all my tribe defend

Dear God, protect all of us

From jealousy!

For jealousy!

OTHELLO

Why, why is this?

Why do you say all of this?

Think'st thou I'ld make a lie of jealousy,

Do you think that I will become so jealous

To follow still the changes of the moon

That I will watch for the moon to change phases

With fresh suspicions? No; to be once in doubt

And get suspicious each time it does? No, if I became doubtful,

Is once to be resolved: exchange me for a goat,

I would then become resolved to end doubt. I would sooner be a goat

When I shall turn the business of my soul

Than spend my energy on

To such exsufflicate and blown surmises,

Such meaningless and trivial guesswork,

Matching thy inference. 'Tis not to make me jealous

Looking to infer what has happened. It will not make me jealous

To say my wife is fair, feeds well, loves company,

To hear that my wife is beautiful, cooks well, enjoys company,

Is free of speech, sings, plays and dances well;

Speaks freely, sings and has fun and dances well –

Where virtue is, these are more virtuous:

These are only great things, and she is great.

Nor from mine own weak merits will I draw

I will not overcompensate for my weakness by creating

The smallest fear or doubt of her revolt;

A fear or doubt of her leaving me.

For she had eyes, and chose me. No, Iago;

She had eyes and was not tricked, and she still chose me. No, Iago,

I'll see before I doubt; when I doubt, prove;

I would look before I begin to doubt, and then if I were to doubt, I would find proof,

And on the proof, there is no more but this,--

And as for proof, there is nothing –

Away at once with love or jealousy!

So my love will do away with jealousy!

IAGO

I am glad of it; for now I shall have reason

I am glad, because now I have reason

To show the love and duty that I bear you

To love you and obey your requests

With franker spirit: therefore, as I am bound,

With a more honest spirit. Therefore, since you have asked,

Receive it from me. I speak not yet of proof.

I will tell you. I do not have proof of anything.

Look to your wife; observe her well with Cassio;

Look at your wife, and look at her when she is with Cassio.

Wear your eye thus, not jealous nor secure:

Behave like this, carefully, but neither jealous nor unaware.

I would not have your free and noble nature,

I would not want your noble and trusting character

Out of self-bounty, be abused; look to't:

From someone else's gain, be taken advantage of. So be wary.

I know our country disposition well;

I know the people of our county well –

In Venice they do let heaven see the pranks

In Venice, they let God see their sins,

They dare not show their husbands; their best conscience

But they never show these sins to their husbands. They think it is best

Is not to leave't undone, but keep't unknown.

When they can sin, but keep it unknown to everyone.

OTHELLO

Dost thou say so?

Do you really think so?

IAGO

She did deceive her father, marrying you;

She already tricked her father by marrying you,

And when she seem'd to shake and fear your looks,

And she acted scared about your appearance

She loved them most.

Even though she loved it most.

OTHELLO

And so she did.

Yes, she did.

IAGO

Why, go to then;

Well, there it is:

She that, so young, could give out such a seeming,

She who was so young put on such an act

To seal her father's eyes up close as oak-

To trick her father

He thought 'twas witchcraft--but I am much to blame;

That he thought it was witchcraft – but I shouldn't say that.

I humbly do beseech you of your pardon

I ask for your forgiveness for speaking

For too much loving you.

Which I do only because I love you too much.

OTHELLO

I am bound to thee for ever.

I owe you forever.

IAGO

I see this hath a little dash'd your spirits.

I see this has upset you a little.

OTHELLO

Not a jot, not a jot.

Not at all, not at all.

IAGO

I' faith, I fear it has.

Truly, I am afraid it has.

I hope you will consider what is spoke

I hope that you know that what I said

Comes from my love. But I do see you're moved:

Came from love. But I see that you are sad.

I am to pray you not to strain my speech

Please do not take what I have said so seriously

To grosser issues nor to larger reach

That you stretch it to greater imaginations and situations

Than to suspicion.

Than the appropriate suspicion it deserves.

OTHELLO

I will not.

I will not.

IAGO

Should you do so, my lord,

If you do, my lord,

My speech should fall into such vile success

Then what I have said has had awful effects

As my thoughts aim not at. Cassio's my worthy friend--

That I did not intend. Cassio is a good friend –

My lord, I see you're moved.

My lord, I see that you are upset.

OTHELLO

No, not much moved:

No, not that upset.

I do not think but Desdemona's honest.

I think that Desdemona is very honest.

IAGO

Long live she so! and long live you to think so!

And may she be her whole life! And may your whole life you think so!

OTHELLO

And yet, how nature erring from itself,--

And yet, one can act against one's true nature –

IAGO

Ay, there's the point: as--to be bold with you--

Ah, that is what I meant. To be bold,

Not to affect many proposed matches

She was not affected by any proposals

Of her own clime, complexion, and degree,

From men who are more similar to her, as in country, skin color, and status,

Whereto we see in all things nature tends--

Which nature tends to respect most –

Foh! one may smell in such a will most rank,

Oh! One can almost sense such a disgusting will

Foul disproportion thoughts unnatural.

In evilly overestimating such unnatural things!

But pardon me; I do not in position

But excuse me, I don't mean

Distinctly speak of her; though I may fear

To speak specifically of her. Though, still, I worry

Her will, recoiling to her better judgment,

That her desires, against her better judgement,

May fall to match you with her country forms

Will compare you to her countrymen

And happily repent.

And choose them instead.

OTHELLO

Farewell, farewell:

Goodbye, goodbye –

If more thou dost perceive, let me know more;

If you see more, let me know,

Set on thy wife to observe: leave me, Iago:

And ask your wife to watch her. Go now, Iago.

IAGO

[Going] My lord, I take my leave.

My lord, I will go now.

OTHELLO

Why did I marry? This honest creature doubtless

Why did I even marry? This honest man must

Sees and knows more, much more, than he unfolds.

See and know much more than he says.

IAGO

[Returning] My lord, I would I might entreat your honour

My lord, I must ask you

To scan this thing no further; leave it to time:

To stop thinking about this thing. Give it time.

Though it be fit that Cassio have his place,

Though it is right that Cassio get his rank back,

For sure, he fills it up with great ability,

After all he is very able and talented,

Yet, if you please to hold him off awhile,

But if you hold him from accepting him for a while

You shall by that perceive him and his means:

You will see how he handles it.

Note, if your lady strain his entertainment

If your lady continues to insist on his return

238

With any strong or vehement importunity;

By strongly begging you –

Much will be seen in that. In the mean time,

You will see a lot in that. Meanwhile,

Let me be thought too busy in my fears--

Think of me as too paranoid –

As worthy cause I have to fear I am--

For I often am –

And hold her free, I do beseech your honour.

And hold her as blameless, please.

OTHELLO

Fear not my government.

Do not worry about my judgment.

IAGO

I once more take my leave.

Again, I will go now.

Exit

OTHELLO

This fellow's of exceeding honesty,

Iago is incredibly honest

And knows all qualities, with a learned spirit,

And speaks wisely of the qualities

Of human dealings. If I do prove her haggard,

Of other men. If I do find out she has been cheating on me,

Though that her jesses were my dear heartstrings,

Even though she is tied to my very heartstrings

I'd whistle her off and let her down the wind,

I will send her off

To pray at fortune. Haply, for I am black

To her own luck. Maybe because I am black

And have not those soft parts of conversation

And do not have the skilled softness of speech

That chamberers have, or for I am declined

That mannered men have, or because I have aged

Into the vale of years,--yet that's not much--

And am now old – yet not too old –

She's gone. I am abused; and my relief

She leaves me. I have been wronged and my only hope

Must be to loathe her. O curse of marriage,

Is to hate her. Marriage is such a curse:

That we can call these delicate creatures ours,

We think we can own these beautiful women,

And not their appetites! I had rather be a toad,

And yet we cannot own their desires! I would rather be a frog

And live upon the vapour of a dungeon,

Living on the germ-ridden air and mold of a dungeon

Than keep a corner in the thing I love

Than to have only part of the woman I love

For others' uses. Yet, 'tis the plague of great ones;

And share her with others. This is the plague of great men:

Prerogatived are they less than the base;

They are less favored than lower men,

'Tis destiny unshunnable, like death:

It's an unshakeable destiny, like death.

Even then this forked plague is fated to us

We are fated to walk down this plagued path

When we do quicken. Desdemona comes:

From our birth. Here is Desdemona.

Re-enter DESDEMONA and EMILIA

If she be false, O, then heaven mocks itself!

If she has lied, then God is mocking himself!

I'll not believe't.

I will not believe it.

DESDEMONA

How now, my dear Othello!

How are you, dear Othello!

Your dinner, and the generous islanders

Your dinner is waiting for you, and the islanders

By you invited, do attend your presence.

Whom you invited want to see you at dinner.

OTHELLO

I am to blame.

It is my fault.

DESDEMONA

Why do you speak so faintly?

Why do you speak so quietly?

Are you not well?

Are you sick?

OTHELLO

I have a pain upon my forehead here.

I have a headache.

DESDEMONA

'Faith, that's with watching; 'twill away again:

That's from the guard and not sleeping. It will go away.

Let me but bind it hard, within this hour

Let me wrap it tightly and in an hour

It will be well.

It will be alright.

OTHELLO

Your napkin is too little:

This is a little too tight.

He puts the handkerchief from him; and it drops

Let it alone. Come, I'll go in with you.

Leave it alone. Come on, I will go with you.

DESDEMONA

I am very sorry that you are not well.

I am sorry that you are not feeling well.

Exeunt OTHELLO and DESDEMONA

EMILIA

I am glad I have found this napkin:

I am glad I found this napkin –

This was her first remembrance from the Moor:

It is her first keepsake from the Moor.

My wayward husband hath a hundred times

My evil husband has asked me a hundred times

Woo'd me to steal it; but she so loves the token,

To steal it from her, but she loves it,

For he conjured her she should ever keep it,

Since Othello asked her to keep it,

That she reserves it evermore about her

So she keeps it near her

To kiss and talk to. I'll have the work ta'en out,

In order to talk to it and kiss it. I will have the pattern copied

And give't Iago: what he will do with it

And given to Iago. What he does with it

Heaven knows, not I;

Heaven knows, but I don't.

I nothing but to please his fantasy.

I do whatever I can to please him.

Re-enter Iago

IAGO

How now! what do you here alone?

What's going on? Why are you here alone?

EMILIA

Do not you chide; I have a thing for you.

Do not be mean to me. I have something for you.

IAGO

A thing for me? it is a common thing--

Something for me? Well you give that to everyone...

EMILIA

Ha!

Ha!

IAGO

To have a foolish wife.

O, to have a dumb wife.

EMILIA

O, is that all? What will you give me now

Are you done? What will you give me

For the same handkerchief?

In exchange for the handkerchief?

IAGO

What handkerchief?

What handkerchief?

EMILIA

What handkerchief?

What handkerchief?

Why, that the Moor first gave to Desdemona;

The same one that the Moor gave to Desdemona

That which so often you did bid me steal.

Which you have wanted me to steal.

IAGO

Hast stol'n it from her?

And you stole it?

EMILIA

No, 'faith; she let it drop by negligence.

No, of course not. She let it drop in passing

And, to the advantage, I, being here, took't up.

And, fortunately, I was here, and picked it up.

Look, here it is.

Here it is.

IAGO

A good wench; give it me.

You are a good woman. Give it to me.

EMILIA

What will you do with 't, that you have been so earnest

What will you do with it? Why were you so intent

To have me filch it?

On me taking it?

IAGO

[Snatching it] Why, what's that to you?

How is that your business?

EMILIA

If it be not for some purpose of import,

If it is not for some important business

Give't me again: poor lady, she'll run mad

Then give it back. The poor lady will go mad

When she shall lack it.

When she sees she does not have it.

IAGO

Be not acknown on 't; I have use for it.

Do not admit you know where it is. I need it for a reason.

Go, leave me.

Go, leave me.

Exit EMILIA

I will in Cassio's lodging lose this napkin,

I will place this napkin in Cassio's place

And let him find it. Trifles light as air

And make sure he finds it. Such a little thing

Are to the jealous confirmations strong

Becomes the confirmation of a jealous man's thoughts,

As proofs of holy writ: this may do something.

As if they were holy proof. This might work.

The Moor already changes with my poison:

The Moor is already affected by what I said to him.

Dangerous conceits are, in their natures, poisons.

Evil ideas are really just like poisons:

Which at the first are scarce found to distaste,

At first, they aren't even distasted,

But with a little act upon the blood.

But then they get into the blood.

Burn like the mines of Sulphur. I did say so:

There they burn like mines of sulphur.

Look, where he comes!

Look, here he comes!

Re-enter OTHELLO

Not poppy, nor mandragora,

No flower

Nor all the drowsy syrups of the world,

Or medicine in all the world

Shall ever medicine thee to that sweet sleep

Will ever force you into the sweet sleep

Which thou owedst yesterday.

That you had yesterday.

OTHELLO

Ha! ha! false to me?

Ah! Is she cheating on me?

IAGO

Why, how now, general! no more of that.

What? Now, general, no more of that!

OTHELLO

Avaunt! be gone! thou hast set me on the rack:

Go away! You have place me on the torture rack.

I swear 'tis better to be much abused

It is better to be taken advantage of completely

Than but to know't a little.

Than to know about it at all.

IAGO

How now, my lord!

What are you saying, my lord!

OTHELLO

What sense had I of her stol'n hours of lust?

Did I know anything of the hours she spent cheating on me?

I saw't not, thought it not, it harm'd not me:

I didn't see it or think it, and it didn't hurt me.

I slept the next night well, was free and merry;

I slept well, and was happy.

I found not Cassio's kisses on her lips:

I never tasted Cassio on her lips.

He that is robb'd, not wanting what is stol'n,

Whoever is robbed but does not notice it

Let him not know't, and he's not robb'd at all.

Should never be told, since he is not really robbed at all.

IAGO

I am sorry to hear this.

I am sorry to hear this.

OTHELLO

I had been happy, if the general camp,

I would have been happier if the entire squadron,

Pioners and all, had tasted her sweet body,

Even the lowest ranking soldiers, had had sex with her,

So I had nothing known. O, now, for ever

As long as I didn't know. And now, forever,

Farewell the tranquil mind! farewell content!

Goodbye peaceful mind! Goodbye happiness!

Farewell the plumed troop, and the big wars,

Goodbye to the soldiers and wars

That make ambition virtue! O, farewell!

That make one great! O, goodbye!

Farewell the neighing steed, and the shrill trump,

Goodbye to the neighing horse and loud trumpet,

The spirit-stirring drum, the ear-piercing fife,

The patriotic drum, the flute,

The royal banner, and all quality,

The royal flag and all the glory,

Pride, pomp and circumstance of glorious war!

The pride, festivity, and situations of war!

And, O you mortal engines, whose rude throats

And you, the cannons whose sounds

The immortal Jove's dead clamours counterfeit,

Rival Jove's thunderbolts,

Farewell! Othello's occupation's gone!

Goodbye! My career is ruined!

IAGO

Is't possible, my lord?

Is that possible, my lord?

OTHELLO

Villain, be sure thou prove my love a whore,

Villain, you had better be sure that you can prove my love is a whore.

Be sure of it; give me the ocular proof:

Be sure of it and give me visible proof,

Or by the worth of man's eternal soul,

Or I swear by a man's eternal soul

Thou hadst been better have been born a dog

That you would rather have been born a dog

Than answer my waked wrath!

Than stand in front of my anger!

IAGO

Is't come to this?

Has it come to this?

OTHELLO

Make me to see't; or, at the least, so prove it,

Make me see it, or at the least, prove it

That the probation bear no hinge nor loop

So that there is no possible explanation

To hang a doubt on; or woe upon thy life!

That doubts it, or your life will be destroyed!

IAGO

My noble lord,--

My noble lord –

OTHELLO

If thou dost slander her and torture me,

If you are speaking poorly of her in order to torture me,

Never pray more; abandon all remorse;

Then you should stop praying. Do not think you can repent.

On horror's head horrors accumulate;

On your head evil deeds will be numbered,

Do deeds to make heaven weep, all earth amazed;

So do such awful things that heaven cries and all of the earth is stunned.

For nothing canst thou to damnation add

Nothing can add to the damnation

Greater than that.

You would already receive.

IAGO

O grace! O heaven forgive me!

O God! O God forgive me!

Are you a man? have you a soul or sense?

Are you still a man, and do you still have sense?

God be wi' you; take mine office. O wretched fool.

Please, I resign my rank. I am a fool,

That livest to make thine honesty a vice!

For living to tell the truth and then seeing that it is a vice!

O monstrous world! Take note, take note, O world,

O awful world! O world, be forewarned:

To be direct and honest is not safe.

It is not safe to be honest and straightforward.

I thank you for this profit; and from hence

Thank you for teaching me this, and from now on

I'll love no friend, sith love breeds such offence.

I will give such love to no one, since it only hurts them.

OTHELLO

Nay, stay: thou shouldst be honest.

No, stay, you should be honest.

IAGO

I should be wise, for honesty's a fool

No, I should be wise. Honesty is foolish

And loses that it works for.

And loses the friendship it works to serve.

OTHELLO

By the world,

By God,

I think my wife be honest and think she is not;

I think my wife is honest and dishonest,

I think that thou art just and think thou art not.

And that you are trustworthy and untrustworthy.

I'll have some proof. Her name, that was as fresh

I need proof. Her name, that was as pure

253

As Dian's visage, is now begrimed and black

As the Goddess Diana, is now tainted and as black

As mine own face. If there be cords, or knives,

As my face. As long as there are ropes or knives

Poison, or fire, or suffocating streams,

Or poison or fire or streams to drown in,

I'll not endure it. Would I were satisfied!

I won't stand for this. I wish I knew the truth!

IAGO

I see, sir, you are eaten up with passion:

Sir, you are consumed by passion and strong feeling,

I do repent me that I put it to you.

And I feel sorry that I did this.

You would be satisfied?

You really want to know?

OTHELLO

Would! nay, I will.

Want! No, I will know.

IAGO

And may: but, how? how satisfied, my lord?

And you might, but how? How will you know, my lord?

Would you, the supervisor, grossly gape on--

Will you try to hide and watch –

254

Behold her topp'd?

Watch her have sex?

OTHELLO

Death and damnation! O!

Curses!

IAGO

It were a tedious difficulty, I think,

It seems like it would be very difficult

To bring them to that prospect: damn them then,

To make sure you do that. Damn them

If ever mortal eyes do see them bolster

If anyone else's eyes see them

More than their own! What then? how then?

Do what they shouldn't be! So what can we do?

What shall I say? Where's satisfaction?

What can I say, how can you find proof?

It is impossible you should see this,

It seems impossible that you will see them having sex,

Were they as prime as goats, as hot as monkeys,

Even if they were as ready as goats or as hot as monkeys,

As salt as wolves in pride, and fools as gross

As horny as wolves, and as foolish as

As ignorance made drunk. But yet, I say,

255

Drunken morons. But, I wonder,

If imputation and strong circumstances,

If calculations and circumstantial evidence,

Which lead directly to the door of truth,

Which in inference lead towards the truth,

Will give you satisfaction, you may have't.

Might give you the proof you need, you would accept it.

OTHELLO

Give me a living reason she's disloyal.

Give me a good reason that she is disloyal to me.

IAGO

I do not like the office:

I do not like this task,

But, sith I am enter'd in this cause so far,

But, since I am already this far in,

Prick'd to't by foolish honesty and love,

Led to it by foolish honesty and my love for you,

I will go on. I lay with Cassio lately;

I will continue. I slept near Cassio lately

And, being troubled with a raging tooth,

And, in pain from a toothache,

I could not sleep.

I could not sleep.

There are a kind of men so loose of soul,

Some men have a loose soul

That in their sleeps will mutter their affairs:

That causes them to talk in their sleep –

One of this kind is Cassio:

Cassio is a man like that.

In sleep I heard him say 'Sweet Desdemona,

While he was asleep I heard him say, "Sweet Desdemona,

Let us be wary, let us hide our loves;'

Let us be careful and hide our love"

And then, sir, would he gripe and wring my hand,

And then, sir, he grabbed and held onto my hand,

Cry 'O sweet creature!' and then kiss me hard,

Crying "Sweet darling!" and then kissing me hard

As if he pluck'd up kisses by the roots

As if he were taking the kisses out by force

That grew upon my lips: then laid his leg

From my lips. Then he placed his leg

Over my thigh, and sigh'd, and kiss'd; and then

Over my thigh, and sighed, and kisse me again,

Cried 'Cursed fate that gave thee to the Moor!'

And cried out "How awful that you belong to the Moor!"

OTHELLO

O monstrous! monstrous!

O awful! awful!

257

IAGO

Nay, this was but his dream.

No, this was only a dream.

OTHELLO

But this denoted a foregone conclusion:

But it marks something that already happened.

'Tis a shrewd doubt, though it be but a dream.

It's a good reason to doubt, even though it is only a dream.

IAGO

And this may help to thicken other proofs

It may help support other proofs,

That do demonstrate thinly.

If they are not very convincing on their own.

OTHELLO

I'll tear her all to pieces.

I will destroy her!

IAGO

Nay, but be wise: yet we see nothing done;

No, be smart. We do not know anything yet,

She may be honest yet. Tell me but this,

She might be honest. Tell me this:

Have you not sometimes seen a handkerchief

Have you seen a handkerchief

Spotted with strawberries in your wife's hand?

Spotted with strawberries, held by your wife?

OTHELLO

I gave her such a one; 'twas my first gift.

I gave it to her, it was my first gift to her.

IAGO

I know not that; but such a handkerchief--

I did not know about that, but this handkerchief –

I am sure it was your wife's--did I to-day

I am sure it was your wife's – I saw today,

See Cassio wipe his beard with.

And Cassio wiped his beard with it.

OTHELLO

If it be that--

If that was hers–

IAGO

If it be that, or any that was hers,

If it was hers, or anything else that belonged to her,

It speaks against her with the other proofs.

Then it speaks strongly against her alongside the other proofs.

OTHELLO

O, that the slave had forty thousand lives!

O, if Cassio had forty thousand lives!

One is too poor, too weak for my revenge.

One life is too few for me to get my revenge.

Now do I see 'tis true. Look here, Iago;

Now I see it is true. Look, Iago,

All my fond love thus do I blow to heaven.

I am getting rid of all of my love for Desdemona.

'Tis gone.

It's gone.

Arise, black vengeance, from thy hollow cell!

Come to me, vengeance!

Yield up, O love, thy crown and hearted throne

My Love, give up your spot in my life

To tyrannous hate! Swell, bosom, with thy fraught,

To Hate instead! O, my chest, fill with pain

For 'tis of aspics' tongues!

As if you are full of snakes' tongues!

IAGO

Yet be content.

Please, be calm.

OTHELLO

O, blood, blood, blood!

O, blood!

IAGO

Patience, I say; your mind perhaps may change.

Be patient. Your mind might change.

OTHELLO

Never, Iago: Like to the Pontic sea,

No, Iago, never. Like a river to the sea

Whose icy current and compulsive course

Whose cold stream and steady course

Ne'er feels retiring ebb, but keeps due on

Never fades away but continues on

To the Propontic and the Hellespont,

To the seas in front of it,

Even so my bloody thoughts, with violent pace,

So too my revengeful thoughts violently

Shall ne'er look back, ne'er ebb to humble love,

never look back or calm to love

Till that a capable and wide revenge

Until a they are able to have their full revenge

Swallow them up. Now, by yond marble heaven,

And let that swallow them up. Now, I swear by the sky

Kneels

In the due reverence of a sacred vow

In a sacred, holy vow,

I here engage my words.

To make my words lead to action.

IAGO

Do not rise yet.

Do not get up yet.

Kneels

Witness, you ever-burning lights above,

Heaven, be my witness,

You elements that clip us round about,

Everything that surrounds us daily,

Witness that here Iago doth give up

Witness that I, Iago, give up

The execution of his wit, hands, heart,

The power of my mind, my hands, and my heart

To wrong'd Othello's service! Let him command,

To Othello who has been wronged! Let him command,

And to obey shall be in me remorse,

And I will obey him,

What bloody business ever.

No matter what happens.

They rise

OTHELLO

I greet thy love,

I thank you for your love,

Not with vain thanks, but with acceptance bounteous,

Not vainly, but with devoted acceptance.

And will upon the instant put thee to't:

This instant I will task you:

Within these three days let me hear thee say

Within the next three days, I must hear you say

That Cassio's not alive.

That Cassio is no longer alive.

IAGO

My friend is dead; 'tis done at your request:

My friend will die. At your request it will be done,

But let her live.

But let her live.

OTHELLO

Damn her, lewd minx! O, damn her!

Damn her, evil whore! O, damn her!

Come, go with me apart; I will withdraw,

Go away from me. I will withdraw to my room

To furnish me with some swift means of death

To figure out some way to kill

For the fair devil. Now art thou my lieutenant.

That beautiful demon. You are my lieutenant.

IAGO

I am your own for ever.

I am yours forever.

Exeunt

Scene IV. Before the castle.

Enter DESDEMONA, EMILIA, and Clown

DESDEMONA

Do you know, sirrah, where Lieutenant Cassio lies?

Do you know, sir, where Cassio lies?

Clown

I dare not say he lies any where.

I would not say he lies anywhere.

DESDEMONA

Why, man?

Why would you say that?

Clown

He's a soldier, and for one to say a soldier lies,

Because he is a soldier, and one who says that soldier lies

is stabbing.

might be stabbed.

DESDEMONA

Go to: where lodges he?

Come on now, where does he stay?

Clown

To tell you where he lodges, is to tell you where I lie.

To tell you where he stays is the same as telling you where I lie.

DESDEMONA

Can any thing be made of this?

What does this mean?

Clown

I know not where he lodges, and for me to devise a

I do not know where he stays, so to say that he

lodging and say he lies here or he lies there, were

stays anywhere, here or there, is the same

to lie in mine own throat.

as lying.

DESDEMONA

Can you inquire him out, and be edified by report?

Can you ask about him, and report back to me?

Clown

I will catechise the world for him; that is, make

I will ask the world about him.

questions, and by them answer.

DESDEMONA

Seek him, bid him come hither: tell him I have

Find him and ask him to come to me. Tell him that I have

moved my lord on his behalf, and hope all will be well.

influenced Othello to take him back and that I hope all will be well.

Clown

To do this is within the compass of man's wit: and

This is within my intelligence, and

therefore I will attempt the doing it.

therefore I will do it.

Exit

DESDEMONA

Where should I lose that handkerchief, Emilia?

Where did I lose my handkerchief, Emilia?

EMILIA

I know not, madam.

I don't know, madam.

DESDEMONA

Believe me, I had rather have lost my purse

Believe me, I would have rather lost my purse

Full of crusadoes: and, but my noble Moor

Full of money. It's a good thing that the noble Moor

Is true of mind and made of no such baseness

Is so honest and not made of such evilness

As jealous creatures are, it were enough

As jealous men are – or else that would be enough

To put him to ill thinking.

To make him think awful things.

EMILIA

Is he not jealous?

He does not get jealous?

DESDEMONA

Who, he? I think the sun where he was born

Who, Othello? I think the sun where he was born was so hot

Drew all such humours from him.

That it sapped him from those feelings.

EMILIA

Look, where he comes.

Look, here he comes.

DESDEMONA

I will not leave him now till Cassio

I will not leave him until he calls Cassio

Be call'd to him.

To him.

Enter OTHELLO

How is't with you, my lord?

How are you, my lord?

OTHELLO

Well, my good lady.

I am well, good lady.

Aside

O, hardness to dissemble!--

It is so hard to pretend! –

How do you, Desdemona?

How are you, Desdemona?

DESDEMONA

Well, my good lord.

I am well, my lord.

OTHELLO

Give me your hand: this hand is moist, my lady.

Give me your hand – it is moist with love, my lady.

DESDEMONA

It yet hath felt no age nor known no sorrow.

It has gotten old and has not been sad at all.

OTHELLO

This argues fruitfulness and liberal heart:

This hand says that you have a giving heart and are fertile.

Hot, hot, and moist: this hand of yours requires

Hot, hot and moist – with a hand like this you need to

A sequester from liberty, fasting and prayer,

Take a break from freedom. You need to fast and pray

Much castigation, exercise devout;

And become devout,

For here's a young and sweating devil here,

Since a young, horny devil could be near,

That commonly rebels. 'Tis a good hand,

One that rebels against their devotion. This is a good hand,

A frank one.

An honest one.

DESDEMONA

You may, indeed, say so;

You are right –

For 'twas that hand that gave away my heart.

This hand gave you my heart.

OTHELLO

A liberal hand: the hearts of old gave hands;

A free hand – long ago, hearts gave hands,

But our new heraldry is hands, not hearts.

But now people give each other their hands, but not their hearts.

270

DESDEMONA

I cannot speak of this. Come now, your promise.

I have nothing to say about that. Now then, you have a promise for me.

OTHELLO

What promise, chuck?

What promise, dear?

DESDEMONA

I have sent to bid Cassio come speak with you.

I have sent away to ask Cassio to speak with you.

OTHELLO

I have a salt and sorry rheum offends me;

I have a cold and a cough bothers me –

Lend me thy handkerchief.

Can you lend me your handkerchief?

DESDEMONA

Here, my lord.

Here it is, my lord.

OTHELLO

That which I gave you.

The one I gave you, I mean.

DESDEMONA

I have it not about me.

I don't have it with me.

OTHELLO

Not?

No?

DESDEMONA

No, indeed, my lord.

No, I don't, my lord.

OTHELLO

That is a fault.

This is not good.

That handkerchief

That handkerchief

Did an Egyptian to my mother give;

Was given to my mother by an Egyptian –

She was a charmer, and could almost read

She was a magician and could almost read

The thoughts of people: she told her, while she kept it,

People's thoughts. She told her, while she kept it,

'Twould make her amiable and subdue my father

That it would make her obedient to my father

Entirely to her love, but if she lost it

Entirely, but that if she ever lost it

Or made gift of it, my father's eye

Or gave it away, my father

Should hold her loathed and his spirits should hunt

Would hate her and his desires would hunt

After new fancies: she, dying, gave it me;

After other women. When she was dying, she gave it to me

And bid me, when my fate would have me wive,

And told me that when I found a wife,

To give it her. I did so: and take heed on't;

To give it to her. I did, so look:

Make it a darling like your precious eye;

Treat it like your own child to your eye;

To lose't or give't away were such perdition

To lose it or give it away is a sin

As nothing else could match.

That nothing could match.

DESDEMONA

Is't possible?

Is that true?

OTHELLO

'Tis true: there's magic in the web of it:

Yes, there is magic in its threads.

A sibyl, that had number'd in the world

A witch, who had lived in the world

The sun to course two hundred compasses,

For two hundred years

In her prophetic fury sew'd the work;

Sewed it in a prophetic fury.

The worms were hallow'd that did breed the silk;

She used holy worms for the silk

And it was dyed in mummy which the skilful

And it was dyed in the mummified

Conserved of maidens' hearts.

preserves of virgins' hearts.

DESDEMONA

Indeed! is't true?

Really! It's true?

OTHELLO

Most veritable; therefore look to't well.

Yes, very true. So keep an eye on it.

DESDEMONA

Then would to God that I had never seen't!

Then I wish I had never seen it!

OTHELLO

Ha! wherefore?

Ha! Why do you say that?

DESDEMONA

Why do you speak so startingly and rash?

Why do you speak so aggressively?

OTHELLO

Is't lost? is't gone? speak, is it out

Is it lost? Gone? Tell me, is it

o' the way?

no longer here?

DESDEMONA

Heaven bless us!

Heaven help me!

OTHELLO

Say you?

What are you saying?

DESDEMONA

It is not lost; but what an if it were?

It is not lost, but what if it was?

OTHELLO

How!

How!

DESDEMONA

I say, it is not lost.

I will say it again, it's not lost.

OTHELLO

Fetch't, let me see't.

Then get it and let me see it.

DESDEMONA

Why, so I can, sir, but I will not now.

Well I could, but I will not now.

This is a trick to put me from my suit:

This is a trick to keep me from my request.

Pray you, let Cassio be received again.

Please, let Cassio be reinstated.

OTHELLO

Fetch me the handkerchief: my mind misgives.

Please get the handkerchief, my mind doubts.

DESDEMONA

Come, come;

Come, now.

You'll never meet a more sufficient man.

You will never meet a more able soldier.

OTHELLO

The handkerchief!

The handkerchief!

DESDEMONA

I pray, talk me of Cassio.

Please, talk to me about Cassio.

OTHELLO

The handkerchief!

The handkerchief!

DESDEMONA

A man that all his time

He has spent all his time

Hath founded his good fortunes on your love,

Centering himself on his love for you,

Shared dangers with you,--

And even went through dangerous situations with you–

OTHELLO

The handkerchief!

The handkerchief!

DESDEMONA

In sooth, you are to blame.

Truly, you are to blame for acting poorly.

OTHELLO

Away!

Go away!

Exit

EMILIA

Is not this man jealous?

And you said this man is not jealous?

DESDEMONA

I ne'er saw this before.

I never saw him act like this before.

Sure, there's some wonder in this handkerchief:

But yes, there is something special about the handkerchief.

I am most unhappy in the loss of it.

I am very upset that I lost it.

EMILIA

'Tis not a year or two shows us a man:

Only a year or two will truly teach you about a man.

They are all but stomachs, and we all but food;

They are all desire, and we are all they desire –

To eat us hungerly, and when they are full,

They want to take us, and then when they are satisfied,

They belch us. Look you, Cassio and my husband!

They treat us poorly. Here is Cassio and Iago!

Enter CASSIO and IAGO

IAGO

There is no other way; 'tis she must do't:

There is no other way – she must help you.

And, lo, the happiness! go, and importune her.

And here she is, what luck! Go and beg her.

DESDEMONA

How now, good Cassio! what's the news with you?

How are you, good Cassio! What is the news?

CASSIO

Madam, my former suit: I do beseech you

Madam, only my previous case. I beg you

That by your virtuous means I may again

That from your friendship that I may again

Exist, and be a member of his love

Return and enter into Othello's love,

Whom I with all the office of my heart

Who I with all of my heart

Entirely honour: I would not be delay'd.

Honor – I do not want to wait longer.

If my offence be of such mortal kind

If what I have done is so horrible

That nor my service past, nor present sorrows,

That neither my past service nor present sorrows

Nor purposed merit in futurity,

Nor my future potential merit

Can ransom me into his love again,

Can win me back to him,

But to know so must be my benefit;

Then it would be best that I know.

So shall I clothe me in a forced content,

I will force myself to accept it,

And shut myself up in some other course,

And will stop myself from looking for another way

To fortune's alms.

To regain this fortune.

DESDEMONA

Alas, thrice-gentle Cassio!

Oh, gentle Cassio!

My advocation is not now in tune;

My pleading is not working.

My lord is not my lord; nor should I know him,

Othello is not acting like himself,

Were he in favour as in humour alter'd.

But as if he has been changed.

So help me every spirit sanctified,

So God must help me,

As I have spoken for you all my best

For I have spoken to you as best I cant

And stood within the blank of his displeasure

And have stood in front of him as he showed how displeased he was

For my free speech! you must awhile be patient:

At my words! You must be patient:

What I can do I will; and more I will

Whatever I can do I will do, more than

Than for myself I dare: let that suffice you.

I should dare. Let that be enough for you now.

IAGO

Is my lord angry?

Is Othello angry?

EMILIA

He went hence but now,

He just left,

And certainly in strange unquietness.

And certainly seemed like he was in an unsettled mood.

IAGO

Can he be angry? I have seen the cannon,

Can he really be angry? I have seen the cannon

When it hath blown his ranks into the air,

Blow his men into the air

And, like the devil, from his very arm

And, like the devil, even

Puff'd his own brother:--and can he be angry?

Kill his own brother – and he is angry now?

Something of moment then: I will go meet him:

It must be from something important. I will go see him.

There's matter in't indeed, if he be angry.

There must be something serious if he is indeed angry.

DESDEMONA

I prithee, do so.

Please, do so.

Exit IAGO

Something, sure, of state,

It must be a national item,

Either from Venice, or some unhatch'd practise

Something from Venice, or else some plot

Made demonstrable here in Cyprus to him,

That here in Cyprus he discovered,

Hath puddled his clear spirit: and in such cases

And this must have clouded his mind. In such cases,

Men's natures wrangle with inferior things,

Men fight with the small, trivial things,

Though great ones are their object. 'Tis even so;

When the more important ones are their true object. It's true for us too,

For let our finger ache, and it indues

When our finger hurts, it makes

Our other healthful members even to that sense

The rest of our body align with that pain

Of pain: nay, we must think men are not gods,

And hurt as well. No, we must not think men are gods,

Nor of them look for such observances

Nor think that they will always act as if

As fit the bridal. Beshrew me much, Emilia,

It is their wedding day. O curse me, Emilia,

I was, unhandsome warrior as I am,

I am such a poor soldier, and I

Arraigning his unkindness with my soul;

Blamed him for his unkindness,

But now I find I had suborn'd the witness,

When really I was judging him

And he's indicted falsely.

And thinking of him wrongly.

EMILIA

Pray heaven it be state-matters, as you think,

I pray that it is state matters, like you think,

And no conception nor no jealous toy

And no imagination or jealousy

Concerning you.

That is about you.

DESDEMONA

Alas the day! I never gave him cause.

I would rue that day! I never gave him a reason for such thoughts.

EMILIA

But jealous souls will not be answer'd so;

But jealous men do not need reason.

They are not ever jealous for the cause,

They are not jealous for a cause,

But jealous for they are jealous: 'tis a monster

But simply because they are jealous. It's a monster

Begot upon itself, born on itself.

That creates itself.

DESDEMONA

Heaven keep that monster from Othello's mind!

God, keep that monster away from Othello!

EMILIA

Lady, amen.

Amen to that.

DESDEMONA

I will go seek him. Cassio, walk hereabout:

I will go to him. Cassio, stay here –

If I do find him fit, I'll move your suit

If I find him able to talk to, I will plead your case

And seek to effect it to my uttermost.

With all my strength.

CASSIO

I humbly thank your ladyship.

I humbly thank you.

Exeunt DESDEMONA and EMILIA

Enter BIANCA

BIANCA

Save you, friend Cassio!

Hello, Cassio!

CASSIO

What make you from home?

How are you so far from home?

How is it with you, my most fair Bianca?

How are you, my beautiful Bianca?

I' faith, sweet love, I was coming to your house.

Truly, sweet love, I was on my way to you.

BIANCA

And I was going to your lodging, Cassio.

And I was on my way to your house, Cassio.

What, keep a week away? seven days and nights?

What, should I stay away from you for a full week? Seven days and nights?

Eight score eight hours? and lovers' absent hours,

One hundred and sixty eight hours? And these are the hours of lovers apart,

More tedious than the dial eight score times?

Which are much longer than regular ones.

O weary reckoning!

O what a tedious waiting!

CASSIO

Pardon me, Bianca:

Forgive me, Bianca –

I have this while with leaden thoughts been press'd:

I have been depressed with heavy thoughts,

But I shall, in a more continuate time,

But hopefully I will soon

Strike off this score of absence. Sweet Bianca,

Make up this absent time. Sweet Bianca,

Giving her DESDEMONA's handkerchief

Take me this work out.

Could you copy this pattern for me?

BIANCA

O Cassio, whence came this?

Cassio, where did this come from?

This is some token from a newer friend:

This must be a gift from a newer girl.

To the felt absence now I feel a cause:

Now I know why you were absent.

Is't come to this? Well, well.

Has it come to this?

CASSIO

Go to, woman!

Go do it, woman!

Throw your vile guesses in the devil's teeth,

Get rid of your evil guesses and send them back

From whence you have them. You are jealous now

To where you got them. You are jealous

That this is from some mistress, some remembrance:

That this is from some new mistress of mine:

No, in good troth, Bianca.

It's not, truly, Bianca.

BIANCA

Why, whose is it?

Then whose is it?

CASSIO

I know not, sweet: I found it in my chamber.

I don't know, my sweet. I found it in my room.

I like the work well: ere it be demanded--

I like the stitching, and before I have to give it back –

As like enough it will--I'ld have it copied:

Which I certainly will – I would like to have it copied for me.

Take it, and do't; and leave me for this time.

Take it and stitch it for me, and leave me for now.

BIANCA

Leave you! wherefore?

Leave you! Why?

CASSIO

I do attend here on the general;

I am waiting here for Othello,

And think it no addition, nor my wish,

And I do not think it will help me

To have him see me woman'd.

If he sees me with a woman.

BIANCA

Why, I pray you?

Why?

CASSIO

Not that I love you not.

Though I do love you.

BIANCA

But that you do not love me.

But you don't love me.

I pray you, bring me on the way a little,

Please, bring me along with you

And say if I shall see you soon at night.

And tell me if I will see you later.

CASSIO

'Tis but a little way that I can bring you;

I can only bring you a little ways

For I attend here: but I'll see you soon.

Since I must wait here. I will see you soon.

BIANCA

'Tis very good; I must be circumstanced.

Alright, fine. I will obey the circumstance.

Exeunt

Act IV

Scene I. Cyprus. Before the castle.

Enter OTHELLO and IAGO

IAGO

Will you think so?

Do you think so?

OTHELLO

Think so, Iago!

Think so! Iago!

IAGO

What,

What,

To kiss in private?

Did they kiss in private?

OTHELLO

An unauthorized kiss.

A wrong, secret kiss.

IAGO

Or to be naked with her friend in bed

Or perhaps they were naked together in bed

An hour or more, not meaning any harm?

For an hour or so, but didn't do anything?

OTHELLO

Naked in bed, Iago, and not mean harm!

Naked in bed, and not do anything! Absurd!

It is hypocrisy against the devil:

That would be like the devil being a hypocrite and not really doing evil.

They that mean virtuously, and yet do so,

If they meant to not have sex, and yet laid together like that,

The devil their virtue tempts, and they tempt heaven.

Then they are asking to be tempted, and condemned.

IAGO

So they do nothing, 'tis a venial slip:

Then if they do not do anything, it is only a minor slip-up.

But if I give my wife a handkerchief,--

But, if I give my wife a handkerchief–

OTHELLO

What then?

Then what?

IAGO

Why, then, 'tis hers, my lord; and, being hers,

Well, then it is hers, my lord. And since it is hers,

She may, I think, bestow't on any man.

She can give it to anyone.

OTHELLO

She is protectress of her honour too:

She is also the owner of her honor, though –

May she give that?

Can she give that to anyone?

IAGO

Her honour is an essence that's not seen;

Her honor is a quality, not a tangible object.

They have it very oft that have it not:

Many times people do not even have the honor they think they do.

But, for the handkerchief,--

But a handkerchief–

OTHELLO

By heaven, I would most gladly have forgot it.

By God, I wish I could forget about it

Thou said'st, it comes o'er my memory,

What you said clouds my thinking

As doth the raven o'er the infected house,

And, like a raven flying over a cursed house,

Boding to all--he had my handkerchief.

Foreshadows evil. He has my handkerchief!

IAGO

Ay, what of that?

So, what of it?

OTHELLO

That's not so good now.

That is no good.

IAGO

What,

Well

If I had said I had seen him do you wrong?

What if I said that I had seen him do something wrong?

Or heard him say,--as knaves be such abroad,

Or if I heard him say – like evil men,

Who having, by their own importunate suit,

Who of their own forceful manipulation

Or voluntary dotage of some mistress,

Or the love of some woman

Convinced or supplied them, cannot choose

Get what they are after, cannot help themselves

But they must blab--

But talk about it–

OTHELLO

Hath he said any thing?

Did he say something?

IAGO

He hath, my lord; but be you well assured,

He did, my lord, but you should know

No more than he'll unswear.

That he will only deny it.

OTHELLO

What hath he said?

What did he say?

IAGO

'Faith, that he did--I know not what he did.

Well, that he did– I don't know what he did.

OTHELLO

What? what?

What? Tell me.

IAGO

Lie--

That he laid

OTHELLO

With her?

With her?

IAGO

With her, on her; what you will.

With her, on her, whatever you think.

OTHELLO

Lie with her! lie on her! We say lie on her, when

Lay with her! On her! I would rather hear, instead of "lie on her"

they belie her. Lie with her! that's fulsome.

that people were lying about her. Lay with her! That's disgusting.

--Handkerchief--confessions--handkerchief!--To

–Handkerchief–confessions–handkerchief! He must

confess, and be hanged for his labour;--first, to be

confess and then be hung for his confession. –No, first

hanged, and then to confess.--I tremble at it.

hung, and then he can confess. – I am shaking with anger.

Nature would not invest herself in such shadowing

Nature would not let me feel like this, in such

passion without some instruction. It is not words

passion, if there was no truth to the matter. Simple words

that shake me thus. Pish! Noses, ears, and lips.

can't shake me like this. Bah! Noses, ears, lips.

--Is't possible?--Confess--handkerchief!--O devil!--

Is it possible? – Confess – handkerchief! – O devil!

Falls in a trance

IAGO

Work on,

Keep going,

My medicine, work! Thus credulous fools are caught;

My poisonous imaginations that I gave him! Naively trusting fools are easily caught

And many worthy and chaste dames even thus,

And many worthy, pure women are,

All guiltless, meet reproach. What, ho! my lord!

Even though they are blameless, punished. What, Othello!

My lord, I say! Othello!

Othello!

Enter CASSIO

How now, Cassio!

Hello, Cassio!

CASSIO

What's the matter?

What is going on?

IAGO

My lord is fall'n into an epilepsy:

Othello has fallen into an epileptic fit.

This is his second fit; he had one yesterday.

This is his second one – the first one was yesterday.

CASSIO

Rub him about the temples.

Rub his temples.

IAGO

No, forbear;

No, just wait –

The lethargy must have his quiet course:

The fit should run its course.

If not, he foams at mouth and by and by

If it doesn't, he begins to foam at the mouth

Breaks out to savage madness. Look he stirs:

And become mad. Look, he wakes.

Do you withdraw yourself a little while,

Go away for a little while,

He will recover straight: when he is gone,

He will recover quickly. When he is gone,

I would on great occasion speak with you.

I greatly need to talk to you.

Exit CASSIO

How is it, general? have you not hurt your head?

General, how are you? Did you hurt your head?

OTHELLO

Dost thou mock me?

Are you mocking me?

IAGO

I mock you! no, by heaven.

Mocking you! Of course not.

Would you would bear your fortune like a man!

But I wish you could bear your misfortune like a man!

OTHELLO

A horned man's a monster and a beast.

A man who has been cheated on is more of a monster and an animal.

IAGO

There's many a beast then in a populous city,

Well there are many animals, then, in a crowded city,

And many a civil monster.

And many monsters are still polite.

OTHELLO

Did he confess it?

Did he confess to it?

IAGO

Good sir, be a man;

Good sir, act like a man.

Think every bearded fellow that's but yoked

Every married fellow

May draw with you: there's millions now alive

Has the same situation you do. There are millions

That nightly lie in those unproper beds

Who go to bed each night with their cheating wives

Which they dare swear peculiar: your case is better.

Whom they think are loyal to them. Your situation is better.

O, 'tis the spite of hell, the fiend's arch-mock,

O, it is indeed a curse, the worst kind of mocking,

To lip a wanton in a secure couch,

To kiss a loose woman

And to suppose her chaste! No, let me know;

And believe she is pure! No, I would rather know,

And knowing what I am, I know what she shall be.

And then I will know what I really am and what she really is.

OTHELLO

O, thou art wise; 'tis certain.

You are certainly wise.

IAGO

Stand you awhile apart;

Go away from the situation for a little

Confine yourself but in a patient list.

And calm down in patience.

Whilst you were here o'erwhelmed with your grief--

While you were overwhelmed here in a fit of sadness –

A passion most unsuiting such a man--

Which is not the proper response for a man –

Cassio came hither: I shifted him away,

Cassio came here. I ushered him away

And laid good 'scuse upon your ecstasy,

And made up an excuse for your fit,

Bade him anon return and here speak with me;

But asked him to come back and talk with me,

The which he promised. Do but encave yourself,

Which he agreed to do. So hide yourself

And mark the fleers, the gibes, and notable scorns,

And make a note of all of the sneers and scorns

That dwell in every region of his face;

That will show up on his face.

For I will make him tell the tale anew,

I will make him tell the story again –

Where, how, how oft, how long ago, and when

Where, how, how often, when it started, and when

He hath, and is again to cope your wife:

He plans again to go to your wife.

I say, but mark his gesture. Marry, patience;

Again, make a note of his actions. Be patient,

Or I shall say you are all in all in spleen,

Or I will think that you are taken up by your rage

And nothing of a man.

And not really a man.

OTHELLO

Dost thou hear, Iago?

Do you hear me, Iago?

I will be found most cunning in my patience;

I will be quiet and cunning in my patience,

But--dost thou hear?--most bloody.

But – and hear this – still very violent when the time comes.

IAGO

That's not amiss;

That's not a wrong thing,

But yet keep time in all. Will you withdraw?

But it must be in the right time. Now go away.

OTHELLO retires

Now will I question Cassio of Bianca,

I will ask Cassio about Bianca,

A housewife that by selling her desires

A prostitute that sells sex

Buys herself bread and clothes: it is a creature

So that she can buy food and clothes. She

That dotes on Cassio; as 'tis the strumpet's plague

Loves Cassio – it is the loose woman's curse

To beguile many and be beguiled by one:

To convince many to love her, but to be in love with one.

He, when he hears of her, cannot refrain

When he hears talk about her, he won't be able to stop

From the excess of laughter. Here he comes:

Laughing. Here he comes.

Re-enter CASSIO

As he shall smile, Othello shall go mad;

He will smile, and Othello will go crazy.

And his unbookish jealousy must construe

His unhinged jealousy will interpret

Poor Cassio's smiles, gestures and light behavior,

Cassio's smiles, actions, and happy behavior

Quite in the wrong. How do you now, lieutenant?

Wrongly. How are you, lieutenant?

CASSIO

The worser that you give me the addition

I am worse when you call me by that rank

Whose want even kills me.

Since I want it back so badly.

IAGO

Ply Desdemona well, and you are sure on't.

Beg Desdemona well, and you will get it.

Speaking lower

Now, if this suit lay in Bianca's power,

Now if it were up to Bianca,

How quickly should you speed!

303

You would have it back so quickly!

CASSIO

Alas, poor caitiff!

Ah, poor awful woman.

OTHELLO

Look, how he laughs already!

Look how he laughs!

IAGO

I never knew woman love man so.

I never knew a woman who was so in love with a man.

CASSIO

Alas, poor rogue! I think, i' faith, she loves me.

That poor rogue! I think that she really does love me.

OTHELLO

Now he denies it faintly, and laughs it out.

Now he denies it quietly and tries to laugh it away.

IAGO

Do you hear, Cassio?

Have you heard this, Cassio?

OTHELLO

Now he importunes him

Now Iago is asking him

To tell it o'er: go to; well said, well said.

To tell the story again. Well played.

IAGO

She gives it out that you shall marry hey:

She says that you are to marry –

Do you intend it?

Do you intend to do this?

CASSIO

Ha, ha, ha!

Ha ha ha!

OTHELLO

Do you triumph, Roman? do you triumph?

Do you think you have won, really?

CASSIO

I marry her! what? a customer! Prithee, bear some

I marry her! What? I am only a customer! Please, give

charity to my wit: do not think it so unwholesome.

my intelligence some credit – I am not that dumb.

Ha, ha, ha!

Ha ha ha!

OTHELLO

So, so, so, so: they laugh that win.

Well, well, well – the true winner has the last laugh.

IAGO

'Faith, the cry goes that you shall marry her.

Really! The word is that you are going to marry her.

CASSIO

Prithee, say true.

Please, speak honestly.

IAGO

I am a very villain else.

I am, and would be a villain to say otherwise.

OTHELLO

Have you scored me? Well.

Have you made her pregnant as well? Fine.

CASSIO

This is the monkey's own giving out: she is

Then this is made up by her, that monkey. She

persuaded I will marry her, out of her own love and

thinks I will marry her because she loves me and

flattery, not out of my promise.

flatters herself, but it is not backed up by me.

OTHELLO

Iago beckons me; now he begins the story.

Iago is motioning that Cassio is beginning the story.

CASSIO

She was here even now; she haunts me in every place.

She was just here – she follows me everywhere.

I was the other day talking on the sea-bank with

The other day I was talking on the shore with

certain Venetians; and thither comes the bauble,

a few Venetians and here comes that fool,

and, by this hand, she falls me thus about my neck--

takes me by the hand, and puts her arms around me like this–

OTHELLO

Crying 'O dear Cassio!' as it were: his gesture imports it.

It looks like he is motioning how she cried out his name.

CASSIO

So hangs, and lolls, and weeps upon me; so hales,

She hangs on me, and cries over me, and shakes me like this,

and pulls me: ha, ha, ha!

and pulls on me like this. Ha ha ha!

OTHELLO

Now he tells how she plucked him to my chamber. O,

Now he is telling how she took him to my room. O,

I see that nose of yours, but not that dog I shall

I see your nose, but I cannot yet see the dog that I will

throw it to.

throw it to.

CASSIO

Well, I must leave her company.

Well, I must stay away from her.

IAGO

Before me! look, where she comes.

Then look out, for here she comes.

CASSIO

'Tis such another fitchew! marry a perfumed one.

It's a whore like all of the others, wearing perfume.

Enter BIANCA

What do you mean by this haunting of me?

Why do you keep following me?

BIANCA

Let the devil and his dam haunt you! What did you

I hope the devil and his wife haunt you! Why did

mean by that same handkerchief you gave me even now?

you give me that handkerchief earlier?

I was a fine fool to take it. I must take out the

I was a fool to take it. And I must copy it for you?

work?--A likely piece of work, that you should find

A likely story, that you would find it

it in your chamber, and not know who left it there!

in your room and not know who put it there!

This is some minx's token, and I must take out the

This is some token from another woman, and you want me to

work? There; give it your hobby-horse: wheresoever

copy it? There, take it, give it back to the other woman

you had it, I'll take out no work on't.

For I will not copy it for you.

CASSIO

How now, my sweet Bianca! how now! how now!

Oh don't be like that, sweet Bianca!

OTHELLO

By heaven, that should be my handkerchief!

By God, that is my handkerchief!

BIANCA

An you'll come to supper to-night, you may; an you

If you want to have dinner with me tonight, you may.

will not, come when you are next prepared for.

If you do not want to, then come some other time.

Exit

IAGO

After her, after her.

Go after her.

CASSIO

'Faith, I must; she'll rail in the street else.

Truly, I must or else she will scream in the streets.

IAGO

Will you sup there?

Will you eat there tonight?

CASSIO

'Faith, I intend so.

Yes, I think so.

IAGO

Well, I may chance to see you; for I would very fain

Well I might see you then. I would very much like

speak with you.

to speak with you.

CASSIO

Prithee, come; will you?

Please do come.

IAGO

Go to; say no more.

Go after her and say no more now.

Exit CASSIO

OTHELLO

[Advancing] How shall I murder him, Iago?

How should I kill him, Iago?

IAGO

Did you perceive how he laughed at his vice?

So you saw how he laughed at his sins?

OTHELLO

O Iago!

O Iago!

IAGO

And did you see the handkerchief?

Did you see the handkerchief?

OTHELLO

Was that mine?

Was that mine?

IAGO

Yours by this hand: and to see how he prizes the

Yes, yours. And you can see how highly he prizes

foolish woman your wife! she gave it him, and he

your foolish wife, for she gave it to him and he

hath given it his whore.

gave it to his whore.

OTHELLO

I would have him nine years a-killing.

I would like to kill him for nine years straight.

A fine woman! a fair woman! a sweet woman!

She is such a fine, sweet woman!

IAGO

Nay, you must forget that.

No, forget about that.

OTHELLO

Ay, let her rot, and perish, and be damned to-night;

Yes, she can rot and die and be damned,

for she shall not live: no, my heart is turned to

because she will no longer live. No, my heart has turned

stone; I strike it, and it hurts my hand. O, the

to stone and it hurts my hand when I hit it. The

world hath not a sweeter creature: she might lie by

world has not seen a sweeter woman – she could sleep

an emperor's side and command him tasks.

with the emperor himself and still tell him what to do.

IAGO

Nay, that's not your way.

No, that is not who you are.

OTHELLO

Hang her! I do but say what she is: so delicate

Damn her! I am only saying what she is in reality. She

with her needle: an admirable musician: O! she

is a good seamstress and a wonderful musician – she

will sing the savageness out of a bear: of so high

could calm a bear with her voice – and she has such

and plenteous wit and invention:--

a clever mind –

IAGO

She's the worse for all this.

All the worse that she ended up like this.

OTHELLO

O, a thousand thousand times: and then, of so

A thousand times worse – O and she has

gentle a condition!

such a sweet personality.

IAGO

Ay, too gentle.

Too sweet, perhaps.

OTHELLO

Nay, that's certain: but yet the pity of it, Iago!

True, but that's the sadness of it, Iago!

O Iago, the pity of it, Iago!

Iago, how sad, Iago!

IAGO

If you are so fond over her iniquity, give her

If you love her so much even when she cheats on you, then give her

patent to offend; for, if it touch not you, it comes

permission to keep doing it. If it does not bother you, it won't be an issue

near nobody.

for anyone else.

OTHELLO

I will chop her into messes: cuckold me!

I will chop her into bits! How dare she cheat on me!

IAGO

O, 'tis foul in her.

It's very evil.

OTHELLO

With mine officer!

With my own officer!

IAGO

That's fouler.

Even worse.

OTHELLO

Get me some poison, Iago; this night: I'll not

Iago, get me some poison tonight. I will not

expostulate with her, lest her body and beauty

argue at all with her so that her beauty

unprovide my mind again: this night, Iago.

cannot tempt me to change my mind Tonight, Iago.

IAGO

Do it not with poison, strangle her in her bed, even

Don't do it with poison, but strangle her in her bed, the same

the bed she hath contaminated.

one that she ruined.

OTHELLO

Good, good: the justice of it pleases: very good.

Yes, I appreciate the fitting justice of it.

IAGO

And for Cassio, let me be his undertaker: you

As for Cassio, leave him to me. You

shall hear more by midnight.

Will hear from me by midnight.

OTHELLO

Excellent good.

Excellent.

A trumpet within

What trumpet is that same?

What trumpet is that?

IAGO

Something from Venice, sure. 'Tis Lodovico

It sounds like someone from Venice. It is Lodovico

Come from the duke: and, see, your wife is with him.

Sent from the duke – and look, your wife is with him.

Enter LODOVICO, DESDEMONA, and Attendants

LODOVICO

Save you, worthy general!

God bless you, worthy General!

OTHELLO

With all my heart, sir.

And all of us, sir.

LODOVICO

The duke and senators of Venice greet you.

The duke and senators from Venice send their greetings.

Gives him a letter

OTHELLO

I kiss the instrument of their pleasures.

I will gladly read and obey their requests.

Opens the letter, and reads

DESDEMONA

And what's the news, good cousin Lodovico?

What is the news, good cousin Lodovico?

IAGO

I am very glad to see you, signior.

I am glad to see you, sir.

Welcome to Cyprus.

Welcome to Cyprus.

LODOVICO

I thank you. How does Lieutenant Cassio?

Thank you, How is Lieutenant Cassio?

IAGO

Lives, sir.

Alive, sir.

DESDEMONA

Cousin, there's fall'n between him and my lord

Cousin, there has been a falling out between him and my lord.

An unkind breach: but you shall make all well.

It's an awful thing, but you will fix it.

OTHELLO

Are you sure of that?

Are you sure?

DESDEMONA

My lord?

What do you mean, my lord?

OTHELLO

[Reads] 'This fail you not to do, as you will--'

Do not fail to do this, since then you will –

LODOVICO

He did not call; he's busy in the paper.

He didn't speak, he's reading.

Is there division 'twixt my lord and Cassio?

So there has been a fight between Othello and Cassio?

DESDEMONA

A most unhappy one: I would do much

A sad one, yes. I would do whatever I can

To atone them, for the love I bear to Cassio.

To have them forgive each other since I love Cassio.

OTHELLO

Fire and brimstone!

O, damnation!

DESDEMONA

My lord?

Excuse me?

OTHELLO

Are you wise?

Are you sane?

DESDEMONA

What, is he angry?

Wait, is Othello angry?

LODOVICO

May be the letter moved him;

Perhaps the letter has upset him.

For, as I think, they do command him home,

I think that they are requesting him to come home,

Deputing Cassio in his government.

Placing Cassio in charge.

DESDEMONA

Trust me, I am glad on't.

Oh, well that is good news.

OTHELLO

Indeed!

Is it really!

DESDEMONA

My lord?

Othello?

OTHELLO

I am glad to see you mad.

I am glad that you are getting angry.

DESDEMONA

Why, sweet Othello,--

Othello, why?

OTHELLO

[Striking her] Devil!

You devil!

DESDEMONA

I have not deserved this.

I haven't done anything to deserve this.

LODOVICO

My lord, this would not be believed in Venice,

My lord, no one in Venice would believe this,

Though I should swear I saw't: 'tis very much:

Even if I swore that I saw it. This is too much.

Make her amends; she weeps.

Apologize, she is crying.

OTHELLO

O devil, devil!

O she is the debil!

If that the earth could teem with woman's tears,

The whole earth could be filled with this woman's tears

Each drop she falls would prove a crocodile.

And I would still believe she is falsely crying.

Out of my sight!

Get out of my sight!

DESDEMONA

I will not stay to offend you.

I will not stay here to upset you then.

Going

LODOVICO

Truly, an obedient lady:

She is truly an obedient woman.

I do beseech your lordship, call her back.

I beg you, Othello, call her back.

OTHELLO

Mistress!

Madam!

DESDEMONA

My lord?

Yes, my lord?

OTHELLO

What would you with her, sir?

What do you want with her, sir?

LODOVICO

Who, I, my lord?

What do I want?

OTHELLO

Ay; you did wish that I would make her turn:

Yes, you asked me to have her come back.

Sir, she can turn, and turn, and yet go on,

She can turn around and around and

And turn again; and she can weep, sir, weep;

Keep turning. She can cry and cry.

And she's obedient, as you say, obedient,

And she is so obedient, just as you say,

Very obedient. Proceed you in your tears.

Very obedient. Go on and cry.

Concerning this, sir,--O well-painted passion!--

Now about this letter – O what fake crying! –

I am commanded home. Get you away;

It commands me to return home. Get away from me,

I'll send for you anon. Sir, I obey the mandate,

I will send for you to return soon. Sir, I will obey this order

And will return to Venice. Hence, avaunt!

And return to Venice. Away, go away!

Exit DESDEMONA

Cassio shall have my place. And, sir, tonight,

Cassio will take my spot and, sir, tonight,

I do entreat that we may sup together:

Please come and eat with me.

You are welcome, sir, to Cyprus.--Goats and monkeys!

You are welcome to Cyprus. –Horny animals everywhere!

Exit

LODOVICO

Is this the noble Moor whom our full senate

Is this the same noble Moor whom everyone in the government

Call all in all sufficient? Is this the nature

Calls the most able of the soldiers? Is this the same character

Whom passion could not shake? whose solid virtue

That passion could never shake? Whose goodness

The shot of accident, nor dart of chance,

No accident or chance misfortune

Could neither graze nor pierce?

Could destroy?

IAGO

He is much changed.

He has changed a lot.

LODOVICO

Are his wits safe? is he not light of brain?

Is he still sane? Or has he lost his mind?

IAGO

He's that he is: I may not breathe my censure

He is what he is. I will not voice any criticism

What he might be: if what he might he is not,

About what he might be – if he is not what he should be,

I would to heaven he were!

Than I wish he were!

LODOVICO

What, strike his wife!

He struck his wife!

IAGO

'Faith, that was not so well; yet would I knew

Yes, that was not very good. But I wish I knew

That stroke would prove the worst!

That that was the worst thing he could do!

LODOVICO

Is it his use?

Does he usually do things like that?

Or did the letters work upon his blood,

325

Or did the letters make him angry

And new-create this fault?

And lead him to this new sin?

IAGO

Alas, alas!

Oh it's so bad!

It is not honesty in me to speak

It is not honest for me to say

What I have seen and known. You shall observe him,

What I have seen and known before. You watch him

And his own courses will denote him so

And his actions will tell you all you need to know so

That I may save my speech: do but go after,

That I do not have to say anything. But follow him,

And mark how he continues.

And watch his lifestyle.

LODOVICO

I am sorry that I am deceived in him.

I am very sad that I was wrong about him.

Exeunt

Scene II. A room in the castle.

Enter OTHELLO and EMILIA

OTHELLO

You have seen nothing then?

So you have not seen anything?

EMILIA

Nor ever heard, nor ever did suspect.

No, and I didn't hear or suspect anything either.

OTHELLO

Yes, you have seen Cassio and she together.

But you did see Cassio with her.

EMILIA

But then I saw no harm, and then I heard

But there was nothing wrong there, and I heard

Each syllable that breath made up between them.

Every word they said between them

OTHELLO

What, did they never whisper?

They never whispered?

EMILIA

Never, my lord.

Never, my lord.

OTHELLO

Nor send you out o' the way?

And never sent you away?

EMILIA

Never.

Never.

OTHELLO

To fetch her fan, her gloves, her mask, nor nothing?

Not to get her fan or gloves or hat or anything?

EMILIA

Never, my lord.

Never, my lord.

OTHELLO

That's strange.

That is very strange.

EMILIA

I durst, my lord, to wager she is honest,

My lord, I think she is very honest

Lay down my soul at stake: if you think other,

And would bet my soul on it. If you think otherwise,

Remove your thought; it doth abuse your bosom.

Please rethink it – it ruins your credibility.

If any wretch have put this in your head,

Whoever has put this into your head,

Let heaven requite it with the serpent's curse!

May heaven curse his head!

For, if she be not honest, chaste, and true,

If Desdemona is not honest, pure, and true,

There's no man happy; the purest of their wives

Than no man may ever be happy. The purest of their wives

Is foul as slander.

Are then evil.

OTHELLO

Bid her come hither: go.

Please ask her to come to me.

Exit EMILIA

She says enough; yet she's a simple bawd

She speaks well for Desdemona – though one would be a stupid prostitute

That cannot say as much. This is a subtle whore,

Who could not lie as well as that. Desdemona is a tricky whore,

A closet lock and key of villanous secrets

She is full of evil secrets that are locked in her,

And yet she'll kneel and pray; I have seen her do't.

And all the while she will kneel and pray. I've seen it.

Enter DESDEMONA with EMILIA

DESDEMONA

My lord, what is your will?

My lord, what do you want?

OTHELLO

Pray, chuck, come hither.

Please, darling, come here.

DESDEMONA

What is your pleasure?

What would you like?

OTHELLO

Let me see your eyes;

Let me see your eyes,

Look in my face.

Look at me.

DESDEMONA

What horrible fancy's this?

What awful game is this.

OTHELLO

[To EMILIA] Some of your function, mistress;

Go to your work, mistress.

Leave procreants alone and shut the door;

Leave us alone to have sex, and shut the door.

Cough, or cry 'hem,' if any body come:

Cough or cry out if anyone comes,

Your mystery, your mystery: nay, dispatch.

Since that is your job. Now, go.

Exit EMILIA

DESDEMONA

Upon my knees, what doth your speech import?

I beg you, what do you mean?

I understand a fury in your words.

There is anger in your words,

But not the words.

But not in the words themselves.

OTHELLO

Why, what art thou?

Who are you?

DESDEMONA

Your wife, my lord; your true

Your wife, lord, your honest

And loyal wife.

And loyal wife.

OTHELLO

Come, swear it, damn thyself

Come and swear it to me. Damn yourself by lying

Lest, being like one of heaven, the devils themselves

So that the devils will not confuse you for an angel

Should fear to seize thee: therefore be double damn'd:

And thus fail to take you. Be double-damned

Swear thou art honest.

And swear your honesty.

DESDEMONA

Heaven doth truly know it.

God knows I am.

OTHELLO

Heaven truly knows that thou art false as hell.

God knows that you have been as evil as hell.

DESDEMONA

To whom, my lord? with whom? how am I false?

To whom, my lord? With whom? How have I been unfaithful?

OTHELLO

O Desdemona! away! away! away!

O Desdemona go away!

DESDEMONA

Alas the heavy day! Why do you weep?

This is such a sad day! Why do you weep?

Am I the motive of these tears, my lord?

Did I force you to cry, my lord?

If haply you my father do suspect

If you suspect that my father

An instrument of this your calling back,

Is the reason you have been called back,

Lay not your blame on me: If you have lost him,

Then do not blame me. If he hates you,

Why, I have lost him too.

Then I hate him too.

OTHELLO

Had it pleased heaven

If heaven wanted

To try me with affliction; had they rain'd

To test me through pain, if they had placed

All kinds of sores and shames on my bare head,

All kinds of sores and illnesses on my body,

Steep'd me in poverty to the very lips,

Or had made me incredibly poor,

Given to captivity me and my utmost hopes,

Or had given me to slavery so that I could not even hope for freedom,

I should have found in some place of my soul

I would have found in my soul

A drop of patience: but, alas, to make me

An ability to be patient. But instead, He has made me

A fixed figure for the time of scorn

Into a man built for being mocked

To point his slow unmoving finger at!

And for others to point their fingers at!

Yet could I bear that too; well, very well:

I could even handle that, though,

But there, where I have garner'd up my heart,

If it did not have to do with my heart's foundations, my wife,

Where either I must live, or bear no life;

The person whom I depend on,

The fountain from the which my current runs,

And the fountain my lineage must come from,

Or else dries up; to be discarded thence!

Or it dries up and is ruined!

Or keep it as a cistern for foul toads

Now this fountain is a container for ugly toads

To knot and gender in! Turn thy complexion there,

To copulate in! Turn your gaze to this,

Patience, thou young and rose-lipp'd cherubin,--

O Patience, you young and rose-lipped angel,

Ay, there, look grim as hell!

Look how awful it is!

DESDEMONA

I hope my noble lord esteems me honest.

I wish my noble lord would know that I am honest.

OTHELLO

O, ay; as summer flies are in the shambles,

O yes, you are as honest as the summer flies in the woods

That quicken even with blowing. O thou weed,

That leave each time the wind blows. O you weed,

Who art so lovely fair and smell'st so sweet

Who is so beautiful and smell so good,

That the sense aches at thee, would thou hadst

That one aches to see and smell you – it would be better if

ne'er been born!

you were never born!

DESDEMONA

Alas, what ignorant sin have I committed?

Please, what sin that I do not know about have I committed?

OTHELLO

Was this fair paper, this most goodly book,

Was this beautiful woman, like a good and holy book,

Made to write 'whore' upon? What committed!

Created in order for someone to write "whore" on it? What you committed!

Committed! O thou public commoner!

Committed! O you public prostitute!

I should make very forges of my cheeks,

My cheeks would burn like ovens

That would to cinders burn up modesty,

And devour all modesty in their flames

Did I but speak thy deeds. What committed!

If I spoke aloud what you did. What you did!

Heaven stops the nose at it and the moon winks,

Heaven holds its nose at you, and the moon closes its eyes,

The bawdy wind that kisses all it meets

And the playful wind that kisses everything

Is hush'd within the hollow mine of earth,

Has been calmed and quieted into the earth,

And will not hear it. What committed!

And refuses to hear it. What you did!

Impudent strumpet!

Bold whore!

DESDEMONA

By heaven, you do me wrong.

By God, you are treating me wrongly.

OTHELLO

336

Are you not a strumpet?

Aren't you a whore?

DESDEMONA

No, as I am a Christian:

No, I am a Christian,

If to preserve this vessel for my lord

If I keep my body only for you

From any other foul unlawful touch

And do not allow any evil touch,

Be not to be a strumpet, I am none.

If that is the definition of someone who is not a whore, then I am not one.

OTHELLO

What, not a whore?

You aren't a whore?

DESDEMONA

No, as I shall be saved.

No, by my own salvation I swear.

OTHELLO

Is't possible?

Is it possible?

DESDEMONA

O, heaven forgive us!

God forgive us!

OTHELLO

I cry you mercy, then:

I ask for your forgiveness then:

I took you for that cunning whore of Venice

I mistook you for the tricky whore from Venice

That married with Othello.

Who married Othello.

Raising his voice

You, mistress,

You, mistress,

That have the office opposite to Saint Peter,

That have watched the gates of this room like Saint Peter's opposite,

And keep the gate of hell!

Watching the gates of hell!

Re-enter EMILIA

You, you, ay, you!

You, yes, you!

We have done our course; there's money for your pains:

We have finished. Here is money for your work.

I pray you, turn the key and keep our counsel.

Please, lock the door and keep silent about our conversation.

Exit

EMILIA

Alas, what does this gentleman conceive?

What is Othello thinking?

How do you, madam? how do you, my good lady?

Madam, how are you, my lady?

DESDEMONA

'Faith, half asleep.

I am dazed.

EMILIA

Good madam, what's the matter with my lord?

O madam, what is the matter with Othello?

DESDEMONA

With who?

With who?

EMILIA

Why, with my lord, madam.

With your lord, madam.

DESDEMONA

Who is thy lord?

Who is my lord?

EMILIA

He that is yours, sweet lady.

He that belongs to you, sweet lady.

DESDEMONA

I have none: do not talk to me, Emilia;

I own no one. Don't talk to me, Emilia.

I cannot weep; nor answer have I none,

I can't cry and I have no answers

But what should go by water. Prithee, tonight

Except for my tears. Please, tonight

Lay on my bed my wedding sheets: remember;

Make my bed with the wedding sheets. Do this

And call thy husband hither.

And call for my husband.

EMILIA

Here's a change indeed!

This is a strange change!

Exit

DESDEMONA

'Tis meet I should be used so, very meet.

It must be fair for him to treat me like this.

How have I been behaved, that he might stick

How have I acted that he might complain

The small'st opinion on my least misuse?

About even the smallest problem with me?

Re-enter EMILIA with IAGO

IAGO

What is your pleasure, madam?

What would you like, madam?

How is't with you?

How are you?

DESDEMONA

I cannot tell. Those that do teach young babes

I don't know. Parents teach children

Do it with gentle means and easy tasks:

Gently, with easy suggestions.

He might have chid me so; for, in good faith,

He could have treated me like that, for honestly

I am a child to chiding.

I am only a child to being upbraided.

IAGO

What's the matter, lady?

What is the matter, lady?

EMILIA

Alas, Iago, my lord hath so bewhored her.

Iago, Othello has claimed she is a whore.

Thrown such despite and heavy terms upon her,

He has called her such awful names and said such awful things

As true hearts cannot bear.

For hearts to try to bear.

DESDEMONA

Am I that name, Iago?

Am I what he says, Iago?

IAGO

What name, fair lady?

And what is that, fair lady?

DESDEMONA

Such as she says my lord did say I was.

The name she says he called me.

EMILIA

He call'd her whore: a beggar in his drink

He called her a whore. A poor drunkard

Could not have laid such terms upon his callat.

Could not have been so mean to his woman.

IAGO

Why did he so?

342

Why did he say this?

DESDEMONA

I do not know; I am sure I am none such.

I don't know. I am sure I am not one.

IAGO

Do not weep, do not weep. Alas the day!

Don't cry, don't cry. O awful day!

EMILIA

Hath she forsook so many noble matches,

She spurned so many good matches with noble men,

Her father and her country and her friends,

As well as her father, country, and friends,

To be call'd whore? would it not make one weep?

All to be called a whore? Isn't that enough to make one cry?

DESDEMONA

It is my wretched fortune.

It is my poor luck.

IAGO

Beshrew him for't!

Well curse him for saying it!

How comes this trick upon him?

How did he get such an idea?

DESDEMONA

Nay, heaven doth know.

Only God knows.

EMILIA

I will be hang'd, if some eternal villain,

I swear on my life that some villain,

Some busy and insinuating rogue,

Some meddling and tricky man,

Some cogging, cozening slave, to get some office,

Some lying slave, all for self-gain,

Have not devised this slander; I'll be hang'd else.

Made up this slanderous falsehood. I swear on my life.

IAGO

Fie, there is no such man; it is impossible.

No, no such person exists. That's impossible.

DESDEMONA

If any such there be, heaven pardon him!

If there is, may heaven forgive him!

EMILIA

A halter pardon him! and hell gnaw his bones!

A hangman's noose will forgive him! And may hell have his body!

Why should he call her whore? who keeps her company?

Why would he call her a whore? Who spends time with her?

What place? what time? what form? what likelihood?

Where? When? How?

The Moor's abused by some most villanous knave,

The Moor has been tricked by a villainous enemy,

Some base notorious knave, some scurvy fellow.

A notorious criminal, some evil fellow.

O heaven, that such companions thou'ldst unfold,

O heaven, I wish we could discover who these people are

And put in every honest hand a whip

And give every honest man a whip

To lash the rascals naked through the world

So they could beat these rascals everywhere they go,

Even from the east to the west!

Across the whole world!

IAGO

Speak within door.

Speak quietly.

EMILIA

O, fie upon them! Some such squire he was

O curses on them! It;s the same bastard

That turn'd your wit the seamy side without,

345

Who changed your mind to the wrong side

And made you to suspect me with the Moor.

And made you think I slept with the Moor.

IAGO

You are a fool; go to.

You fool, go away.

DESDEMONA

O good Iago,

O Iago,

What shall I do to win my lord again?

What can I do to win back Othello?

Good friend, go to him; for, by this light of heaven,

Good friend, go to him. By the sun above,

I know not how I lost him. Here I kneel:

I don't know how I lost him. I'm begging you:

If e'er my will did trespass 'gainst his love,

If I ever wrong him or his love for me,

Either in discourse of thought or actual deed,

Either in what I thought or did,

Or that mine eyes, mine ears, or any sense,

Or if my eyes, ears, or anything about me

Delighted them in any other form;

Took pleasure in someone else,

Or that I do not yet, and ever did,

Or that I do not and have not

And ever will--though he do shake me off

And never will – even though he might

To beggarly divorcement--love him dearly,

Divorce me and make me poor – love him fully,

Comfort forswear me! Unkindness may do much;

Than I hope I never have comfort! Being mean can do a lot,

And his unkindness may defeat my life,

And his meanness might end my life,

But never taint my love. I cannot say 'whore:'

But it will never ruin my love. I cannot say "whore,"

It does abhor me now I speak the word;

It disgusts me to even say the word.

To do the act that might the addition earn

To do the act that would gain me that title –

Not the world's mass of vanity could make me.

I wouldn't do it for all the fame in the world.

IAGO

I pray you, be content; 'tis but his humour:

Please, be happy. This is only a mood,

The business of the state does him offence,

And the state business is angering him,

And he does chide with you.

He is only taking it out on you.

DESDEMONA

If 'twere no other--

If that's all it is—

IAGO

'Tis but so, I warrant.

It is, I promise.

Trumpets within

Hark, how these instruments summon to supper!

Listen! The trumpets are calling out for dinner.

The messengers of Venice stay the meat;

The messengers from Venice are waiting to eat.

Go in, and weep not; all things shall be well.

Go to them, do not cry, and everything will be alright.

Exeunt DESDEMONA and EMILIA

Enter RODERIGO

How now, Roderigo!

Hello Roderigo!

RODERIGO

I do not find that thou dealest justly with me.

You are not being fair with me.

IAGO

What in the contrary?

Why do you say that?

RODERIGO

Every day thou daffest me with some device, Iago;

Every day you mess with me somehow, Iago,

and rather, as it seems to me now, keepest from me

and now, it seems to me, you keep me from

all conveniency than suppliest me with the least

making any advantage that would give me

advantage of hope. I will indeed no longer endure

the slightest hope. I will not put up with it any longer

it, nor am I yet persuaded to put up in peace what

and I am not persuaded to just accept what

already I have foolishly suffered.

I have already suffered.

IAGO

Will you hear me, Roderigo?

Will you hear me out, Roderigo?

RODERIGO

'Faith, I have heard too much, for your words and

I have already listened to you too much. Your words

performances are no kin together.

and actions do not fit together.

IAGO

You charge me most unjustly.

You charge me wrongly.

RODERIGO

With nought but truth. I have wasted myself out of

I charge you only with the truth. I have exhausted

my means. The jewels you have had from me to

Everything I have. The jewels that you made me

deliver to Desdemona would half have corrupted a

send to Desdemona would have tempted a

votarist: you have told me she hath received them

nun. You told me she received them

and returned me expectations and comforts of sudden

and would return to me certain comforts

respect and acquaintance, but I find none.

and signs of respect, but I got nothing.

IAGO

Well; go to; very well.

Fine, go on.

RODERIGO

Very well! go to! I cannot go to, man; nor 'tis

Fine! Go on! I cannot go on, and it is not

not very well: nay, I think it is scurvy, and begin

fine. No, it is anything but fine, and I think I

to find myself fobbed in it.

am being toyed with!

IAGO

Very well.

Fine.

RODERIGO

I tell you 'tis not very well. I will make myself

I am telling you that it is not fine. I will make sure

known to Desdemona: if she will return me my

that Desdemona knows about me. If she sends my

jewels, I will give over my suit and repent my

jewels back to me, I will give up my case and apologize

unlawful solicitation; if not, assure yourself I

for pursuing her. If she will not send them back, I

will seek satisfaction of you.

will get my repayment from you.

IAGO

You have said now.

So you say.

RODERIGO

Ay, and said nothing but what I protest intendment of doing.

Yes, and I say nothing except that which I will do.

351

IAGO

Why, now I see there's mettle in thee, and even from

Well, I see that there's some fight in you, and from

this instant to build on thee a better opinion than

this moment I am building a better opinion of you

ever before. Give me thy hand, Roderigo: thou hast

than before. Give me your hand, Roderigo. You have

taken against me a most just exception; but yet, I

complained against me very rightly, but still, I

protest, I have dealt most directly in thy affair.

have dealt very fairly with you.

RODERIGO

It hath not appeared.

It doesn't look like it.

IAGO

I grant indeed it hath not appeared, and your

I agree, it doesn't look like it, and you

suspicion is not without wit and judgment. But,

are smart to be suspicious. But,

Roderigo, if thou hast that in thee indeed, which I

Roderigo, if you are really a more aggressive person, which I

have greater reason to believe now than ever, I mean

am beginning to think you are, and have

352

purpose, courage and valour, this night show it: if

bravery and courage, show it tonight. If

thou the next night following enjoy not Desdemona,

tomorrow night you are not sleeping with Desdemona,

take me from this world with treachery and devise

than find a way through treachery to take

engines for my life.

this world away from me.

RODERIGO

Well, what is it? is it within reason and compass?

Well, what do you want me to do? Is it within my abilities, and is it reasonable?

IAGO

Sir, there is especial commission come from Venice

Sir, there has been a special commission from Venice

to depute Cassio in Othello's place.

to put Cassio in charge and recall Othello.

RODERIGO

Is that true? why, then Othello and Desdemona

Really? Than Othello and Desdemona

return again to Venice.

must go back to Venice.

IAGO

O, no; he goes into Mauritania and takes away with

No, he will go to Mauritania with

him the fair Desdemona, unless his abode be

beautiful Desdemona unless he

lingered here by some accident: wherein none can be

is kept here through some accidental situation. The best situation

so determinate as the removing of Cassio.

for him to stay would be to get rid of Cassio.

RODERIGO

How do you mean, removing of him?

What do you mean, "get rid of him"?

IAGO

Why, by making him uncapable of Othello's place;

Well, by making him unable to lead –

knocking out his brains.

in other words, to knock out his brains and kill him.

RODERIGO

And that you would have me to do?

And you want me to do that?

IAGO

Ay, if you dare do yourself a profit and a right.

Yes, if you dare do something that will help you.

He sups to-night with a harlotry, and thither will I

He is dining tonight with a prostitute, where I

go to him: he knows not yet of his honorable

will meet him. He doesn't know about his appointment

fortune. If you will watch his going thence, which

yet. You must watch when he leaves. I will

I will fashion to fall out between twelve and one,

make sure he leaves between twelve and one

you may take him at your pleasure: I will be near

and then you can snatch him. I will be nearby

to second your attempt, and he shall fall between

to help you, and between the two of us we can take him.

us. Come, stand not amazed at it, but go along with

Come now, stop standing so stunned but come with

me; I will show you such a necessity in his death

me. I will give you such reasons for his death

that you shall think yourself bound to put it on

that you will find it your obligation to kill

him. It is now high suppertime, and the night grows

him. It is almost suppertime and we are wasting

to waste: about it.

time. Let's go.

RODERIGO

I will hear further reason for this.

I want to hear more about this.

355

IAGO

And you shall be satisfied.

You will hear as much as you want.

Exeunt

Scene III. Another room In the castle.

Enter OTHELLO, LODOVICO, DESDEMONA, EMILIA and Attendants

LODOVICO

I do beseech you, sir, trouble yourself no further.

Please sir, do not trouble yourself anymore.

OTHELLO

O, pardon me: 'twill do me good to walk.

O, excuse me. It would be good for me to take a walk.

LODOVICO

Madam, good night; I humbly thank your ladyship.

Madam, goodnight. I humbly thank you.

DESDEMONA

Your honour is most welcome.

Your welcome.

OTHELLO

Will you walk, sir?

Will you walk with me, sir?

O,--Desdemona,--

O – Desdemona –

DESDEMONA

My lord?

Yes, my lord?

OTHELLO

Get you to bed on the instant; I will be returned

Go to your bed immediately. I will come back

forthwith: dismiss your attendant there: look it be done.

soon. Dismiss your attendants as well. Make sure it is done.

DESDEMONA

I will, my lord.

I will my lord.

Exeunt OTHELLO, LODOVICO, and Attendants

EMILIA

How goes it now? he looks gentler than he did.

How is it going? He looks a bit more gentle than he did.

DESDEMONA

He says he will return incontinent:

He says he will return shortly

He hath commanded me to go to bed,

And he commanded me to go to bed

And bade me to dismiss you.

And dismiss you.

EMILIA

Dismiss me!

Dismiss me!

DESDEMONA

It was his bidding: therefore, good Emilia,

It was what he asked. So, good Emilia,

Give me my nightly wearing, and adieu:

Give me my pajamas and good night.

We must not now displease him.

I do not want to upset him now.

EMILIA

I would you had never seen him!

I wish you had never met him!

DESDEMONA

So would not I my love doth so approve him,

I don't wish that – I love him regardless,

That even his stubbornness, his cheques, his frowns--

And even his stubbornness and meanness –

Prithee, unpin me,--have grace and favour in them.

Please, pin this for me – have a beauty to them.

EMILIA

I have laid those sheets you bade me on the bed.

I put the sheets you asked for on the bed.

DESDEMONA

All's one. Good faith, how foolish are our minds!

It doesn't matter. How foolish our minds are!

If I do die before thee prithee, shroud me

If I die with you around, please wrap me

In one of those same sheets.

In one of these sheets in my coffin.

EMILIA

Come, come you talk.

Come now, don't talk like that.

DESDEMONA

My mother had a maid call'd Barbara:

My mother had a maid named Barbara.

She was in love, and he she loved proved mad

She was in love, and the man she loved was crazy

And did forsake her: she had a song of 'willow;'

And left her. She knew a song called "Willow,"

An old thing 'twas, but it express'd her fortune,

An old song, but it meant a lot to her

And she died singing it: that song to-night

And she died singing it. Tonight that song

360

Will not go from my mind; I have much to do,

Will be in my head. I have a lot to do,

But to go hang my head all at one side,

But all the while I hang my head to the side

And sing it like poor Barbara. Prithee, dispatch.

And sing like Barbara. Please, go now.

EMILIA

Shall I go fetch your night-gown?

Shall I fetch your nightgown?

DESDEMONA

No, unpin me here.

No, just unpin me here.

This Lodovico is a proper man.

Lodovico is a handsome man.

EMILIA

A very handsome man.

Yes, very handsome.

DESDEMONA

He speaks well.

He speaks well, also.

EMILIA

I know a lady in Venice would have walked barefoot

I know a lady from Venice who would have walked barefoot

to Palestine for a touch of his nether lip.

all the way to Palestine just to kiss his lip.

DESDEMONA

[Singing] The poor soul sat sighing by a sycamore tree,

The poor woman sat crying by the sycamore tree,

Sing all a green willow:

Everyone sing with the willow:

Her hand on her bosom, her head on her knee,

Her hand on her chest, her head on her knee,

Sing willow, willow, willow:

Sing willow, willow, willow:

The fresh streams ran by her, and murmur'd her moans;

The fresh streams ran past her and murmured like she did,

Sing willow, willow, willow;

Sing willow, willow, willow:

Her salt tears fell from her, and soften'd the stones;

Her tears fell and softened the stones–

Lay by these:--

Put them here –

Singing

Sing willow, willow, willow;

Sing willow, willow, willow–

Prithee, hie thee; he'll come anon:--

Please, get going, he will come soon –

Singing

Sing all a green willow must be my garland.

Everyone sing with the willow, a willow my necklace,

Let nobody blame him; his scorn I approve,-

Let nobody blame him for he is right to hate me–

Nay, that's not next.--Hark! who is't that knocks?

No, that doesn't come next – Listen! Who is knocking?

EMILIA

It's the wind.

It's only the wind.

DESDEMONA

[Singing] I call'd my love false love; but what

I told me lover he didn't really love me but what

said he then?

Did he say?

Sing willow, willow, willow:

Sing willow, willow, willow:

If I court moe women, you'll couch with moe men!

If I chase more women, you will sleep with more men!

So, get thee gone; good night, Mine eyes do itch;

So get going, goodnight. My eyes itch–

Doth that bode weeping?

Does that mean I will soon start crying?

EMILIA

'Tis neither here nor there.

It doesn't mean anything.

DESDEMONA

I have heard it said so. O, these men, these men!

I have heard something about it before. O, these men!

Dost thou in conscience think,--tell me, Emilia,--

Do you honestly think – be true, Emilia –

That there be women do abuse their husbands

That women hurt their husbands

In such gross kind?

Just as much?

EMILIA

There be some such, no question.

Some do, undoubtedly.

DESDEMONA

Wouldst thou do such a deed for all the world?

Would you ever do such a thing for all the money in the world?

EMILIA

Why, would not you?

Why, would you?

DESDEMONA

No, by this heavenly light!

No, I swear by heaven!

EMILIA

Nor I neither by this heavenly light;

Well I wouldn't by heaven's light either,

I might do't as well i' the dark.

But I might in the dark.

DESDEMONA

Wouldst thou do such a deed for all the world?

Is there anything in the world that could make you do it?

EMILIA

The world's a huge thing: it is a great price.

The world is a big, expensive thing

For a small vice.

For a small sin.

DESDEMONA

In troth, I think thou wouldst not.

Truly, I don't think you would do it.

EMILIA

In troth, I think I should; and undo't when I had

Actually, I might do it, and then undo it when it was

done. Marry, I would not do such a thing for a

done. I wouldn't do such a thing for

joint-ring, nor for measures of lawn, nor for

a ring or for a garden, not for

gowns, petticoats, nor caps, nor any petty

dresses or petticoats or caps or any small

exhibition; but for the whole world,--why, who would

thing, but for the wholed world... why, would wouldn't

not make her husband a cuckold to make him a

cheat on her husband if afterwards she could make him

monarch? I should venture purgatory for't.

a king? I would risk purgatory for it.

DESDEMONA

Beshrew me, if I would do such a wrong

Curse me if I would do such a thing,

For the whole world.

Even for the whole world.

EMILIA

Why the wrong is but a wrong i' the world: and

Well it is only wrong insofar as it is in the world, and

having the world for your labour, tis a wrong in your

if your wrong ends up winning you the whole world, than it is wrong

own world, and you might quickly make it right.

in your world – you might as well make it right, then.

DESDEMONA

I do not think there is any such woman.

I don't think such a woman exists.

EMILIA

Yes, a dozen; and as many to the vantage as would

They do, dozens of them, as many as would exist

Store the world they played for.

In the world they did it for.

But I do think it is their husbands' faults

But I do think it is the husbands' faults

If wives do fall: say that they slack their duties,

If wives cheat on them. Say that the husbands stop their duties to us as their wives

And pour our treasures into foreign laps,

And instead sleep with other women,

Or else break out in peevish jealousies,

Or say they become annoyingly jealous,

Throwing restraint upon us; or say they strike us,

And make us stick to rules they impose, or say they hit us

Or scant our former having in despite;

Or stop letting us have access to money –

Why, we have galls, and though we have some grace,

Well, we have backbones, and even though we might be gracious,

Yet have we some revenge. Let husbands know

We can take our revenge. Husbands should know

Their wives have sense like them: they see and smell

That their wives are like them: they see and smell

And have their palates both for sweet and sour,

And have tastes for sweet and sour

As husbands have. What is it that they do

Just like their husbands. Why do they

When they change us for others? Is it sport?

Exchange us for other women? For fun?

I think it is: and doth affection breed it?

I think so. For lust and affection?

I think it doth: is't frailty that thus errs?

That too. Is it their weaknesses that makes them fall?

It is so too: and have not we affections,

Yes, that too: but don't we have lust as well,

Desires for sport, and frailty, as men have?

And desire for fun, and weaknesses, just like men do?

Then let them use us well: else let them know,

Then we should use them also, or else we should let them know

The ills we do, their ills instruct us so.

That if we do something wrong, it is because they do.

DESDEMONA

Good night, good night: heaven me such uses send,

368

Goodnight, goodnight. I pray God will help me use this information

Not to pick bad from bad, but by bad mend!

Not so that I learn from the bad, but so that I can avoid becoming like that!

Exeunt

Act V

Scene I. Cyprus. A street.

Enter IAGO and RODERIGO

IAGO

Here, stand behind this bulk; straight will he come:

Stand here behind the wall and he will come here soon.

Wear thy good rapier bare, and put it home:

Keep your sword unsheathed, and then drive it in him.

Quick, quick; fear nothing; I'll be at thy elbow:

Do it quickly and do not fear, I will be beside you.

It makes us, or it mars us; think on that,

This will help us or it will hurt us, so think about that

And fix most firm thy resolution.

And carry through with determination.

RODERIGO

Be near at hand; I may miscarry in't.

Be close, I may miss him.

IAGO

Here, at thy hand: be bold, and take thy stand.

Here, stay close. Be bold and take a stand.

Retires

RODERIGO

I have no great devotion to the deed;

I don't really want to do this,

And yet he hath given me satisfying reasons:

But he gave me strong reasons.

'Tis but a man gone. Forth, my sword: he dies.

One man gone. First my sword in him, and then he dies.

IAGO

I have rubb'd this young quat almost to the sense,

I have inflamed this pimple until it is ready to pop,

And he grows angry. Now, whether he kill Cassio,

And he is getting angry. Now. whether he kills Cassio

Or Cassio him, or each do kill the other,

Or Cassio kills him, or they kill each other–

Every way makes my gain: live Roderigo,

Every combination can work for me. But if Roderigo lives,

He calls me to a restitution large

Then he will ask me to repay him

Of gold and jewels that I bobb'd from him,

For the gold and jewels I stole from him

As gifts to Desdemona;

As if they were gifts to Desdemona.

It must not be: if Cassio do remain,

That shouldn't happen. If Cassio remains,

He hath a daily beauty in his life

Then his natural handsomeness

That makes me ugly; and, besides, the Moor

Makes me comparatively look ugly. And besides, the Moor

May unfold me to him; there stand I in much peril:

Might talk to him about what I have been telling him. That would be dangerous for me.

No, he must die. But so: I hear him coming.

No, he must die as well. I hear him coming.

Enter CASSIO

RODERIGO

I know his gait, 'tis he.--Villain, thou diest!

I know those steps, it's Cassio. –Villain! Die!

Makes a pass at CASSIO

CASSIO

That thrust had been mine enemy indeed,

That is the thrust of an enemy,

But that my coat is better than thou know'st

But I have armor underneath my coat,

I will make proof of thine.

And now we will see how strong your clothing is.

Draws, and wounds RODERIGO

RODERIGO

O, I am slain!

O, I am dead!

IAGO from behind wounds CASSIO in the leg, and exit

CASSIO

I am maim'd for ever. Help, ho! murder! murder!

I am injured forever! Help! Murder! Murder!

Falls

Enter OTHELLO

OTHELLO

The voice of Cassio: Iago keeps his word.

That's the voice of Cassio. Iago has kept his word.

RODERIGO

O, villain that I am!

O I am such a villain!

OTHELLO

It is even so.

That's true.

CASSIO

O, help, ho! light! a surgeon!

O, help! Get a light! Get a surgeon!

OTHELLO

'Tis he:--O brave Iago, honest and just,

It's he. O brave Iago, honest and just,

That hast such noble sense of thy friend's wrong!

You have such a noble understanding of your friend's hurt!

Thou teachest me. Minion, your dear lies dead,

You teach me well. Whore, here, dead, is your lover,

And your unblest fate hies: strumpet, I come.

And your fate is coming soon.

Forth of my heart those charms, thine eyes, are blotted;

Your eyes have been shut out of my heart.

Thy bed, lust-stain'd, shall with lust's blood be spotted.

You stained the bed with lust, now your lusting blood will stain it.

Exit

Enter LODOVICO and GRATIANO

CASSIO

What, ho! no watch? no passage? murder! murder!

What! No guard? No one here? Murder!

GRATIANO

'Tis some mischance; the cry is very direful.

Something is wrong – that cry sounds very bad.

CASSIO

O, help!

Help!

LODOVICO

Hark!

Listen!

RODERIGO

O wretched villain!

O evil man!

LODOVICO

Two or three groan: it is a heavy night:

Two or three are groaning there. It is a dark night,

These may be counterfeits: let's think't unsafe

These might be fake. It might be unsafe

To come in to the cry without more help.

To go to the cry without more help with us.

RODERIGO

Nobody come? then shall I bleed to death.

Nobody is coming? I will bleed to death!

LODOVICO

Hark!

Listen!

Re-enter IAGO, with a light

GRATIANO

Here's one comes in his shirt, with light and weapons.

Here comes someone with no coat on, with a light and with weapons.

IAGO

Who's there? whose noise is this that ones on murder?

Who is htere? Who is shouting "murder"?

LODOVICO

We do not know.

We don't know.

IAGO

Did not you hear a cry?

Did you hear the cries?

CASSIO

Here, here! for heaven's sake, help me!

Here, here, help me!

IAGO

What's the matter?

What is the matter?

GRATIANO

This is Othello's ancient, as I take it.

That is Othello's ensign, I think

LODOVICO

The same indeed; a very valiant fellow.

It is, and he is a good man.

IAGO

What are you here that cry so grievously?

Who is crying so loudly here?

CASSIO

Iago? O, I am spoil'd, undone by villains!

Iago? O I am hurt, destroyed by criminals!

Give me some help.

Get me help!

IAGO

O me, lieutenant! what villains have done this?

O, lieutenant! What criminals have done this?

CASSIO

I think that one of them is hereabout,

I think one is nearby,

And cannot make away.

And can't get away.

IAGO

O treacherous villains!

O evil men!

What are you there? come in, and give some help.

Why are you standing there? Come in and help.

To LODOVICO and GRATIANO

RODERIGO

O, help me here!

O help me here!

CASSIO

That's one of them.

That must be one of them.

IAGO

O murderous slave! O villain!

Murderer! Villain!

Stabs RODERIGO

RODERIGO

O damn'd Iago! O inhuman dog!

O damn you Iago, you inhuman dog!

IAGO

Kill men i' the dark!--Where be these bloody thieves?--

How awful to kill men in the dark! – Where are the other thieves? –

How silent is this town!--Ho! murder! murder!--

And this is such a quiet town! – Murder! murder!–

What may you be? are you of good or evil?

Who is coming? Friend or foe?

LODOVICO

As you shall prove us, praise us.

Judge us and see we are friends.

IAGO

Signior Lodovico?

Sir Lodovico?

LODOVICO

He, sir.

I am he, sir.

IAGO

I cry you mercy. Here's Cassio hurt by villains.

I beg you for mercy. Cassio is here, injured by criminals.

GRATIANO

Cassio!

Cassio!

IAGO

How is't, brother!

How did this happen! My brother!

CASSIO

My leg is cut in two.

My leg is sliced into two.

IAGO

Marry, heaven forbid!

O, God forbid!

Light, gentlemen; I'll bind it with my shirt.

Bring the light, gentlemen. I will cover the wound with my shirt.

Enter BIANCA

BIANCA

What is the matter, ho? who is't that cried?

What is the matter? Who is crying out?

IAGO

Who is't that cried!

Who has cried!

BIANCA

O my dear Cassio! my sweet Cassio! O Cassio,

O my dear Cassio! Cassio! O Cassio,

Cassio, Cassio!

Cassio, Cassio!

IAGO

O notable strumpet! Cassio, may you suspect

Notorious prostitute! Cassio, do you know

Who they should be that have thus many led you?

Who attacked you?

CASSIO

No.

No.

GRATIANO

I am to find you thus: I have been to seek you.

I am sorry to see you like this, I have been trying to find you.

IAGO

Lend me a garter. So. O, for a chair,

Give me your sash. O, if only we had a chair

To bear him easily hence!

To carry him away on.

BIANCA

Alas, he faints! O Cassio, Cassio, Cassio!

No, he is fainting! O Cassio, Cassio, Cassio!

IAGO

Gentlemen all, I do suspect this trash

Gentlemen, I think that this trashy girl

To be a party in this injury.

Is part of this situation.

Patience awhile, good Cassio. Come, come;

Be patient, good Cassio. Come, come,

Lend me a light. Know we this face or no?

Put a light on this. Does anyone recognize this face?

Alas my friend and my dear countryman

O, it is my friend and countryman

Roderigo! no:--yes, sure: O heaven! Roderigo.

Roderigo! It can't be – yes, it is, oh no! Roderigo.

GRATIANO

What, of Venice?

From Venice?

IAGO

Even he, sir; did you know him?

That's him, sir – did you know him?

GRATIANO

Know him! ay.

Know him! Yes.

IAGO

383

Signior Gratiano? I cry you gentle pardon;

Sir Gratiano? I ask for your pardon.

These bloody accidents must excuse my manners,

These bloody events have made me forget my manners,

That so neglected you.

And I ignored you.

GRATIANO

I am glad to see you.

I am glad to see you.

IAGO

How do you, Cassio? O, a chair, a chair!

Cassio, are you alright? Bring a chair!

GRATIANO

Roderigo!

Roderigo!

IAGO

He, he 'tis he.

Yes, it's him.

A chair brought in

O, that's well said; the chair!

O, good, the chair!

GRATIANO

Some good man bear him carefully from hence;

Some strong men need to carry him carefully.

I'll fetch the general's surgeon.

I will get the general's surgeon.

To BIANCA

For you, mistress,

As for you, mistress,

Save you your labour. He that lies slain here, Cassio,

Calm down. Cassio, the man who is dead here

Was my dear friend: what malice was between you?

Was a friend of mine. What argument was between you?

CASSIO

None in the world; nor do I know the man.

None in the world: I don't even know him.

IAGO

[To BIANCA] What, look you pale? O, bear him out o' the air.

Why do you look so pale? O carry him away.

CASSIO and RODERIGO are borne off

Stay you, good gentlemen. Look you pale, mistress?

Stay and look, good gentlemen. Are you pale, mistress?

Do you perceive the gastness of her eye?

Do you all see how afraid she looks?

Nay, if you stare, we shall hear more anon.

If you watch her, we will hear more soon.

Behold her well; I pray you, look upon her:

Watch her well, please, watch her well:

Do you see, gentlemen? nay, guiltiness will speak,

Do you see, men? Her guiltiness will speak

Though tongues were out of use.

Even if she is silent.

Enter EMILIA

EMILIA

'Las, what's the matter? what's the matter, husband?

Oh no, what is the matter? Husband, what is the matter?

IAGO

Cassio hath here been set on in the dark

Cassio has been attached in the dark

By Roderigo and fellows that are scaped:

By Roderigo and others who escaped.

He's almost slain, and Roderigo dead.

He is hurt badly, and Roderigo is dead.

EMILIA

Alas, good gentleman! alas, good Cassio!

O my! Good gentlemen! O no, good Cassio!

IAGO

This is the fruit of whoring. Prithee, Emilia,

This is what happens when you visit whores. Please, Emilia,

Go know of Cassio where he supp'd to-night.

Go find out where Cassio had dinner tonight.

To BIANCA

What, do you shake at that?

Why are you shaking?

BIANCA

He supp'd at my house; but I therefore shake not.

He ate at my house, but I am not shaking.

IAGO

O, did he so? I charge you, go with me.

O he did? You must come with me.

EMILIA

Fie, fie upon thee, strumpet!

Curses on you, whore!

BIANCA

I am no strumpet; but of life as honest

I am no whore. I am as honest

As you that thus abuse me.

As all of you who curse me.

EMILIA

As I! foh! fie upon thee!

As me! No! Curses on you!

IAGO

Kind gentlemen, let's go see poor Cassio dress'd.

Gentlemen, let us visit Cassio as he is tended to.

Come, mistress, you must tell's another tale.

Come mistress, you must tell your story.

Emilia run you to the citadel,

Emilia, run to the castle

And tell my lord and lady what hath happ'd.

And tell my lord and lady what happened.

Will you go on? I pray.

Will you go now? Please.

Aside

This is the night

Tonight

That either makes me or fordoes me quite.

Either makes my fortunes or ruins me.

Exeunt

Scene II. A bedchamber in the castle: DESDEMONA in bed asleep; a light burning.

Enter OTHELLO

OTHELLO

It is the cause, it is the cause, my soul,--

I have good reason, I have good reason –

Let me not name it to you, you chaste stars!--

I won't say it to you, O pure stars! –

It is the cause. Yet I'll not shed her blood;

I have good reason. I won't make her bleed

Nor scar that whiter skin of hers than snow,

Nor will I scar her skin that is as white as snow,

And smooth as monumental alabaster.

And as smooth as alabaster stone.

Yet she must die, else she'll betray more men.

Yet if she doesn't die she will betray even more men.

Put out the light, and then put out the light:

I will put out the light of the candle, and then the light of her life.

If I quench thee, thou flaming minister,

If I put you out, you flaming candle,

I can again thy former light restore,

I can always light you again

Should I repent me: but once put out thy light,

If I feel sorry for it. But once I put out Desdemona's light,

Thou cunning'st pattern of excelling nature,

That beautiful, cunning woman,

I know not where is that Promethean heat

Then I do not know what heat

That can thy light relume. When I have pluck'd the rose,

Can relit her life. When I have picked that rose,

I cannot give it vital growth again.

I cannot give it life again.

It must needs wither: I'll smell it on the tree.

It must wither. I will smell it once more while it is alive on the tree.

Kissing her

Ah balmy breath, that dost almost persuade

Sweet breath, you almost persuade me

Justice to break her sword! One more, one more.

Not to kill you and not to carry out the deserved justice. One more kiss.

Be thus when thou art dead, and I will kill thee,

If you look like this when you are dead, then I will kill you

And love thee after. One more, and this the last:

And I will love you afterwards. One more kiss, and this is the last one.

So sweet was ne'er so fatal. I must weep,

Something so sweet was never so fatal. I must cry,

But they are cruel tears: this sorrow's heavenly;

But I must be cruel as well. This is a Godly sorrow

It strikes where it doth love. She wakes.

Which punishes the one it loves. She is waking up.

DESDEMONA

Who's there? Othello?

390

Who is there? Othello?

OTHELLO

Ay. Desdemona.

Yes, Desdemona.

DESDEMONA

Will you come to bed, my lord?

Will you please come to bed, my lord?

OTHELLO

Have you pray'd to-night, Desdemona?

Have you prayed tonight, Desdemona?

DESDEMONA

Ay, my lord.

yes, my lord.

OTHELLO

If you bethink yourself of any crime

If you can think of any crime

Unreconciled as yet to heaven and grace,

That you have not asked for forgiveness for,

Solicit for it straight.

Do that now.

DESDEMONA

Alas, my lord, what do you mean by that?

My lord, what do you mean?

OTHELLO

Well, do it, and be brief; I will walk by:

Do it, and be quick. I will wait,

I would not kill thy unprepared spirit;

For I will not kill someone who is not spiritually ready.

No; heaven forfend! I would not kill thy soul.

No, by God I would not want your soul to go to hell.

DESDEMONA

Talk you of killing?

You are talking about killing?

OTHELLO

Ay, I do.

I am.

DESDEMONA

Then heaven

God

Have mercy on me!

Have mercy on me!

OTHELLO

Amen, with all my heart!

Amen to that!

DESDEMONA

If you say so, I hope you will not kill me.

Since you say so, I hope you will not kill me.

OTHELLO

Hum!

Hmm!

DESDEMONA

And yet I fear you; for you are fatal then

Yet I am afraid of you, for you are deadly and dangerous

When your eyes roll so: why I should fear I know not,

When your eyes are so red. I don't know why I am afraid,

Since guiltiness I know not; but yet I feel I fear.

Since I am not guilty of anything, but I still feel fear.

OTHELLO

Think on thy sins.

Think about your sins.

DESDEMONA

They are loves I bear to you.

The only one is the love I have for you.

OTHELLO

Ay, and for that thou diest.

And that is why you will die.

DESDEMONA

That death's unnatural that kills for loving.

It isn't right to kill someone for loving.

Alas, why gnaw you so your nether lip?

O, why are you biting your lip?

Some bloody passion shakes your very frame:

A strong, evil emotion is shaking your body.

These are portents; but yet I hope, I hope,

This is some bad omen, but still I hope

They do not point on me.

That it does not bode poorly for me.

OTHELLO

Peace, and be still!

Be quiet and still!

DESDEMONA

I will so. What's the matter?

I will. What is the matter?

OTHELLO

That handkerchief which I so loved and gave thee

The handkerchief that I loved and gave to you,

Thou gavest to Cassio.

You gave to Cassio.

DESDEMONA

No, by my life and soul!

I didn't, I swear by my life and soul!

Send for the man, and ask him.

Send for him and ask him.

OTHELLO

Sweet soul, take heed,

Sweet soul, be careful,

Take heed of perjury; thou art on thy deathbed.

Be careful not to lie, for you are on your deathbed.

DESDEMONA

Ay, but not yet to die.

Yes, but I have not died yet.

OTHELLO

Yes, presently:

Soon,

Therefore confess thee freely of thy sin;

So confess your sin openly:

For to deny each article with oath

It won't help you to swear against each accusation,

Cannot remove nor choke the strong conception

That won't remove the thought that makes me

That I do groan withal. Thou art to die.

Groan in pain. You are going to die.

DESDEMONA

Then Lord have mercy on me!

Lord have mercy on me!

OTHELLO

I say, amen.

Again, I say Amen.

DESDEMONA

And have you mercy too! I never did

And you have mercy on me too! I never did anything

Offend you in my life; never loved Cassio

To offend you. I never loved Cassio

But with such general warranty of heaven

Except with the rule of heaven that towards anyone

As I might love: I never gave him token.

I could love. I never gave him that handkerchief.

OTHELLO

By heaven, I saw my handkerchief in's hand.

By God, I saw it in his hand,

O perjured woman! thou dost stone my heart,

You lying woman! You turn my heart to stone,

And makest me call what I intend to do

And make me call what I am about to do

A murder, which I thought a sacrifice:

A murder, when I thought it was a sacrifice.

I saw the handkerchief.

I saw the handkerchief.

DESDEMONA

He found it then;

He must have found it then.

I never gave it him: send for him hither;

I never gave it to him. Send for him,

Let him confess a truth.

And let him confess the truth.

OTHELLO

He hath confess'd.

He already confessed.

DESDEMONA

What, my lord?

What, my lord?

OTHELLO

That he hath used thee.

That he had sex with you.

DESDEMONA

How? unlawfully?

What? That he had sex with me?

OTHELLO

Ay.

Yes.

DESDEMONA

He will not say so.

He will not say that.

OTHELLO

No, his mouth is stopp'd;

No, not now. His mouth won't say anything

Honest Iago hath ta'en order for't.

Since honest Iago has taken care of him.

DESDEMONA

O! my fear interprets: what, is he dead?

O no! I am afraid to interpret that. Is he dead?

OTHELLO

Had all his hairs been lives, my great revenge

If he had as many lives as he had hairs, I would have had

Had stomach for them all.

A desire to take revenge on all of them.

DESDEMONA

Alas! he is betray'd and I undone.

No! Someone has betrayed him, and I am ruined.

OTHELLO

Out, strumpet! weep'st thou for him to my face?

You whore! You dare cry over him in front of me.

DESDEMONA

O, banish me, my lord, but kill me not!

My lord, banish me but do not kill me!

OTHELLO

Down, strumpet!

Sit down, whore!

DESDEMONA

Kill me to-morrow: let me live to-night!

Kill me tomorrow, but let me live tonight!

OTHELLO

Nay, if you strive--

No, if you struggle–

DESDEMONA

But half an hour!

Just half an hour more!

OTHELLO

Being done, there is no pause.

There is no sense in pausing now.

DESDEMONA

But while I say one prayer!

Let me say one prayer!

OTHELLO

It is too late.

It is too late.

He stifles her

EMILIA

[Within] My lord , my lord! what, ho! my lord, my lord!

400

My lord, my lord! What! Hello! My lord!

OTHELLO

What noise is this? Not dead? not yet quite dead?

What noise is this? Are you not dead yet? Yet?

I that am cruel am yet merciful;

I might be cruel, but I am still merciful enough

I would not have thee linger in thy pain: So, so.

That I would not want you to be in pain.

EMILIA

[Within] What, ho! my lord, my lord!

What! My lord! My lord!

OTHELLO

Who's there?

Who is it?

EMILIA

[Within] O, good my lord, I would speak a word with you!

O my lord, I must tell you something!

OTHELLO

Yes: 'tis Emilia. By and by. She's dead.

It is Emilia. I'm coming. Ok, she's dead.

'Tis like she comes to speak of Cassio's death.--

She is likely coming here to tell me about Cassio's death.–

The noise was here. Ha! no more moving?

The noise of the fight was near here. Now! No more moving?

Still as the grave. Shall she come in? were't good?--

She is as still as a grave. Should Emilia come in? Is that a good idea?–

I think she stirs again:--no. What's best to do?

I think she is moving again. No. What should I do?

If she come in, she'll sure speak to my wife:

If she comes in, she will want to speak to my wife:

My wife! my wife! what wife? I have no wife.

My wife! my wife! what wife? I have no wife.

O insupportable! O heavy hour!

O this is an unbearable and sad time!

Methinks it should be now a huge eclipse

I would have guessed that a huge eclipse

Of sun and moon, and that the affrighted globe

Of the sun and the moon would have occurred

Should yawn at alteration.

Now that Desdemona is off of the planet.

EMILIA

[Within] I do beseech you

Please,

That I may speak with you, O, good my lord!

I must speak to you, my lord!

OTHELLO

I had forgot thee: O, come in, Emilia;

I forgot about you, come in Emilia.

Soft; by and by. Let me the curtains draw.

Wait and let me draw the curtains.

Where art thou?

Where are you?

Unlocks the door

Enter EMILIA

What's the matter with thee now?

Now what's the matter?

EMILIA

O, my good lord, yonder's foul murders done!

My lord, awful murders have occurred!

OTHELLO

What, now?

What, just now?

EMILIA

But now, my lord.

Just now, my lord.

OTHELLO

It is the very error of the moon;

It must be because of the moon:

She comes more nearer earth than she was wont,

It has come closer to the earth than it usually does,

And makes men mad.

And it drives men crazy.

EMILIA

Cassio, my lord, hath kill'd a young Venetian

My lord, Cassio has killed a young Venetian

Call'd Roderigo.

Named Roderigo.

OTHELLO

Roderigo kill'd!

Roderigo dead!

And Cassio kill'd!

And Cassio dead!

EMILIA

No, Cassio is not kill'd.

No, Cassio is not yet dead.

OTHELLO

Not Cassio kill'd! then murder's out of tune,

Cassio is not dead? Then the murder is wrong,

And sweet revenge grows harsh.

And my revenge is ruined.

DESDEMONA

O, falsely, falsely murder'd!

O I have been wrongly murdered!

EMILIA

Alas, what cry is that?

O what is that cry!

OTHELLO

That! what?

What? That?

EMILIA

Out, and alas! that was my lady's voice.

Oh no! It was my lady's voice!

Help! help, ho! help! O lady, speak again!

Help! Help! Help! O lady, speak again!

Sweet Desdemona! O sweet mistress, speak!

Sweet Desdemona! My mistress speak!

DESDEMONA

A guiltless death I die.

I die without blame.

EMILIA

O, who hath done this deed?

Who has done this to you?

DESDEMONA

Nobody; I myself. Farewell

Nobody, I did it to myself. Goodbye

Commend me to my kind lord: O, farewell!

And give my love to my lord. Goodbye!

Dies

OTHELLO

Why, how should she be murder'd?

How was she murdered?

EMILIA

Alas, who knows?

Who knows?

OTHELLO

You heard her say herself, it was not I.

You heard her say it was not me.

EMILIA

She said so: I must needs report the truth.

Yes, that's what she said. I must report this.

OTHELLO

She's, like a liar, gone to burning hell:

She lied even as she was going to hell.

'Twas I that kill'd her.

It was me. I killed her.

EMILIA

O, the more angel she,

O then she is an angel for it

And you the blacker devil!

And you are a devil for it!

OTHELLO

She turn'd to folly, and she was a whore.

She cheated on me and became a whore.

EMILIA

Thou dost belie her, and thou art a devil.

You are lying about her. You are a devil.

OTHELLO

She was false as water.

She was as unfaithful as water.

EMILIA

Thou art rash as fire, to say

You are mean and angry like fire if you

That she was false: O, she was heavenly true!

Think she was unfaithful. She was purely true to you!

OTHELLO

Cassio did top her; ask thy husband else.

Cassio had sex with her, ask your husband.

O, I were damn'd beneath all depth in hell,

I would damn myself to the depths of hell

But that I did proceed upon just grounds

If I did not do what I did from certain grounds of proof.

To this extremity. Thy husband knew it all.

Your husband knew everything.

EMILIA

My husband!

My husband!

OTHELLO

Thy husband.

Your husband.

EMILIA

That she was false to wedlock?

He said she was unfaithful?

OTHELLO

Ay, with Cassio. Nay, had she been true,

Yes, with Cassio. If she had remained faithful,

If heaven would make me such another world

Heaven could have created another world

Of one entire and Perfect chrysolite,

Of perfect crystal

I'ld not have sold her for it.

And I would not have sold her for it.

EMILIA

My husband!

My husband!

OTHELLO

Ay, 'twas he that told me first:

Yes, he told me about it first.

An honest man he is, and hates the slime

He is an honest man and hates the effects

That sticks on filthy deeds.

Of evil actions.

EMILIA

My husband!

My husband!

OTHELLO

What needs this iteration, woman? I say thy husband.

Why do you keep repeating this, woman? Yes, your husband.

EMILIA

O mistress, villany hath made mocks with love,

O my lady. a villain has mocked your love.

My husband say that she was false!

My husband said that she was unfaithful!

OTHELLO

He, woman;

Yes, woman,

I say thy husband: dost understand the word?

Your husband. Do you understand that word, "husband"?

My friend, thy husband, honest, honest Iago.

My friend, your husband, the honest Iago.

EMILIA

If he say so, may his pernicious soul

If he said that, then his evil soul

Rot half a grain a day! he lies to the heart:

Should rot in hell! He is lying completely.

She was too fond of her most filthy bargain.

She loved her awful marriage to you.

410

OTHELLO

Ha!

Ha!

EMILIA

Do thy worst:

Do your worst.

This deed of thine is no more worthy heaven

You can kill me and it will not get you into heaven,

Than thou wast worthy her.

Just like you weren't worthy of her to begin with.

OTHELLO

Peace, you were best.

You would be best if you shut up.

EMILIA

Thou hast not half that power to do me harm

You can't hurt me, I can endure much more

As I have to be hurt. O gull! O dolt!

Than you can do to me. You fool!

As ignorant as dirt! thou hast done a deed--

As dumb as dirt! You have done an awful thing–

I care not for thy sword; I'll make thee known,

I do not care about your sword. I'll make sure others know what you did

Though I lost twenty lives.--Help! help, ho! help!

Even if I lost my life twenty times. – Help! help! help!

The Moor hath kill'd my mistress! Murder! murder!

The Moor killed my lady! Murder! murder!

Enter MONTANO, GRATIANO, IAGO, and others

MONTANO

What is the matter? How now, general!

What is the matter? What is going on, general?

EMILIA

O, are you come, Iago? you have done well,

O have you come too, Iago? You have done very well,

That men must lay their murders on your neck.

Since men are claiming you are the reason for murdering others.

GRATIANO

What is the matter?

What is going on?

EMILIA

Disprove this villain, if thou be'st a man:

Tell this criminal that he is wrong, if you are a man.

He says thou told'st him that his wife was false:

He says that you told him his wife was unfaithful,

I know thou didst not, thou'rt not such a villain:

And I know that you did not. You can't be such a criminal.

Speak, for my heart is full.

Speak, I am too full of emotion.

IAGO

I told him what I thought, and told no more

I told him what I thought, and nothing else.

Than what he found himself was apt and true.

He found the proof and truth behind the rest of it.

EMILIA

But did you ever tell him she was false?

But did you tell him she was unfaithful?

IAGO

I did.

I did.

EMILIA

You told a lie, an odious, damned lie;

Then you lied, an awful, cursed lie.

Upon my soul, a lie, a wicked lie.

On my soul, a wicked lie.

She false with Cassio!--did you say with Cassio?

She unfaithful with Cassio! Is that what you said?

IAGO

With Cassio, mistress. Go to, charm your tongue.

With Cassio, mistress. Now hold your tongue and be quiet.

EMILIA

I will not charm my tongue; I am bound to speak:

I will not be quiet, I must speak.

My mistress here lies murder'd in her bed,--

My lady has been murdered in her bed–

All

O heavens forfend!

God forbid!

EMILIA

And your reports have set the murder on.

And your lies led to the murder.

OTHELLO

Nay, stare not, masters: it is true, indeed.

Stop staring, sirs. It's true.

GRATIANO

'Tis a strange truth.

This is unbelievable.

MONTANO

O monstrous act!

A horrifying act!

EMILIA

Villany, villany, villany!

Evil, evil, evil!

I think upon't, I think: I smell't: O villany!--

I can't stop thinking about it. I even smell the evil!

I thought so then:--I'll kill myself for grief:--

I suspected as much – I will kill myself for sorrow–

O villany, villany!

O evil!

IAGO

What, are you mad? I charge you, get you home.

Have you gone mad? I order you, go home.

EMILIA

Good gentlemen, let me have leave to speak:

Good men, give me permission to speak.

'Tis proper I obey him, but not now.

It is usually appropriate to obey him, but not now.

Perchance, Iago, I will ne'er go home.

Maybe, Iago, I will never go home to you.

OTHELLO

O! O! O!

O, O, O!

He falls on the bed

EMILIA

Nay, lay thee down and roar;

Go ahead and lay down and moan,

For thou hast kill'd the sweetest innocent

For you have killed the most beautiful and innocent woman

That e'er did lift up eye.

Who ever lived.

OTHELLO

[Rising] O, she was foul!

She was evil!

I scarce did know you, uncle: there lies your niece,

I barely knew you, Uncle Gratiano, but there is your niece,

Whose breath, indeed, these hands have newly stopp'd:

Whose breath I have recently stopped by choking her.

I know this act shows horrible and grim.

I know this sounds horrible.

GRATIANO

Poor Desdemona! I am glad thy father's dead:

Poor Desdemona! I am glad your father is dead:

Thy match was mortal to him, and pure grief

The marriage was too much for him and from his sadness

Shore his old thread in twain: did he live now,

He died before his time. If he were alive now,

This sight would make him do a desperate turn,

Seeing this would cause him to do desperate things.

Yea, curse his better angel from his side,

Yes, he would even curse his goodness

And fall to reprobation.

And end up in hell.

OTHELLO

'Tis pitiful; but yet Iago knows

This is sad, but Iago knows

That she with Cassio hath the act of shame

That she and Cassio have slept together

A thousand times committed; Cassio confess'd it:

A thousand times. Cassio confessed to it.

And she did gratify his amorous works

And she returned her favor to his love

With that recognizance and pledge of love

With a pledge of her own love by giving him

Which I first gave her; I saw it in his hand:

What I first gave to her. I saw it in his hand:

It was a handkerchief, an antique token

It was my handkerchief, an old token

My father gave my mother.

That my father game to my mother.

EMILIA

O heaven! O heavenly powers!

O heaven! O God!

IAGO

Come, hold your peace.

Stop, be quiet.

EMILIA

'Twill out, 'twill out: I peace!

The truth will come out! Me keep quiet?

No, I will speak as liberal as the north:

No, I will as openly as I want.

Let heaven and men and devils, let them all,

God and men and devils, all of them

All, all, cry shame against me, yet I'll speak.

Can say that I am shameful for speaking, but I will.

IAGO

Be wise, and get you home.

Be smart and go home.

EMILIA

I will not.

I will not.

IAGO offers to stab EMILIA

GRATIANO

Fie!

What!

Your sword upon a woman?

You draw your sword to attack a woman?

EMILIA

O thou dull Moor! that handkerchief thou speak'st of

You stupid Moor! That handkerchief you were talking about

I found by fortune and did give my husband;

Was the same one I found and gave to Iago.

For often, with a solemn earnestness,

He often, and very seriously,

More than indeed belong'd to such a trifle,

Giving an importance to it that such a small thing does not have,

He begg'd of me to steal it.

Begged me to steal it.

IAGO

Villanous whore!

Evil whore!

EMILIA

She give it Cassio! no, alas! I found it,

You think she gave it to Cassio! No! I found it

And I did give't my husband.

And gave it to Iago.

IAGO

Filth, thou liest!

You trash, you are lying!

EMILIA

By heaven, I do not, I do not, gentlemen.

By God, I am not lying, gentlemen.

O murderous coxcomb! what should such a fool

You murderous, conceited man! How did such a fool

Do with so good a woman?

Get such a wonderful woman?

OTHELLO

Are there no stones in heaven

Why won't God throw down stones at Iago

But what serve for the thunder?--Precious villain!

Like the ones that make the noise of thunder? – You villain!

He runs at IAGO IAGO, from behind, stabs EMILIA, and exit

GRATIANO

The woman falls; sure, he hath kill'd his wife.

This woman has fallen: he has killed his wife.

EMILIA

Ay, ay: O, lay me by my mistress' side.

Yes, yes, place me next to my mistress.

GRATIANO

He's gone, but his wife's kill'd.

He is gone, but his wife is dead.

MONTANO

'Tis a notorious villain. Take you this weapon,

He is the worst kind of criminal. Take this weapon

Which I have here recover'd from the Moor:

Which I have taken from the Moor,

Come, guard the door without; let him not pass,

And come, guard the door outside. Do not let the Moor pass,

But kill him rather. I'll after that same villain,

But kill him if he tries to leave. I will go after Iago;

For 'tis a damned slave.

He is a damn slave.

Exeunt MONTANO and GRATIANO

OTHELLO

I am not valiant neither,

I am not very strong

But ever puny whipster gets my sword:

If every little wimp can take my sword.

But why should honour outlive honesty?

But why should my reputation go on longer than my honesty?

Let it go all.

It's all gone.

EMILIA

What did thy song bode, lady?

Lady, what did your song mean?

Hark, canst thou hear me? I will play the swan.

Can you hear me? I will be like a swan

And die in music.

And die singing.

Singing

Willow, willow, willow,--

Willow, willow, willow–

Moor, she was chaste; she loved thee, cruel Moor;

Moor, she was pure and loved you, cruel Moor.

So come my soul to bliss, as I speak true;

I swear by my soul I speak truly,

So speaking as I think, I die, I die.

And as I speak my honest thoughts, I die.

Dies

OTHELLO

I have another weapon in this chamber;

I have another sword in this room.

It is a sword of Spain, the ice-brook's temper:--

It is a Spanish sword, tempered by ice water –

O, here it is. Uncle, I must come forth.

Here it is. Uncle, I am coming out.

GRATIANO

[Within] If thou attempt it, it will cost thee dear:

If you do, it will cost you your life.

Thou hast no weapon, and perforce must suffer.

You do not have a weapon and so you will suffer.

OTHELLO

Look in upon me then and speak with me,

Look in at me and speak to me,

Or, naked as I am, I will assault thee.

Or, weaponless, I will attack you.

Re-enter GRATIANO

GRATIANO

What is the matter?

What is it?

OTHELLO

423

Behold, I have a weapon;

Look, I have a sword,

A better never did itself sustain

One better than any that laid

Upon a soldier's thigh: I have seen the day,

On a soldier's leg. I have,

That, with this little arm and this good sword,

With this single arm and this good sword,

I have made my way through more impediments

Fought through more obstacles,

Than twenty times your stop: but, O vain boast!

Twenty times more, than your guard. But what an arrogant comment!

Who can control his fate? 'tis not so now.

It is not like I can control my fate.

Be not afraid, though you do see me weapon'd;

Don't be afraid, even though I have a weapon.

Here is my journey's end, here is my butt,

This is the end of my journey,

And very sea-mark of my utmost sail.

The last place my sail will take me.

Do you go back dismay'd? 'tis a lost fear;

Are you backing away in fear? It is not necessary.

Man but a rush against Othello's breast,

Rush against my chest,

And he retires. Where should Othello go?

And I will back down. Where should Othello go?

Now, how dost thou look now? O ill-starr'd wench!

O, look at you, Desdemona, your cruel fate!

Pale as thy smock! when we shall meet at compt,

As pale as your nightgown! When we shall meet at the end of time,

This look of thine will hurl my soul from heaven,

This look of yours will throw my soul out of heaven

And fiends will snatch at it. Cold, cold, my girl!

And demons will take it. Cold, cold, my wife!

Even like thy chastity. O cursed slave!

You are as white as your purity. O I am accursed!

Whip me, ye devils,

Devils, whip me,

From the possession of this heavenly sight!

And keep me from looking at this angel!

Blow me about in winds! roast me in sulphur!

Blow on me with the winds of hell! Roast me in sulphur!

Wash me in steep-down gulfs of liquid fire!

Wash me in lava fire!

O Desdemona! Desdemona! dead!

O Desdemona! Desdemona! dead!

Oh! Oh! Oh!

Oh, Oh, Oh!

Enter LODOVICO. MONTANO, CASSIO carried in a chair, and Officers with IAGO, prisoner

LODOVICO

Where is this rash and most unfortunate man?

Where is this poor, reckless man?

OTHELLO

That's he that was Othello: here I am.

You are speaking of him who was Othello. I am him.

LODOVICO

Where is that viper? bring the villain forth.

Where is that snake, Iago? Bring him forward.

OTHELLO

I look down towards his feet; but that's a fable.

I look down at your feet, but it is a fable that the devil has cloven hooves.

If that thou best a devil, I cannot kill thee.

If you are the devil truly, I will not be able to kill you.

Wounds IAGO

LODOVICO

Wrench his sword from him.

Take his sword away.

IAGO

I bleed, sir; but not kill'd.

I bleed, sir, but am not dead.

OTHELLO

I am not sorry neither: I'ld have thee live;

I am not sorry about that. I want you to live,

For, in my sense, 'tis happiness to die.

Since to me, death is happiness.

LODOVICO

O thou Othello, thou wert once so good,

Othello, you used to be so good,

Fall'n in the practise of a damned slave,

But then you fell victim to the words of this damn slave.

What shall be said to thee?

What can we say about you?

OTHELLO

Why, any thing:

Anything.

An honourable murderer, if you will;

Call me an honorable murderer if you want.

For nought I did in hate, but all in honour.

I did nothing out of hate, but everything from a sense of honor.

LODOVICO

This wretch hath part confess'd his villany:

This villain has confessed part of his plans.

Did you and he consent in Cassio's death?

Did you and him plan together for Cassio's death?

OTHELLO

Ay.

Yes.

CASSIO

Dear general, I never gave you cause.

But general, I never have you reason to think poorly of me.

OTHELLO

I do believe it, and I ask your pardon.

I believe you, and I ask that you forgive me.

Will you, I pray, demand that demi-devil

Will you please make this half-devil speak

Why he hath thus ensnared my soul and body?

And say why he tricked my soul and body?

IAGO

Demand me nothing: what you know, you know:

Ask nothing from me. You know what you know

From this time forth I never will speak word.

And I will not say anything every again.

LODOVICO

What, not to pray?

Not even to pray?

GRATIANO

Torments will ope your lips.

Torture might make you talk.

OTHELLO

Well, thou dost best.

Do whatever is best.

LODOVICO

Sir, you shall understand what hath befall'n,

Sir, you will soon understand everything that has happened,

Which, as I think, you know not. Here is a letter

Which you do not, yet. Here is a letter

Found in the pocket of the slain Roderigo;

That we found in Roderigo's pocket,

And here another: the one of them imports

And here is another. One talks about the

The death of Cassio to be undertook

Death of Cassio and how it was meant to be accomplished

By Roderigo.

By Roderigo.

OTHELLO

O villain!

That villain!

CASSIO

Most heathenish and most gross!

So ungodly and disgusting!

LODOVICO

Now here's another discontented paper,

And here is another letter

Found in his pocket too; and this, it seems,

From his pocket. This one, it seems,

Roderigo meant to have sent this damned villain;

Was from Roderigo, and he meant to give it to Iago

But that belike Iago in the interim

But then Iago

Came in and satisfied him.

Came in and killed him.

OTHELLO

O the pernicious caitiff!

O evil scoundrel!

How came you, Cassio, by that handkerchief

Cassio, how did that handkerchief come to you

That was my wife's?

That was my wife's?

CASSIO

I found it in my chamber:

It was in my room

And he himself confess'd but even now

And Iago just confessed

That there he dropp'd it for a special purpose

That he dropped it there for his own purposes

Which wrought to his desire.

Which he used for his desires.

OTHELLO

O fool! fool! fool!

Fool! fool! fool!

CASSIO

There is besides in Roderigo's letter,

In Roderigo's letter,

How he upbraids Iago, that he made him

He criticizes Iago for making him

Brave me upon the watch; whereon it came

Anger me during the watch where I

That I was cast: and even but now he spake,

Was assigned, and he even admitted just now,

After long seeming dead, Iago hurt him,

Though he looked like he was dead, that Iago hurt him

Iago set him on.

And tricked him to do it.

LODOVICO

You must forsake this room, and go with us:

You must leave this room and come with us.

Your power and your command is taken off,

Your rank has been removed,

And Cassio rules in Cyprus. For this slave,

And Cassio has been placed in charge of Cyprus. As for Iago,

If there be any cunning cruelty

If there is any cunning torture

That can torment him much and hold him long,

That can keep him in pain for a while but alive just as long,

It shall be his. You shall close prisoner rest,

He will get it. You will stay as a prisoner

Till that the nature of your fault be known

Until your crimes are known

To the Venetian state. Come, bring him away.

In the Venetian government. Bring him away.

OTHELLO

Soft you; a word or two before you go.

Wait, I want to say a word before going.

I have done the state some service, and they know't.

I have worked for the government, and they know that.

No more of that. I pray you, in your letters,

432

Nothing more needs said there. I ask that in your letters,

When you shall these unlucky deeds relate,

When you talk about these bad events,

Speak of me as I am; nothing extenuate,

Talk about me as I am in reality. Do not exaggerate

Nor set down aught in malice: then must you speak

And do not write about me in anger. Describe me

Of one that loved not wisely but too well;

As someone who did not love wisely, but did love a lot,

Of one not easily jealous, but being wrought

And say that I was prone to jealousy, but was manipulated

Perplex'd in the extreme; of one whose hand,

In the extreme, and say that my hand

Like the base Indian, threw a pearl away

Like a foolish Indian, threw away a pearl

Richer than all his tribe; of one whose subdued eyes,

Worth more than his whole tribe. Write that my calm eyes,

Albeit unused to the melting mood,

Not used to being sad,

Drop tears as fast as the Arabian trees

Give off tears faster than trees from Arabia

Their medicinal gum. Set you down this;

That are known to let drip their sap. Write this,

And say besides, that in Aleppo once,

And say also that once in Aleppo,

Where a malignant and a turban'd Turk

Where a dangerous Turk wearing a turban

Beat a Venetian and traduced the state,

Beat a Venetian man and slandered the country,

I took by the throat the circumcised dog,

I took the Turk by the throat

And smote him, thus.

And killed him like this.

Stabs himself

LODOVICO

O bloody period!

What a bloody ending!

GRATIANO

All that's spoke is marr'd.

Everything that has been said is bad.

OTHELLO

I kiss'd thee ere I kill'd thee: no way but this;

I kissed you before I killed you. Now it is fitting

Killing myself, to die upon a kiss.

That killing myself, I die kissing you.

Falls on the bed, and dies

CASSIO

This did I fear, but thought he had no weapon;

I was afraid of this, but I thought he did not have a weapon.

For he was great of heart.

He was a passionate man.

LODOVICO

[To IAGO] O Spartan dog,

You dog,

More fell than anguish, hunger, or the sea!

Crueler than sadness, hunger, and the sea!

Look on the tragic loading of this bed;

Look at the dead bodies piled onto this bed:

This is thy work: the object poisons sight;

This is your work. This is a poisonous sight,

Let it be hid. Gratiano, keep the house,

Someone cover it. Gratiano, take care of the house

And seize upon the fortunes of the Moor,

And take the Moor's estate,

For they succeed on you. To you, lord governor,

For it all goes to you. And you, Cassio,

Remains the censure of this hellish villain;

Must punish this criminal.

The time, the place, the torture: O, enforce it!

Enforce the time, the place, and the kind of torture.

Myself will straight aboard: and to the state

I am returning to Venice immediately to tell them

This heavy act with heavy heart relate.

In sadness the awful events that happened here

Exeunt

About BookCaps

We all need refreshers every now and then. Whether you are a student trying to cram for that big final, or someone just trying to understand a book more, BookCaps can help. We are a small, but growing company, and are adding titles every month.

Visit www.bookcaps.com to see more of our books, or contact us with any questions.

Printed in Great Britain
by Amazon